Kubernetes Programming with Go

Programming Kubernetes Clients
and Operators Using
Go and the Kubernetes API

Philippe Martin

Apress®

Kubernetes Programming with Go: Programming Kubernetes Clients and Operators Using Go and the Kubernetes API

Philippe Martin
Blanquefort, France

ISBN-13 (pbk): 978-1-4842-9025-5
https://doi.org/10.1007/978-1-4842-9026-2

ISBN-13 (electronic): 978-1-4842-9026-2

Managing Director, Apress Media LLC: Welmoed Spahr
Acquisitions Editor: Divya Modi
Development Editor: James Markham
Coordinating Editor: Divya Modi
Copy Editor: Kim Burton Wiseman

Cover designed by eStudioCalamar

Cover image designed by Freepik (www.freepik.com)

Distributed to the book trade worldwide by Springer Science+Business Media New York, 1 New York Plaza, New York, NY 10004. Phone 1-800-SPRINGER, fax (201) 348-4505, e-mail orders-ny@springer-sbm.com, or visit www.springeronline.com. Apress Media, LLC is a California LLC and the sole member (owner) is Springer Science + Business Media Finance Inc (SSBM Finance Inc). SSBM Finance Inc is a **Delaware** corporation.

For information on translations, please e-mail booktranslations@springernature.com; for reprint, paperback, or audio rights, please e-mail bookpermissions@springernature.com.

Apress titles may be purchased in bulk for academic, corporate, or promotional use. eBook versions and licenses are also available for most titles. For more information, reference our Print and eBook Bulk Sales web page at http://www.apress.com/bulk-sales.

Any source code or other supplementary material referenced by the author in this book is available to readers on GitHub via the book's product page, located at https://github.com/Apress/Kubernetes-Programming-with-Go-by-Philippe-Martin. For more detailed information, please visit http://www.apress.com/source-code.

Printed on acid-free paper

To Mélina and Elsa, my constant source of truth

Table of Contents

About the Author

Philippe Martin has been working with Kubernetes for five years, first by creating an Operator to deploy video CDNs into the cloud, later helping companies deploy their applications into Kubernetes, then writing a Client to help developers work in a Kubernetes environment. Philippe has passed the CKAD, CKA, and CKS certifications. He has extensive experience with distributed systems and open-source software: he started his career 20 years ago creating thin clients based on the Linux kernel and open-source components. He is currently working at Red Hat on the Development Tools team.

Philippe has been active in the development of Kubernetes, especially its documentation, and participates in the translation of the official documentation into French, has edited two reference books about the Kubernetes API and **kubectl**, and is responsible for the French translation of the Kubernetes Dashboard. He participated in Google Season of Docs to create the new Kubernetes API Reference section of the official documentation and is maintaining it.

About the Technical Reviewers

Bartosz Majsak writes code for fun and profit while proudly wearing a red fedora (also known as the Red Hat). He has been long-time open-source contributor and Java developer turned into Golang aficionado. Bartosz is overly enthusiastic about coffee, open source, and speaking at conferences, not necessarily in that order. One thing that perhaps proves he is not a total geek is his addiction to alpine skiing (and running).

Prasanth is a Blockchain Certified Professional, Professional Scrum Master, and Microsoft Certified Trainer who is passionate about helping others learn how to use and gain benefits from the latest technologies. He is a thought leader and practitioner in Blockchain, Cloud, and Scrum. He also handles the Agile Methodology, Cloud, and Blockchain technology community initiatives within TransUnion through coaching, mentoring, and grooming techniques.

Prasanth is an adjunct professor and a technical speaker. He was selected as a speaker at the China International Industry Big Data Expo 2018 by the Chinese government and also was invited to the International Blockchain Council by the Government of Telangana and Goa. In addition, he received accolades from the Chinese government for his presentation at China International Industry Big Data Expo 2018. Prasanth has published his Patent, entitled "Digital Educational Certificate Management System Using IPFS-Based Blockchain."

To date, he has interacted extensively, reaching more than 50,000 students, mostly within the technical domain. Prasanth is a working group member of the CryptoCurrency Certification Consortium, the Scrum Alliance, the Scrum Organization, and the International Institute of Business Analysis.

Acknowledgments

I would like to thank the whole Anevia "CDN" team who started working with me on Kubernetes back in 2018: David, Ansou, Hossam, Yassine, Étienne, Jason, and Michaël. Special thanks to Damien Lucas for initiating this project and for having trusted us with this challenge.

My discovery of Kubernetes has been much easier and pleasant thanks to the TGIK channel and its numerous episodes, hosted by Joe Beda, Kris Nova, and many others. Plus, thanks to all the Kubernetes community for such a great ecosystem!

Introduction

Back in 2017, I was working for a company building video streaming software. At the end of that year, a small team, including me, got assigned a new job to work on deploying the Video CDN developed by the company on Kubernetes. We decided to explore the concept of Custom Resources and Operators to deploy this CDN.

The current Kubernetes release was 1.9, the concept of Custom Resource Definition had just been released in 1.7, and the sample-controller repository was the only documentation we knew of to help build an Operator. The Kubernetes ecosystem, being especially lively, had tools appearing in the following months, specifically the Kubebuilder SDK. Thus, our project was launched.

From that moment on, I spent numerous days exploring how to build Operators and other programs interacting with the Kubernetes API. But the damage was done: I had started to learn Kubernetes programming from specific to general, and it took me a long time to fully understand the innards of the Kubernetes API.

I have written this book in the hope that it can teach new Kubernetes developers how to program, from general to specific, with the Kubernetes API in Go.

Chapters at a Glance

The target reader for this book has some experience working with REST APIs, accessing them either by HTTP or using clients for specific languages; and has some knowledge of the Kubernetes platform, essentially as a user—for example, some experience deploying such APIs or frontend applications with the help of YAML manifests.

- Chapter 1 of the book explores the Kubernetes API and how it implements the principles of REST. It especially focuses on the Group-Version-Resource organization and the Kind concept proposed by the API.

- Chapter 2 continues by covering the operations proposed by the API and the details of each operation, using the HTTP protocol.

- Chapters 3 to 5 describe the common and "low-level" Go libraries to work with the Kubernetes API: the API and API Machinery Libraries.

- Chapters 6 and 7 cover the Client-go Library—the high-level library to work with the Kubernetes API in Go—and how to unit test code using this library.

At this point in the book, the reader should be comfortable with building Go applications working with native resources of the Kubernetes API.

- Chapters 8 and 9 introduce the concept of Custom Resources and how to work with them in Go.

- Chapters 10 to 12 cover the implementation of Kubernetes Operators using the **controller-runtime** library.

- Chapter 13 explores the Kubebuilder SDK, a tool to help develop and deploy Kubernetes Operators.

By the end of the book, the reader should be able to start building Kubernetes operators in Go and have a very good understanding of what happens behind the scenes.

CHAPTER 1

Kubernetes API Introduction

Kubernetes is a platform to orchestrate containers operating in the declarative mode. There are one-thousand-and-one ways to describe how the Kubernetes platform is constructed. This book focuses on programming with the platform.

The entry point of the Kubernetes platform is the API. This chapter explores the Kubernetes architecture by highlighting the central role of the Kubernetes API. It then focuses on the HTTP REST nature of the Kubernetes API, and on the extensions added to organize the many resources managed by it.

Finally, you will learn how to navigate the reference documentation effectively to be able to extract the maximum quantity of useful information daily.

Kubernetes Platform at a Glance

On one side of the chain, the user declares the high-level resources to build applications to deploy: Deployments, Ingresses, and so on.

In the middle, controllers are activated to transform these resources into low-level resources (Pods), and the scheduler distributes these resources into nodes. On the other side of the chain, the node agents deploy the low-level resources onto nodes.

The main elements of the Kubernetes platform (commonly called the control-plane) are highlighted in Figure 1-1 and described in the following:

1. The API server – this is the central point on the control-plane; the user and the various pieces of the control-plane contact this API to create, get, delete, update, and watch resources.

2. The etcd database – this is only accessible by the API Server, is used to persist the data relative to resources.

© Philippe Martin 2023
P. Martin, *Kubernetes Programming with Go*, https://doi.org/10.1007/978-1-4842-9026-2_1

3. The Controller manager – this runs the controllers that transform
    high-level resources declared by the user into low-level resources
    to be deployed on nodes. The controllers are connected to the API
    Server, watching for high-level resources and creating, deleting,
    and updating low-level resources to satisfy the specifications
    declared in high-level resources.

4. Scheduler – this distributes the low-level resources on the various
    nodes. The Scheduler is connected to the API Server to watch for
    unaffected resources and connect them to nodes.

5. Kubelet – this is an agent running on all nodes of the cluster,
    and each agent manages the workloads affected to its node. The
    kubelet is connected to the API Server to watch for Pods resources
    affected to its node and to deploy the associated containers using
    the local container runtime.

6. Kube proxy – this is an agent running on all nodes of the cluster,
    and each agent manages the network configurations affected to
    its node. The kube proxy is connected to the API Server to watch
    for Service resources and to configure associated network rules on
    its node.

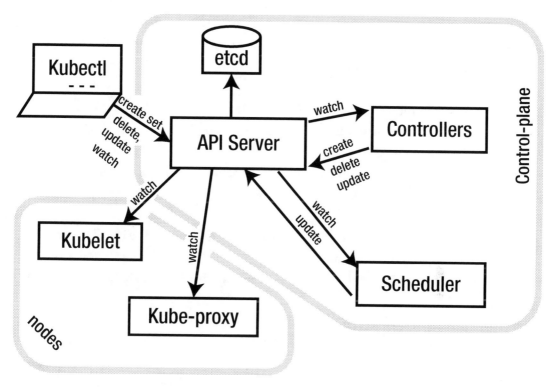

Figure 1-1. *The architecture of Kubernetes*

OpenAPI Specification

The Kubernetes API is an HTTP REST API. The Kubernetes team provides a specification for this API in the OpenAPI format, either in v2 format at `https://github.com/kubernetes/kubernetes/tree/master/api/openapi-spec` or in Kubernetes v1.24, in v3 format, at `https://github.com/kubernetes/kubernetes/tree/master/api/openapi-spec/v3`.

These specifications also are accessible from the API Server at these paths: **/openapi/v2** and **/openapi/v3**.

An OpenAPI specification is made up of various parts and, among these, are a list of paths and a list of definitions. The paths are the URLs you use to request this API, and for each path, the specification gives the distinct operations such as **get**, **delete**, or **post**. Then for each operation, the specification indicates what are the parameters and body format for the request, and what are the possible response codes and associated body format for the response.

The parameters and bodies for requests and responses can be either simple types or, more generally, structures containing data. The list of definitions includes data structures that help build the parameters and bodies for the operations' requests and responses.

Figure 1-2 is a simplified view of a specification for a User API. This API can accept two different paths: **/user/{userId}** and **/user**. The first path, **/user/{userId}**, can accept two operations, **get** and **delete**, respectively, to receive information about a specific user, given its user ID; and to delete information about a specific user, given its user ID. The second path, **/user**, can accept a single operation, **post**, to add a new user, given its information.

In this API, a definition of a structure **User** is given, describing the information for a user: its ID, first name, and last name. This data structure is used in the response body of the **get** operation on the first path, and in the request body of the **post** operation on the second path.

```
paths:
    /user/{userId}:
        get:
            parameters:
                userId: integer
            requestBody: (empty)
            responses:
                200:
                    User
        delete:
            parameters:
                userId: integer
            requestBody: (empty)
            responses:
                204: (empty)
    /user:
        post:
            parameters: (empty)
            requestBody: User
            responses:
                200:
                    User
definitions:
    User:
        ID: integer
        FirstName: string
        LastName: string
```

Figure 1-2. *A simplified user API specification*

Verbs and Kinds

The Kubernetes API adds two concepts to this specification: the **Kubernetes API Verbs** and the **Kubernetes Kinds**.

The Kubernetes API Verbs are mapped directly to the operations in the OpenAPI specification. The defined verbs are **get**, **create**, **update**, **patch**, **delete**, **list**, **watch**, and **deletecollection**. The correspondence with the HTTP verbs can be found in Table 1-1.

Table 1-1. *Correspondence Between Kubernetes API Verbs and HTTP Verbs*

Kubernetes API Verb	HTTP Verb
get	GET
create	POST
update	PUT
patch	PATCH
delete	DELETE
list	GET
watch	GET
deletecollection	DELETE

The Kubernetes Kinds are a subset of the definitions in the OpenAPI specification. When requests are made to the Kubernetes API, data structures are exchanged through the bodies of requests and responses. These structures share common fields, **apiVersion** and **kind**, to help the participants of the request recognize these structures.

If you wanted to make your User API manage this Kind concept, the **User** structure would contain two additional fields, **apiVersion** and **kind**—for example, with values **v1** and **User**. To determine whether a definition in the Kubernetes OpenAPI specification is a Kubernetes Kind, you can look at the **x-kubernetes-group-version-kind** field of the definition. If this field is defined, the definition is a kind, and it gives you the values of the **apiVersion** and **kind** fields.

Group-Version-Resource

The Kubernetes API is a REST API, and as a result of that it manages *Resources*, and the paths to manage these resources follow the REST naming conventions—that is, by using a plural name to identify a resource and by grouping these resources.

Because the Kubernetes API manages hundreds of resources, they are grouped together, and because the API evolves, the resources are versioned. For these reasons, each resource belongs to a given *Group* and *Version*, and each resource is uniquely identified by a Group-Version-Resource, commonly known as **GVR**.

To find the various resources in the Kubernetes API, you can browse the OpenAPI specification to extract the distinct paths. Legacy resources (e.g., **pods** or **nodes**) will have been introduced early in the Kubernetes API and all belong to the group **core** and the version **v1**.

The paths to manage legacy resources cluster-wide follow the format **/api/v1/<plural_resource_name>**—for example, **/api/v1/nodes** to manage **nodes**. Note that the **core** group is not represented in the path. To manage resources in a given namespace, the path format is **/api/v1/namespaces/<namespace_name>/<plural_resource_name>**—for example, **/api/v1/namespaces/default/pods** to manage **pods** in the **default** namespace.

Newer resources are accessible through paths following the format **/apis/<group>/<version>/<plural_resource_name>** or **/apis/<group>/<version>/namespaces/<namespace_name>/<plural_resource_name>**.

To summarize, the formats of the various paths to access resources are:

- /api/v1/<plural_name> – to access legacy non-namespaced resources

  Ex: **/api/v1/nodes** to access non-namespaced **nodes** resources

  or

  To access legacy namespaced resources cluster-wide

  Ex: **/api/v1/pods** to access **pods** across all namespaces

- /api/v1/namespaces/<ns>/<plural_name> – to access legacy namespaced resources in a specific namespace

  Ex: **/api/v1/namespaces/default/pods** to access **pods** in the **default** namespace

- /apis/<group>/<version>/<plural_name> – to access non-namespaced resources in specific group and version

  Ex: **/apis/storage.k8s.io/v1/storageclasses** to access non-namespaced **storageclasses** (group **storage.k8s.io,** version **v1**) or

To access namespaced resources cluster-wide

Ex: **/apis/apps/v1/deployments** to access **deployments** across all
namespaces

- /apis/<group>/<version>/namespaces/<ns>/<plural_name> – to
  access namespaced resources in a specific namespace

  Ex: **/apis/apps/v1/namespaces/default/deployments** to access
  deployments (group **apps**, version **v1**) in the **default** namespace

Sub-resources

Following the REST API convention, the resources can have sub-resources. A sub-
resource is a resource that belongs to another and can be accessed by specifying its
name after the name of the resource, as follows:

- /api/v1/<plural>/<res-name>/<sub-resource>
  Ex: /api/v1/nodes/node1/status

- /api/v1/namespaces/<ns>/<plural>/<res-name>/<sub-resource>
  Ex: /api/v1/namespaces/ns1/pods/pod1/status

- /apis/<group>/<version>/<plural>/<res-name>/<sub-resource>
  Ex: /apis/storage.k8s.io/v1/volumeattachments/volatt1/status

- /apis/<grp>/<v>/namespaces/<ns>/<plural>/<name>/<sub-res>
  Ex: /apis/apps/v1/namespaces/ns1/deployments/dep1/status

Most Kubernetes resources have a **status** sub-resource. You can see, when writing
operators, that the operator needs to update the status sub-resource to be able to
indicate the state of this resource observed by the operator. The operations that can
be executed in the **status** sub-resource are **get**, **patch**, and **update**. The Pod has more
sub-resources, including **attach**, **binding**, **eviction**, **exec**, **log**, **portforward**, and **proxy**.
These sub-resources are useful for getting information about a specific running pod, or
executing some specific operation on a running pod, and so on.

The resources that can Scale (i.e., deployments, replicasets, etc.) have a **scale** sub-resource. The operations that can be executed in the **scale** sub-resource are **get**, **patch,** and **update**.

Official API Reference Documentation

The official reference documentation of the API can be found at `https://kubernetes.io/docs/reference/kubernetes-api/`. The resources managed by the API are first grouped together by category (i.e., workloads, storage, etc.), and for each category, you can obtain a list of resource names with a short description (Figure 1-3).

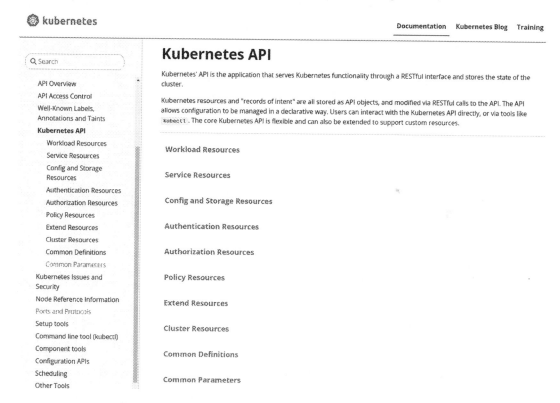

Figure 1-3. *The Kubernetes resources grouped by category*

Note that these categories are not part of the Kubernetes API definition but are used in this website to help inexperienced users find their way into the multitude of available resources.

To be precise, the name displayed is not the resource name in the REST sense, but the associated principal kind, as shown in Figure 1-4. For example, when managing *Pods*, the resource name used in the REST paths is **pods** (i.e., lowercase and plural), and the definition used to exchange information about *Pods* during HTTP requests is named **Pod** (i.e., uppercase and singular). Note that other kinds can be associated with the same resource. In the example in this chapter, the **PodList** kind (used to exchange information about *Lists of Pods*) also exists.

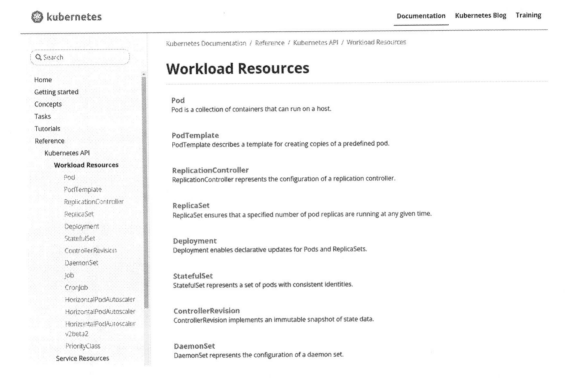

Figure 1-4. *The resources for a specific category, with a short description*

The Deployment Documentation

Let's explore the reference page for the **Deployment** available at this address: https://kubernetes.io/docs/reference/kubernetes-api/workload-resources/ deployment-v1/. The title of the page, **Deployment**, is the principal kind associated with the **deployments** resource shown in Figure 1-5.

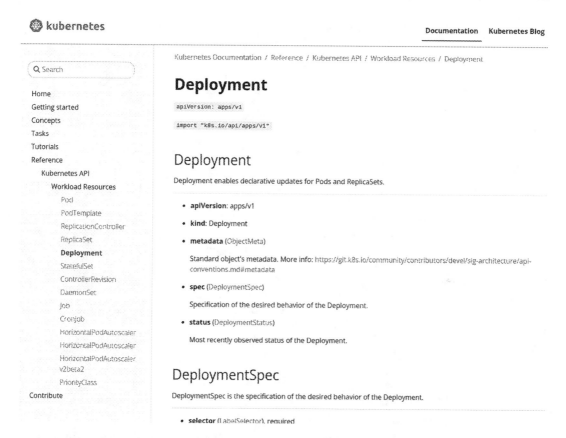

Figure 1-5. *The Deployment documentation page*

The **apiVersion** indicated in the header can help you write a YAML manifest for a *Deployment* resource because you need to specify, for each resource in a Kubernetes manifest, the **apiVersion** and **kind**.

In this case, you know the manifest for a deployment will start with the following:

```
apiVersion: apps/v1
kind: Deployment
```

The next header line indicates the **import** to use when writing Go code. In Chapter 3, you will see how to use this import when describing resources in Go.

After the header, a list of structure definitions is described, also accessible from the table of contents for the Deployment documentation page in Figure 1-6. The first one is the principal kind of the resource, optionally followed by structure definitions that are used in fields of the first kind.

11

Deployment
DeploymentSpec
DeploymentStatus
DeploymentList
Operations
  get read the specified Deployment
  get read status of the specified
  Deployment
  list list or watch objects of kind
  Deployment
  list list or watch objects of kind
  Deployment
  create create a Deployment
  update replace the specified
  Deployment
  update replace status of the specified
  Deployment
  patch partially update the specified
  Deployment
  patch partially update status of the
  specified Deployment
  delete delete a Deployment
  deletecollection delete collection of
  Deployment

Figure 1-6. *Table of contents for the Deployment documentation page*

For example, the Deployment kind contains a **spec** field, of type **DeploymentSpec**, which is described later. Note that **DeploymentSpec** is not a structure directly exchanged during HTTP requests, and for that, it is not a kind and does not contain **kind** or **apiVersion** fields.

Following the principal kind, and its associated definitions, other kinds associated with the resource are displayed. In this case, the **DeploymentList** kind.

Operations Documentation

The next subject in the API Documentation for a resource is the list of possible operations on this resource or its sub-resources, also accessible from the table of contents page (see Figure 1-6). By examining the details for the **create** operation to *Create a Deployment*, as shown in Figure 1-7, you can see the HTTP Request verb and path to use, the parameters to pass during the request, and the possible responses. The HTTP verb to use for the request is **POST** and the path is **/apis/apps/v1/namespaces/ {namespace}/deployments**.

Figure 1-7. *Details for a "create" Deployment operation*

The **{namespace}** part of the path indicates a *path* parameter, which is to be replaced by the name of the namespace on which you want to create the deployment. You can specify the *query* parameters: **dryRun**, **fieldManager**, **fieldValidation**, and **pretty**. These parameters will follow the path with the format **path?dryRun=All**.

The body of the request must be a **Deployment** kind. When using **kubectl**, you are writing *Kubernetes Manifests* that contain this body. In Chapter 3, you will see how to build the body in Go. The possible HTTP codes for the responses are: 200, 201, 202, and 401; and for the 2xx codes, the response body will contain a **Deployment** kind.

The Pod Documentation

Some structures contain many fields. For them, the Kubernetes API documentation categorizes the fields. An example is the documentation of the *Pod* resource.

The documentation page for the Pod resource first contains the description for the principal kind, **Pod**, followed by the description of the **PodSpec** structure. The **PodSpec** structure contains about 40 fields. To help you understand the relationships between these fields and to simplify their exploration, they are arranged into categories. The PodSpec fields' categories are the following: *Containers, Volumes, Scheduling, Lifecycle*, and so on.

Additionally, for fields containing nested fields, descriptions of them are generally displayed inline to avoid a back and forth between structure descriptions. For complex structures, however, the description is reported subsequently on the page, and a link is present next to the field name to be able to access it easily.

This is always the case for the **Spec** and **Status** structures because they are very commonly found in almost all the resources. In addition, this is the case for some structures used in the **Pod** kind—for example, **Container**, **EphemeralContainer**, **LifecycleHandler**, **NodeAffinity**, and so on.

Some structures used in several resources are placed in the *Common Definitions* section, and a link is present next to the field name to access it easily. In Figure 1-8, you can see the *Containers* category inside the description of the PodSpec structure.

PodSpec

PodSpec is a description of a pod.

Containers

- **containers** ([]Container), required

  Patch strategy: merge on key `name`

  List of containers belonging to the pod. Containers cannot currently be added or removed. There must be at least one container in a Pod. Cannot be updated.

- **initContainers** ([]Container)

  Patch strategy: merge on key `name`

  List of initialization containers belonging to the pod. Init containers are executed in order prior to containers being started. If any init container fails, the pod is considered to have failed and is handled according to its restartPolicy. The name for an init container or normal container must be unique among all containers. Init containers may not have Lifecycle actions, Readiness probes, Liveness probes, or Startup probes. The resourceRequirements of an init container are taken into account during scheduling by finding the highest request/limit for each resource type, and then using the max of of that value or the sum of the normal containers. Limits are applied to init containers in a similar fashion. Init containers cannot currently be added or removed. Cannot be updated. More info: https://kubernetes.io/docs/concepts/workloads/pods/init-containers/

- **imagePullSecrets** ([]LocalObjectReference)

  Patch strategy: merge on key `name`

  ImagePullSecrets is an optional list of references to secrets in the same namespace to use for pulling any of the images used by this PodSpec. If specified, these secrets will be passed to individual puller implementations for them to use. For example, in the case of docker, only DockerConfig type secrets are honored. More info: https://kubernetes.io/docs/concepts/containers/images#specifying-imagepullsecrets-on-a-pod

Figure 1-8. *Extract of the PodSpec structure documentation*

You also can see that the fields, **containers** and **initContainers**, are of the same type as **Container**, which is described later on the page and is accessible with a link. The **imagePullSecrets** field is of type **LocalObjectReference**, which is described in the *Common Definitions* section and also is accessible through a link.

One-Page Version of the Documentation

Another version of the API Reference documentation exists and is presented on a single page. This version covers all the versions of the resources served by a Kubernretes version (not just the latest one). This version (if you want, change the last part of the path to navigate to another Kubernetes version) can be found at the following URL:

```
https://kubernetes.io/docs/reference/generated/kubernetes-api/v1.24/
```

Conclusion

In this chapter, you have been able to discover the architecture of the Kubernetes platform, and that the API Server plays a central role. The Kubernetes API is an HTTP REST API, and the resources are categorized into various versioned groups.

Kinds are specific structures used to exchange data between the API server and the clients. You can browse, using the official Kubernetes website, the API specifications in a human-readable form to discover the structure of the various resources and kinds, the different operations available for each resource and sub-resource, and their associated verbs.

CHAPTER 2

Kubernetes API Operations

The previous chapter described that the Kubernetes API follows REST principles and enables users to manipulate resources.

In this chapter, you will learn how to perform various operations by making HTTP requests directly. During your daily work, you probably will not have to interact directly with the HTTP layer, but it is important to understand how the API works at this level so that you can understand how to use more easily it with a higher-level library.

Examining Requests

Before starting to write your own HTTP requests, you can examine with **kubectl** which requests are used when executing **kubectl** commands. This can be achieved by using the verbose flag, **-v**, with a value greater than or equal to **6**. Table 2-1 shows which information is displayed at each level.

For example, if you want to know the URL that is called when getting pods for all namespaces, you can use the following command:

```
$ kubectl get pods --all-namespaces -v6
loader.go:372] Config loaded from file:  /home/user/.kube/config
round_trippers.go:553] GET https://192.168.1.194:6443/api/v1/pods?limit=500
200 OK in 745 milliseconds
```

© Philippe Martin 2023
P. Martin, *Kubernetes Programming with Go*, https://doi.org/10.1007/978-1-4842-9026-2_2

In the output of the command, you can see that the path used is **/api/v1/pods**. Or, when getting pods in a specific namespace, you can see that the path used is **/api/v1/ namespaces/default/pods**:

```
$ kubectl get pods --namespace default -v6
loader.go:372] Config loaded from file:  /home/user/.kube/config
round_trippers.go:553] GET https://192.168.1.194:6443/api/v1/namespaces/
default/pods?limit=500 200 OK in 138 milliseconds
```

Table 2-1. *Verbosity Levels*

Level	Method and URL	Request timing	Events timing	Request headers	Response status	Response headers	Curl cmd	Body length
-v 6	yes	yes	–	–	–	–	–	0
-v 7	yes	–	–	yes	yes	–	–	0
-v 8	yes	–	–	yes	yes	yes	-	≤ 1024
-v 9	yes	yes	yes	–	–	yes	yes	≤ 10240
-v 10	yes	yes	yes	–	–	yes	yes	∞

Making Requests

This section examines all the possible operations you can do with Kubernetes resources.

Using kubectl as a Proxy

You must be authenticated to make requests to the Kubernetes API of a cluster, unless your cluster accepts unauthentified requests, which is unlikely.

A way to run authenticated HTTP requests is to use **kubectl** as a proxy to make it deal with the authentication. For this, the **kubectl proxy** command can be used:

```
$ kubectl proxy
Starting to serve on 127.0.0.1:8001
```

On a new terminal, you can now run your HTTP requests without any authentication. Next, a **HOST** variable to access the proxy is defined:

```
$ HOST=http://127.0.0.1:8001
```

Creating a Resource

You can create a new resource by first creating a Kubernetes manifest describing this resource—for example, to create a Pod, you can write:

```
$ cat > pod.yaml <<EOF
apiVersion: v1
kind: Pod
metadata:
  name: nginx
spec:
  containers:
  - image: nginx
    name: nginx
EOF
```

You then need to pass the resource description into the body of a POST request (note that the **-X POST** flag can be omitted because the **--data-binary** flag is being used). For example, to create a pod resource use:

```
$ curl $HOST/api/v1/namespaces/project1/pods
    -H "Content-Type: application/yaml"
    --data-binary @pod.yaml
```

This is equivalent to running the **kubectl** command:

```
$ kubectl create --namespace project1 -f pod.yaml -o json
```

Note that the namespace is not indicated in the **pod.yaml** file. If you add it, you must specify the same namespace in the YAML file and in the path, or you will get an error—that is, the namespace of the provided object does not match the namespace sent on the request.

Getting Information About a Resource

You can obtain information about a specific resource using a GET request and passing its name as a parameter (and its namespace if it is a namespaced resource) in the path. In this example, you will request the information for the **pod** named **nginx** in the **project1** namespace:

```
$ curl -X GET
    $HOST/api/v1/namespaces/project1/pods/nginx
```

This will return information about the resource in the JSON format, using the kind associated with this resource as a structure; in this example, it is a **Pod** kind. This is equivalent to running the **kubectl** command:

```
$ kubectl get pods --namespace project1 nginx -o json
```

Getting the List of Resources

For namespaced resources, you can get the list of resources either cluster-wide or in a specific namespace. For non-namespaced resources, you can get the list of resources. In any case, you will use a GET request.

Cluster-wide

To get the list of resources cluster-wide, for namespaced or non-namespaced resources; for example, for the pod resource, use the following:

```
$ curl $HOST/api/v1/pods
```

This will return information about the list of pods in all namespaces, using a **PodList** kind. This is equivalent to running the **kubectl** command:

```
$ kubectl get pods --all-namespaces -o json
```

In a Specific namespace

To get the list of resources in a specific namespace, you need to indicate the namespace in the path; for example, for the pod resource, use this:

```
$ curl $HOST/api/v1/namespaces/project1/pods
```

This will return information about the list of pods in the **project1** namespace, using a **PodList** kind. This is equivalent to running the **kubectl** command:

```
$ kubectl get pods --namespace project1 -o json
```

Filtering the Result of a List

When running a *list* request, you get as a result the complete list of resources of this kind, in the specified namespace or cluster-wide, depending on your request.

You may want to filter the result. The most common way to filter resources in Kubernetes is to use *labels*. For this, resources need to have defined labels; then, during a *list* request, you can define some *label selectors*. It also is possible to filter resources based on a limited set of fields by using *field selectors*.

Using Label Selectors

All Kubernetes resources can define labels. For example, when creating pods, you can define some labels with **kubectl**:

```
$ kubectl run nginx1 --image nginx --labels mylabel=foo
$ kubectl run nginx2 --image nginx --labels mylabel=bar
```

This results in pods with labels defined in the metadata part of the resource:

```
$ kubectl get pods nginx1 -o yaml
apiVersion: v1
kind: Pod
metadata:
  labels:
    mylabel: foo
  name: nginx1
[...]
```

```
$ kubectl get pods nginx2 -o yaml
apiVersion: v1
kind: Pod
metadata:
  labels:
```

```
    mylabel: bar
  name: nginx2
[...]
```

Now, when running a *list* request, you can define some *label selectors* to filter these resources by using the **labelSelector** query parameter, which can contain a comma-separated list of selectors.

- Select all the resources defining a specific label, no matter its value; for example, the **mylabel** label:

  ```
  $ curl $HOST/api/v1/namespaces/default/pods?
  labelSelector=mylabel
  ```

- Select all resources not defining a specific label; for example, the **mylabel** label:

  ```
  $ curl $HOST/api/v1/namespaces/default/pods?
  labelSelector=\!mylabel
  ```

Note the exclamation point (!) before the label name—the backslash character (\) is being used because the exclamation point is a special character for the shell.

- Select all resources defining a label with a specific value; for example, **mylabel** having the value **foo**:

  ```
  $ curl $HOST/api/v1/namespaces/default/pods?
  labelSelector=mylabel==foo
  ```

or

  ```
  $ curl $HOST/api/v1/namespaces/default/pods?
  labelSelector=mylabel=foo
  ```

- Select all resources defining a label with a value different from a specific one; for example, the label **mylabel** having a value different from **foo**:

```
$ curl $HOST/api/v1/namespaces/default/pods?
labelSelector=mylabel\!=foo
```

Note the exclamation point (!) before the equal sign (=)—the backslash character (\) is being used because the exclamation point is a special character for the shell.

- Select all resources defining a label with a value in a set of values; for example, the label **mylabel** having one of the values **foo** or **baz**:

```
$ curl $HOST/api/v1/namespaces/default/pods?
labelSelector=mylabel+in+(foo,baz)
```

Note the plus characters (+) that encodes spaces in the URL. The original selector being: **mylabel in (foo,baz)**.

- Select all resources defining a label with a value not in a set of values; for example, the label **mylabel** having a value different from **foo** or **baz**:

```
$ curl $HOST/api/v1/namespaces/default/pods?
labelSelector=mylabel+notin+(foo,baz)
```

Note the plus characters (+) that encodes spaces in the URL. The original selector being: **mylabel not in (foo,baz)**.

You can combine several selectors by separating them with a comma. This will act as an *AND* operator. For example, to select all resources with a label mylabel defined *and* a label otherlabel being equal to **bar**, you can use the following label selector:

```
$ curl $HOST/api/v1/namespaces/default/pods?
labelSelector=mylabel,otherlabel==bar
```

Using Field Selectors

You can filter resources using a limited set of fields. For all resources, you can filter on the **metadata.name** field; and for all namespaced resources, you can filter on the **metadata. namespace** field.

Here is the list of additional fields available for filtering, depending on resources, for Kubernetes 1.23:

```
core.event:

        involvedObject.apiVersion

        involvedObject.fieldPath

        involvedObject.kind

        involvedObject.name

        involvedObject.namespace

        involvedObject.resourceVersion

        involvedObject.uid

        reason

        reportingComponent

        source

        type

    core.namespace:

        status.phase

    core.node:

        spec.unschedulable

    core.pod:

        spec.nodeName

        spec.restartPolicy

        spec.schedulerName

        spec.serviceAccountName
```

```
status.nominatedNodeName

status.phase

status.podIP
```

core.replicationcontroller:

```
status.replicas
```

core.secret:

```
type
```

apps.replicaset:

```
status.replicas
```

batch.job:

```
status.successful
```
certificates.certificatesigningrequest:

```
spec.signerName
```

Now, when running a *list* request, you can indicate some *field selectors* to filter these resources by using the fieldSelector parameter, which can contain a comma-separated list of selectors.

- Select all resources for which a field has a specific value; for example, the field **status.phase** having the value **Running**:

  $ curl $HOST/api/v1/namespaces/default/pods?
  fieldSelector=status.phase==Running

  or

  $ curl $HOST/api/v1/namespaces/default/pods?
  fieldSelector=status.phase=Running

- Select all resources for which a field has a value different from a specific one; for example, the field **status.phase** having a value different from **Running**:

  $ curl $HOST/api/v1/namespaces/default/pods?
      fieldSelector=status.phase\!=Running

Note the exclamation point (!) before the equal sign (=)—the backslash character (\) is being used because the exclamation point is a special character for the shell.

You can combine several selectors by separating them with a comma. This will act as an *AND* operator. For example, to select all pods with a *phase* being equal to Running and a *restart policy* not being Always, you can use this field selector:

```
$ curl $HOST/api/v1/namespaces/default/pods?
    fieldSelector=status.phase==Running,
    spec.restartPolicy\!=Always
```

Deleting a Resource

To delete a resource, you need to specify its name (and namespace for namespaced resources) in the path and use a DELETE request. For example, to delete a pod, use the following:

```
$ curl -X DELETE
    $HOST/api/v1/namespaces/project1/pods/nginx
```

This will return the information about the deleted resource in the JSON format, using the kind associated with the resource—in this case, a **Pod** kind.

This is equivalent to running the kubectl command (except that you cannot get information about the deleted resource, only its name with the **-o name** flag):

```
$ kubectl delete pods --namespace project1 nginx
```

Deleting a Collection of Resources

It also is possible to delete a collection of a given resource in a specific namespace, using a DELETE request; and, for namespaced resources, indicating the namespace in the path:

```
$ curl -X DELETE
    $HOST/api/v1/namespaces/project1/pods
```

This will return the information about the deleted resources in the JSON format, using the List kind associated with the resource; in this example, the **PodList** kind.

This is equivalent to running the kubectl command (except that you cannot get information about the deleted resources, only their names with the **-o name** flag):

```
$ kubectl delete pods --namespace project1 --all
```

Note that it is not possible to delete all resources of a specific kind from all namespaces in a single request the way you could do it with the `kubectl` command: `kubectl delete pods --all-namespaces --all`.

Updating a Resource

It is possible to replace the complete information about a specific resource by using a PUT request and specifying the name (and namespace for namespaced resources) in the path and the new resource information in the body of the request.

To illustrate, you can first define a new deployment, with the following command:

```
$ cat > deploy.yaml <<EOF
apiVersion: apps/v1
kind: Deployment
metadata:
  name: nginx
spec:
  selector:
    matchLabels:
      app: nginx
  template:
    metadata:
      labels:
        app: nginx
    spec:
      containers:
      - image: nginx
        name: nginx
EOF
```

Then, you can create this deployment in the cluster using the following:

```
$ curl
    $HOST/apis/apps/v1/namespaces/project1/deployments
    -H "Content-Type: application/yaml"
    --data-binary @deploy.yaml
```

Next, you can create an updated manifest for the deployment; for example, by updating the image of the container with the following command (this will replace the image name **nginx** with **nginx:latest**):

```
$ cat deploy.yaml |
    sed 's/image: nginx/image: nginx:latest/' >
    deploy2.yaml
```

Finally, you can use the following request to update the deployment into the cluster:

```
$ curl -X PUT
    $HOST/apis/apps/v1/namespaces/project1/deployments/nginx
    -H "Content-Type: application/yaml"
    --data-binary @deploy2.yaml
```

This is equivalent to running the **kubectl** command:

```
$ kubectl replace --namespace project1
    -f deploy2.yaml -o json
```

Managing Conflicts When Updating a Resource

When updating a resource with the previous technique, if another participant makes a modification on the resource between the time you create it and the time you update it, then the modifications made by the other participant will be lost when you update the resource.

To avoid this risk of conflict, you can first read the resource information (using a GET request) to find the value of the **resourceVersion** field in the metadata of the resource, then indicate this **resourceVersion** in the specifications of the resource you want to update.

By sending the PUT request with this **resourceVersion**, the API server will compare the **resourceVersion** values of the received resource and the current one. If the values differ (because another participant has modified the resource in the meantime), the API server will reply with an error: *Operation cannot be fulfilled on [...]: the object has been modified; please apply your changes to the latest version and try again.*

To illustrate, let's create the deployment (be sure to delete it before doing this if you have created it from the previous section):

```
$ curl
    $HOST/apis/apps/v1/namespaces/project1/deployments
    -H "Content-Type: application/yaml"
    --data-binary @deploy.yaml
```

You will receive a response, indicating the **resourceVersion** of the resource you have created; in this example, it is **668867**:

```
{
  "kind": "Deployment",
  "apiVersion": "apps/v1",
  "metadata": {
    "name": "nginx",
    "namespace": "project1",
    "uid": "99d3a1eb-176c-40de-89ec-74313169fe60",
    "resourceVersion": "668867",
    "generation": 1,
  [...]
}
```

After waiting a few seconds, you can execute a GET request to find the latest version, and you will receive the following response:

```
$ curl $HOST/apis/apps/v1/namespaces/project1/deployments/nginx
{
  "kind": "Deployment",
  "apiVersion": "apps/v1",
  "metadata": {
    "name": "nginx",
    "namespace": "project1",
    "uid": "99d3a1eb-176c-40de-89ec-74313169fe60",
    "resourceVersion": "668908",
```

```
    "generation": 1,
  [...]
}
```

You can see that the **resourceVersion** has been incremented and is now **668908**. This happens because the Deployment controller has updated the resource on its own.

Now, if you add the first received version to your YAML manifest and try to update the deployment, you get an error indicating that a conflict has been detected:

```
$ cat > deploy2.yaml <<EOF
apiVersion: apps/v1
kind: Deployment
metadata:
  name: nginx
  resourceVersion: "668867"
spec:
  selector:
    matchLabels:
      app: nginx
  template:
    metadata:
      labels:
        app: nginx
    spec:
      containers:
      - image: nginx
        name: nginx
EOF

$ curl -X PUT
 $HOST/apis/apps/v1/namespaces/project1/deployments/nginx
 -H "Content-Type: application/yaml"
 --data-binary @deploy2.yaml
{
  "kind": "Status",
  "apiVersion": "v1",
  "metadata": {
```

```
  },
  "status": "Failure",
  "message": "Operation cannot be fulfilled on deployments.apps \"nginx\":
the object has been modified; please apply your changes to the latest
version and try again",
  "reason": "Conflict",
  "details": {
    "name": "nginx",
    "group": "apps",
    "kind": "deployments"
  },
  "code": 409
}
```

Now, if you update the YAML manifest with the latest **resourceVersion** by using the following command and running the PUT command again, the operation will succeed:

```
$ sed -i 's/668867/668908/' deploy2.yaml

$ curl -X PUT
 $HOST/apis/apps/v1/namespaces/project1/deployments/nginx
 -H "Content-Type: application/yaml"
 --data-binary @deploy2.yaml
{
  "kind": "Deployment",
  "apiVersion": "apps/v1",
  "metadata": {
    "name": "nginx",
    "namespace": "project1",
    "uid": "99d3a1eb-176c-40de-89ec-74313169fe60",
    "resourceVersion": "671623",
    "generation": 2,
[...]
}
```

Using a Strategic Merge Patch to Update a Resource

When modifying a resource, instead of sending the complete description of it, it is possible to send only the parts that you want to modify by using a *Patch*.

This is possible using a PATCH request with an **application/strategic-merge-patch+json** content-type and specifying the name (and namespace for namespaced resources) in the path and the patch information in the body of the request.

A patch information is an extract of a YAML manifest, which contains only the fields that you want to update. Doing this, the fields you specified in the path will be updated, and the fields not specified in the patch will remain untouched.

To illustrate, you can first create a file containing the patch information using the following:

```
$ cat > deploy-patch.json <<EOF
{
  "spec":{
    "template":{
      "spec":{
        "containers":[{
          "name":"nginx",
          "image":"nginx:alpine"
        }]
}}}}
EOF
```

Then, you can apply this patch to the resource with the following request:

Note the specific **Content-Type** header to use—**application/strategic-merge-patch+json**.

```
$ curl -X PATCH
  $HOST/apis/apps/v1/namespaces/project1/deployments/nginx
  -H
  "Content-Type: application/strategic-merge-patch+json"
  --data-binary @deploy-patch.json
```

This is equivalent to running the **kubectl** command:

```
$ kubectl patch deployment nginx --namespace project1
    --patch-file deploy-patch.json
    --type=strategic
    -o json
```

When a field is a single value (either a simple value like a string, or an object with several fields), the value of the patch replaces the existing value.

Note that if a field is not present in the patch, the original value will not be deleted but will remain untouched.You can specify a value of **null** for a field to delete it from the result.

Patching Array Fields

When a field contains an array of values, the behavior is different from the one for single values.

The default behavior depends on the *Patch strategy* defined for this field in the Kubernetes API specification. For example, you can see in Figure 2-1 that the **env** field of a **container** structure has a Patch strategy of *Merge* on the key **name**. Another possible value for the Patch strategy is *Replace*.

- **env** ([]EnvVar)

  Patch strategy: merge on key `name`

  List of environment variables to set in the container. Cannot be updated.

  EnvVar represents an environment variable present in a Container.

  - **env.name** (string), required

    Name of the environment variable. Must be a C_IDENTIFIER.

  - **env.value** (string)

Figure 2-1. Patch strategy of env field in a container

When the Patch strategy of a field is *Replace*, the resulting array is the one contained in the patch, and the values present in the original array are not considered.

When the Patch strategy of a field is *Merge* on a specific key, the original array and the patch array will be merged. The elements contained in the patch array, but not present in the original array, will be added to the result, and the elements present in both the original and patch arrays will pick up the value of the patch element (elements are the same in both the original and the patch if their *key* has the same value).

Note that the elements present in the original array, but not present in the patch, will remain untouched.

To illustrate, consider an existing deployment with a container that defines these environment variables, and a patch defining these values:

```
Original                Patch
env:                    env:
- name: key1            - name: key1
  value: value1           value: value1bis
- name: key2            - name: key3
  value: value2           value: value3
```

By applying the patch to the existing deployment, the resulting list of environment variables will be the following:

```
Result for Merge strategy
env:
- name: key1
  value: value1bis
- name: key2
  value: value2
- name: key3
  value: value3
```

Special Directives

It is possible to override these default behaviors by using special *Directives* in the patch information.

replace Directive

You can use a **replace** directive either for an object or for an array. When used with an object, the original object will be replaced with the patch object. This means that the fields not in the patch will not be, this time, present in the result; and the arrays of this object will be the exact same arrays of the patch, for which no merge operation will occur.

To declare this directive for an object, you need to add a field **$patch** with the value **replace** to the object. For example, the following patch will replace the **securityContext** for the **nginx** container with a **securityContext** containing only the field **runAsNonRoot**:

```
{
  "spec":{
    "template":{
      "spec":{
        "containers":[{
          "name":"nginx",
          "securityContext": {
            "$patch": "replace",
            "runAsNonRoot": false
}}]}}}}
```

When used with an array, the original array will be replaced by the patch array.

To declare this directive for an array, you need to add an object to this array with a single field **$patch** of value **replace**. For example, the following patch will set the environment variables for the container **nginx** to the single variable, **key1**, regardless of the number of variables defined previously.

```
{
  "spec":{
    "template":{
      "spec":{
        "containers":[{
          "name":"nginx",
          "env": [
            { "$patch": "replace"},
            { "name": "key1", "value": "value1" }
          ]
}]}}}}
```

delete Directive

You can use a **delete** directive either for an object or for an object element of an array. Using this directive for an object is like declaring the value of this object to **null**. For example, this patch will delete the field **securityContext** from the container **nginx**:

```
{
  "spec":{
    "template":{
      "spec":{
        "containers":[{
          "name":"nginx",
          "securityContext": {
            "$patch": "delete"
          }
}]}}}}
```

To delete an element from a list, you need to add the directive to the element you want to **delete**. You will need to indicate the key field (the key indicated for the **Merge** patch strategy). For example, you can use this patch to delete the environment variable named **key1**:

```
{
  "spec":{
    "template":{
      "spec":{
        "containers":[
        {
          "name":"nginx",
          "env": [{
              "name": "key1",
              "$patch": "delete"
          }]
}]}}}}
```

deleteFromPrimitiveList Directive

The **delete** directive is only usable for deleting objects from an array. You can use the **deleteFromPrimitiveList** directive to delete primitive elements from an array by prefixing the field name containing the array with **$deleteFromPrimitiveList/**. For example, to delete the **--debug** argument from a list of the **args** for the **nginx** container, you can use the following patch:

```
{
  "spec":{
    "template":{
      "spec":{
        "containers":[
        {
          "name":"nginx",
          "$deleteFromPrimitiveList/args": [
            "--debug"
          ]
}]}}}}
```

Note that this directive does not work correctly for Kubernetes 1.24 and earlier versions because it keeps the specified values only, instead keeping the other values only.

setElementOrder Directive

The **setElementOrder** directive can be used to sort elements of an array into a different order by prefixing the field name containing the array to sort with **$setElementOrder/**. For example, to reorder **initContainers** of a deployment, you can use this patch:

```
{
  "spec":{
    "template":{
      "spec":{
        "$setElementOrder/initContainers":[
```

```
        { "name": "init2"},
        { "name": "init1"}
    ]}}}}
```

Applying Resources Server-side

As you have seen in the previous sections, you can update resources, but in case of conflicts, you need to write specific directives to indicate how to resolve conflicts. The Kubernetes API has introduced the Server-side Apply as a Beta feature in Kubernetes 1.16, and it has been a stable feature since Kubernetes 1.22.

The Server-side Apply operation is like the **Update** command, with the difference that you can use this command even if the resource does not exist in the cluster, and you must provide a *field manager* when executing the command.

The Server-side Apply operation can be executed using a PATCH request with an **application/apply-patch+yaml** content-type and specifying the name (and namespace for namespaced resources) in the path and the patch information in the body of the request.

On its side, the Kubernetes API will save in a dedicated field (**.metadata.managedFields**) of the resource the list of Apply operations accomplished in this resource.

For each Apply operation saved, each field set by it is marked as "owned" by the field manager provided during the operation. If an Apply operation updates a field that is owned by another field manager, because of a previous Apply operation covering this field, a *conflict* is raised.

It is possible to *force* an Apply operation so that the conflicting fields are established with the new value and the ownership is transferred to the new field manager for them. The ownership is set in objects or primitive elements, as well as in the elements of arrays.

For example, a field manager can define a set of environment variables for a container, and another field manager can define a distinct set of environment variables for the same container of a Pod. Each field manager owns its environment variables. If the first field manager runs a new Apply operation by removing some of its environment variables, these will be removed from the total list, but environment variables of the other field manager will not be affected.

To illustrate this example, you can create the following YAML manifest for a Deployment that defines three environment variables for the Pod's container:

```
# deploy.yaml
apiVersion: apps/v1
kind: Deployment
metadata:
  name: nginx
spec:
  selector:
    matchLabels:
      app: nginx
  template:
    metadata:
      labels:
        app: nginx
    spec:
      containers:
      - image: nginx
        name: nginx
        env:
        - name: key1
          value: value1
        - name: key2
          value: value2
        - name: key3
          value: value3
```

Then, you can apply this manifest by using the Server-side Apply operation (note the content-type header is set to **application/apply-patch+yaml** and the query parameter **fieldManager** is set to **manager1**):

```
$ curl -X PATCH
$HOST/apis/apps/v1/namespaces/project1/deployments/
nginx?fieldManager=manager1
 -H
 "Content-Type: application/apply-patch+yaml"
 --data-binary @deploy.yaml
```

This command will create the Deployment. You can examine the **.metadata. managedFields** of the Deployment resource created with this command (**jq** is used to get an indented form of the JSON):

```
$ kubectl get deploy nginx -o jsonpath={.metadata.managedFields} | jq
[{
  "apiVersion": "apps/v1",
  "fieldsType": "FieldsV1",
  "fieldsV1": {
    "f:spec": {
      "f:template": {
        "f:spec": {
          "f:containers": {
            "k:{\"name\":\"nginx\"}": {
              ".": {},          ❶
              "f:image": {}, ❷
              "f:name": {}    ❸
              "f:env": {
                "k:{\"name\":\"key1\"}": {
                  ".": {}, "f:name": {}, "f:value": {} ❹
                },
                "k:{\"name\":\"key2\"}": {
                  ".": {}, "f:name": {}, "f:value": {} ❺
                },
                "k:{\"name\":\"key3\"}": {
                  ".": {}, "f:name": {}, "f:value": {} ❻
  }}}}}}}},
  "manager": "manager1",  ❼
  "operation": "Apply",    ❽
  "time": "2022-07-14T16:46:48Z"
},
{
  "apiVersion": "apps/v1",
  "fieldsType": "FieldsV1",
  "fieldsV1": {
    "f:status": {
```

```
      "f:availableReplicas": {},
      "f:observedGeneration": {},
      "f:readyReplicas": {},
      "f:replicas": {},
      "f:updatedReplicas": {}
    }
  },
  "manager": "kube-controller-manager",  ❾
  "operation": "Update",                  ❿
  "subresource": "status",
  "time": "2022-07-14T16:46:52Z"
}]
```

You can see in the **managedFields** (abbreviated for clarity) that your operation has been saved as an **Apply** operation, ❽, by the manager, **manager1** ❼; and that this manager owns the element of **container** with the name **nginx** ❶—the fields **image** ❷, **name** ❸, and the elements of **env** with name **key1** ❹, **key2** ❺, and **key3** ❻.

A *Manager* is any program used to edit a resource; for example, **kubectl** when used with an edit or apply command, or a controller or operator managing these resources. You also can see that a second operation of type Update ❿ has been saved and is owned by the **kube-controller-manager** ❾ because the Deployment controller set some values in the status of the Deployment resource when you created it.

Now, a second manager, **manager2**, would like to update the environment variable, **key2**. It can do so by creating the following and running the command (note that the **force** query parameter is set to **true**):

```
-- patch.yaml
apiVersion: apps/v1
kind: Deployment
metadata:
  name: nginx
spec:
  template:
    spec:
      containers:
        - name: nginx
```

```
        env:
        - name: key2
          value: value2bis
```

```
$ curl -X PATCH
"$HOST/apis/apps/v1/namespaces/project1/deployments/nginx?fieldManager=mana
ger2&force=true"
 -H "Content-Type: application/apply-patch+yaml"
 --data-binary @patch.yaml
```

With this operation, **manager2** ❸ now owns the **nginx** element of **container** ❶ and the **key2** element of **env** ❷.

```
{
  "apiVersion": "apps/v1",
  "fieldsType": "FieldsV1",
  "fieldsV1": {
    "f:spec": {
      "f:template": {
        "f:spec": {
          "f:containers": {
            "k:{\"name\":\"nginx\"}": {
              ".": {}, ❶
              "f:env": {
                "k:{\"name\":\"key2\"}": {
                  ".": {}, "f:name": {}, "f:value": {} ❷
                }
              },
              "f:name": {}
  }}}}}},
  "manager": "manager2", ❸
  "operation": "Apply",
  "time": "2022-06-15T17:21:16Z"
},
```

Finally, the first manager, **manager1**, decides to keep only the **key1** environment variable, removing the environment variables **key2** and **key3** from the initial manifest. For this, it will create the following patch and run the command (note that the **force** query parameter is not specified):

```
-- patch2.yaml
apiVersion: apps/v1
kind: Deployment
metadata:
  name: nginx
spec:
  selector:
    matchLabels:
      app: nginx
  template:
    metadata:
      labels:
        app: nginx
    spec:
      containers:
      - image: nginx
        name: nginx
        env:
        - name: key1
          value: value1
```

```
$ curl -X PATCH
"$HOST/apis/apps/v1/namespaces/project1/deployments/
nginx?fieldManager=manager1"
 -H "Content-Type: application/apply-patch+yaml"
 --data-binary @patch2.yaml
```

You can see in the resulting deployment that the following is true:

- The **key2** is still present because it is owned by **manager2**.

- The **key3** is not present anymore because it was owned by **manager1**.

```
$ kubectl get deployments.apps nginx -o yaml
[...]
    spec:
      containers:
      - env:
        - name: key1
          value: value1
        - name: key2
          value: value2bis
        image: nginx
        name: nginx
[...]
```

Watching Resources

The Kubernetes API lets you *watch* resources. This means that your request will not terminate immediately, but it will instead be a long-running request that will send a JSON stream as a response, adding JSON objects to the stream when the watched resources change. A JSON stream is a series of JSON objects separated by new lines—for example:

```
{ "type": "ADDED", "object": ... }
{ "type": "DELETED", "object": ... }
```

The request for watching resources is like the one used to list resources with a **watch** parameter added as a **query** parameter. For example, to watch the pods of the **project1** namespace, you can send this request:

```
$ curl "$HOST/api/v1/namespaces/project1/pods?watch=true"
```

Each JSON object of the stream is called, in Kubernetes terminology, a *Watch Event*, and it will contain two fields: **type** and **object**. The value for the **type** can be **ADDED, MODIFIED, DELETED, BOOKMARK,** or **ERROR**. For each type, the object is as described in Table 2-2.

Table 2-2. *Object Description for Each Type of Watch Event*

Type value	Object description
ADDEDMODIFIED	The new state of the resource, using its kind (e.g., **Pod**).
DELETED	The state of the resource immediately before it is deleted, using its kind (e.g., **Pod**).
BOOKMARK	The resource version, using its kind (e.g., **Pod**), with only the resourceVersion field set. Later in this chapter, you will see in which circumstances this type is used.
ERROR	An object that describes the error.

When this request is executed, you will immediately get a series of **ADDED** JSON objects, describing all the resources present in the cluster at the time of the request; eventually, this is followed by other events when the resources are created, modified, or deleted in the cluster. This is equivalent to running the **kubectl** command, with the difference that the **type** field will not be given and the object's content will be given directly:

```
$ kubectl get pods --namespace project1 --watch -o json
```

Filtering During a Watch Session

It is possible to filter the results returned by a *watch* request by using either label selectors or field selectors, using the same **labelSelectors** and **fieldSelectors** as discussed earlier in the Filtering the Result of a List section.

Watching After Listing Resources

Instead of getting the resources present at the time of the request as part of the *watch* response, you could first run a *list* request to find the list of present resources, then run a *watch* request to obtain the modifications on these resources. By doing this, there is a risk that some modifications may happen between the *list* request and the start of the *watch* request, and that you do not get informed about these modifications.

For this scenario, you can use the **resourceVersion** value returned by the *list* request to indicate at which point in time you want to start your *watch* request. (Note: You need to get the **resourceVersion** into the *List* structure, not from an item.)

As an example, you can first get the list of pods by using the command:

```
$ curl $HOST/api/v1/pods
{
  "kind": "PodList",
  "apiVersion": "v1",
  "metadata": {
    "resourceVersion": "2433789"
  },
  "items": [ ... ]
}
```

As a response to this first request, you get a **resourceVersion** and a list of resources present at the time of the request in the **items** field. Then, you can execute the *watch* request by specifying this **resourceVersion**:

```
$ curl "$HOST/api/v1/namespaces/default/pods?watch=true&resourceVersio
n=2433789"
```

As a result, you will not receive data immediately in the response body that describes the resources present in the cluster; you will receive data only when some resources are modified, added, or deleted.

Restarting a *watch* Request

The *watch* request may be interrupted, and you may want to restart it from the last modification received (or a previous one) during the process.

For this, each resource part of a **DELETE, ADDED,** or **MODIFIED** JSON object in the *watch* response contains a **resourceVersion**, and you can use this to execute a new *watch* request starting just after the specified modification. For example, you can start a *watch* request that is interrupted after a few modifications:

```
$ curl "$HOST/api/v1/namespaces/default/pods?watch=true"
{"type":"ADDED","object":{
  "kind":"Pod","apiVersion":"v1","metadata":{
```

```
    "resourceVersion":"2435623", ...}, ...}}
{"type":"ADDED","object":{
  "kind":"Pod","apiVersion":"v1","metadata":{
    "resourceVersion":"2354893", ...}, ...}}
{"type":"MODIFIED","object":{
  "kind":"Pod","apiVersion":"v1","metadata":{
    "resourceVersion":"2436655", ...}, ...}}
{"type":"DELETED","object":{
  "kind":"Pod","apiVersion":"v1","metadata":{
    "resourceVersion":"2436677", ...}, ...}}
```

Then, you can restart the *watch* request by beginning at any time during the previous request or starting after the latest modification:

```
$ curl "$HOST/api/v1/namespaces/default/pods?watch=true&resourceVersio
n=2436677"
```

Or begin after a previous modification. In this way, you will receive the latest modification again:

```
$ curl "$HOST/api/v1/namespaces/default/pods?watch=true&resourceVersio
n=2436655"
{"type":"DELETED","object":{
  "kind":"Pod","apiVersion":"v1","metadata":{
    "resourceVersion":"2436677", ...}, ...}}
```

Allowing Bookmarks to Efficiently Restart a *watch* Request

As a previous section has shown, it is possible to execute a *watch* session on a subset of resources by using label or field selectors. For example, this request will watch pods with a specific label, **mylabel**, being equal to **foo**:

```
$ curl "$HOST/api/v1/namespaces/project1/pods?
labelSelector=mylabel==foo&watch=true"
```

With this request, you will get events for pods matching your selectors only, not for other pods of the same namespace that do not match your request.

47

When restarting a *watch* request, you will be able to use the **resourceVersion** of a pod that matches the selectors; however, lots of events on other pods could have happened after this one. The API server will have to execute the filtering of all pods' events that have been created in the meantime at the point where you restart the watch on this *old* **resourceVersion**.

Likewise, because the API server is caching these events for a limited time, there is more risk that the old **resourceVersion** is no longer available, compared to the most recent.

For this, you can use the **allowWatchBookmarks** parameter to ask the API server to send **BOOKMARK** events regularly that contain the latest **resourceVersion**; these may be resource versions that are separate from your selection.

The **BOOKMARK** event may contain an object of the kind of your request (e.g., a Pod kind if you are watching for pods), but that includes only the **resourceVersion** field.

```
{"type":"BOOKMARK",
  "object":{
    "kind":"Pod",
    "apiVersion":"v1",
    "metadata":{
      "resourceVersion":"2525115",
      "creationTimestamp":null
    },
    "spec":{
      "containers":null
    },
    "status":{}
  }
}
```

To illustrate, here is a little experiment. First create two (2) pods and watch pods with a selector that will only match the first one. You will get an **ADDED** event for the matching pod, and, after a while, you should get a **BOOKMARK** event (but it is not guaranteed). If, in the meantime, there was no activity on the pods of the namespace, the **resourceVersion** should be the same.

```
$ kubectl run nginx1 --image nginx --labels mylabel=foo
$ kubectl run nginx2 --image nginx --labels mylabel=bar
```

```
$ curl "$HOST/api/v1/namespaces/default/pods?
  labelSelector=mylabel==foo&
  watch=true&
  allowWatchBookmarks=true"
{"type":"ADDED","object":{
  "kind":"Pod","apiVersion":"v1","metadata":{
    "name":"nginx1","resourceVersion":"2520070", ...}, ...}}
{"type":"BOOKMARK","object":{
  "kind":"Pod","apiVersion":"v1","metadata":{
  "resourceVersion":"2520070", ...}, ...}}
```

From another terminal, let's delete the nonmatching pod, **nginx2**, with the command:

```
$ kubectl delete pods nginx2
```

You should not receive any event for this change because the pod does not match the request selector, but after a while, you should receive a new **BOOKMARK** event—this time with a new **resourceVersion**:

```
{"type":"BOOKMARK","object":{
  "kind":"Pod","apiVersion":"v1","metadata":{
  "resourceVersion":"2532566", ...}, ...}}
```

At this point, you can stop the *watch* request from your first terminal.

Next, you can make some modifications on the pods of the namespace—for example, by deleting the **nginx1** pod and recreating the **nginx2** pod:

```
$ kubectl delete pods nginx1
$ kubectl run nginx2 --image nginx --labels mylabel=bar
```

Now, you can restart the *watch* request using the **resourceVersion, 2532566**, to restart the request when it has stopped:

```
curl "$HOST/api/v1/namespaces/default/pods?
  labelSelector=mylabel==foo&
  watch=true&
  allowWatchBookmarks=true&
  resourceVersion=2532566"
```

As a result, you can see that you are getting events for the modifications and deletion of **nginx1** sent when you deleted this pod. You have not lost any event, and you have used a most recent **resourceVersion**, which is more efficient for the API Server.

Paginating Results

When you execute a *list* request, it is possible that the result will contain many elements. In this case, it is preferable to paginate the result by making several requests, and each response will send a limited number of elements.

For this case, the **limit** and **continue** query parameters are used. The first *list* request needs to specify the **limit** parameter to indicate the maximum number of elements to return. The response will contain a **continue** field in the metadata of the **List** structure that contains an opaque token to use in the next request to obtain the next chunk of elements.

```
$ curl "$HOST/api/v1/pods?limit=1"
{
  "kind": "PodList",
  "apiVersion": "v1",
  "metadata": {
    "resourceVersion": "2931316",
    "continue": <continue_token_1>,
    "remainingItemCount": 10
  },
  "items": [{ ... }]
}

$ curl "$HOST/api/v1/pods?limit=1&continue=<continue_token_1>"
{
  "kind": "PodList",
  "apiVersion": "v1",
  "metadata": {
    "resourceVersion": "2931316",
    "continue": <continue_token_2>,
    "remainingItemCount": 9
  },
  "items": [{ ... }]
}
```

Note that you do not need to use the same **limit** value for each chunk. You could make the first request with a limit of **1**, the second one with a limit of **4**, and the third one with a limit of **6**.

Consistency of the Full List

Note that the **resourceVersion** in the *List* structures in both responses are the same (i.e., **"resourceVersion": "2931316"** in the example). When you run the first request, the full response is cached on the server, and you are guaranteed to get a consistent result for the next chunks, independent of the time you get to make the following requests, as well as the modifications made on the resources in the meantime. The resources created, modified, or deleted in the period in-between will not affect the results of the next chunks.

Nevertheless, it is possible that the cache will expire before you can run all the requests. In this case, you will receive an error response with a code **410** and a new **continue** value. Thus, you have two choices:

1. Start a new *List* request without the **continue** parameter to restart the complete list session from the beginning.

2. Make a new request with the returned **continue** value, but in an inconsistent way—that is, the resources added, modified, or deleted since the time the first chunk was returned will influence the responses.

Detecting the Last Chunk

You can see from the metadata of the response that the **remainingItemCount** indicates the number of elements remaining to complete the full response. Note, however, that this information is available only for requests without selectors (either *labels* or *fields* selectors).

When running a paginated *List* request without selectors, the server can know the number of elements in the full list and is able to indicate the number of remaining elements after each request. The server also is able to indicate, when sending the last elements of the full list, that this is the last chunk, by replying with an empty **continue** field in the metadata of the *List* structure.

When running a paginated *List* request with selectors, the server is unable to know in advance the number of elements in the full list. For this reason, it does not send the number of remaining elements after a request, and it sends a **continue** nonempty value even if it happens that the next chunk is empty.

You will need to check whether the returned list is empty or contains less elements than requested in the **limit** field so that you can detect the last chunk.

Getting Results in Various Formats

The Kubernetes API can return the data in various formats. You can ask which format you wish to receive by specifying the **Accept** header in the HTTP request.

Getting Results as a Table

The **kubectl** client (and other clients) displays lists of resources in a tabular format. When running a *List* request, you can ask the API Server to give you the necessary information to build this tabular representation by using the **Accept** header to indicate this specific format:

```
$ curl $HOST/api/v1/pods
-H 'Accept: application/json;as=Table;g=meta.k8s.io;v=v1'
{
  "kind": "Table",
  "apiVersion": "meta.k8s.io/v1",
  "metadata": {
    "resourceVersion": "2995797"
  },
  "columnDefinitions": [ { ... }, { ... }, { ... } ],
  "rows": [ { ... }, { ... } ]
}
```

This helps clients display information in a tabular format for any resource, including custom resources, because a custom resource definition will contain information about which field of the resource to display in which column.

The *kind* of the response will always be **Table** for any resource requested. A first field, **columnDefinitions**, describes each column of the table and a second field, **rows**, gives the column values for each resource of the result.

Column Definitions

A column definition includes the **name**, **type**, **format**, **description,** and **priority** fields. The **name** is intended to be the title of the column. The **type** is an OpenAPI type definition for this column (e.g., **integer**, **number**, **string**, or **boolean**).

The optional **format** is an OpenAPI modifier for the type of the columns, giving more information on the formatting. Formats for **integer** type are **int32** and **int64**, formats for **number** type are **float** and **double**, and formats for **string** type are **byte**, **binary**, **data**, **date-time**, **password**. and **name**. The **name** format value is not part of the OpenAPI specification and is specific to the Kubernetes API. It indicates to the client the primary column that contains the resource name.

The **priority** field is an integer indicating the importance of a column relative to the other ones. Columns with higher values may be omitted when space is limited.

Row Data

A row includes the **cells**, **conditions**, and **object** fields.

The **cells** field is an array the same length of the **columnDefinitions** array and contains values for the resource displayed in the current row. The JSON type and optional format of each element of the array are inferred from the **type** and **format** of the corresponding column definition.

The **conditions** field gives specific attributes for displaying the row. The only defined value as of Kubernetes 1.23 is `'Completed'`, indicating the resource displayed in the row has run to completion and can be given less visual priority.

The object **field** contains, by default, the metadata of the resource displayed in this column. You can add an **includeObject** query parameter to the *List* request to either require no information about the object (**?includeObject=None**), or the complete object (**?includeObject=Object**). The default value for this query parameter is **Metadata**, which requires metadata of the resource only. For example, use the following to return no object information as part of the row data:

```
$ curl $HOST/api/v1/pods?includeObject=None
-H 'Accept: application/json;as=Table;g=meta.k8s.io;v=v1'
```

Using the YAML Format

Earlier in the Creating a Resource section you saw that it is possible to use the YAML format to describe the resource to create using the **Content-Type: application/yaml** header. If you do not specify this header, you will need to describe the resource in the JSON format.

It also is possible to obtain the response of requests in YAML format using the **Accept: application/yaml** header. This is valid for *Get* and *List* requests, but also can be used for requests creating or updating resources that return the new value of them. For example, to get the list of all pods in YAML format use this:

```
$ curl $HOST/api/v1/pods -H 'Accept: application/yaml'
kind: PodList
metadata:
  resourceVersion: "3009983"
items:
  [...]
```

Or, to create a new Pod and get the created Pod in YAML format, use the following:

```
$ curl $HOST/api/v1/namespaces/default/pods
    -H "Content-Type: application/yaml"
    -H 'Accept: application/yaml'
    --data-binary @pod.yaml
```

Note that it is not possible to get the result of a *Watch* request in the YAML format.

Using the Protobuf Format

The Protobuf format also can be used to send data to the API Server or to receive data from it. For this, you need to use the type **application/vnd.kubernetes.protobuf** for the **Content-Type** or **Accept**.

The Kubernetes team discourages the use of the Protobuf format outside of the Kubernetes control plane because they do not guarantee that the Protobuf messages will be as stable as the JSON messages.

If you decide to use the Protobuf format, you need to know that the API Server does not exchange pure Protobuf data, but it adds a header to it to check the compatibility between Kubernetes versions.

The apimachinery library contains Go code to help developers serialize data in various formats, including Protobuf. Chapter 5 describes how to use this library.

Conclusion

This chapter has discussed how to run kubectl to help understand the HTTP requests executed underneath it. Then, it has shown how to create, update, apply, delete, get, list, and watch resources in detail using various HTTP operations. To finish, the chapter has described how to get the results of these operations in several formats: JSON, YAML, and Protobuf, or as a Table.

CHAPTER 3

Working with API Resources in Go

The first two chapters of this book have described how the Kubernetes API is designed, and how to access it using HTTP requests. Specifically, you have seen that resources managed by the API are organized into **Group-Version-Resource**s, and that objects exchanged between the client and the API Server are defined as *Kinds* by the Kubernetes API. The chapter also shows that this data can be encoded in JSON, YAML, or Protobuf during the exchange, depending on the HTTP headers the client has set.

In the next chapters, you will see how to access this API using the Go language. The two important Go libraries needed to work with the Kubernetes API are the apimachinery and the api.

The API Machinery is a generic library that takes care of serializing data between Go structures and objects written in the JSON (or YAML or Protobuf) format. This makes it possible for developers of clients, but also API Servers, to write data using Go structures and transparently use these resources in JSON (or YAML or Protobuf) during the HTTP exchanges.

The API Machinery Library is generic in the sense that it does not include any Kubernetes API resource definitions. It makes the Kubernetes API extendable and makes the API Machinery usable for any other API that would use the same mechanisms—that is, *Kind*s and **Group-Version-Resource**s.

The API Library, for its part, is a collection of Go structures that are needed to work in Go with the resources defined by the Kubernetes API.

API Library Sources and Import

The sources of the API Library can be accessed from `https://github.com/kubernetes/api`. If you want to contribute to this library, note that the sources are not managed from

57

© Philippe Martin 2023
P. Martin, *Kubernetes Programming with Go*, https://doi.org/10.1007/978-1-4842-9026-2_3

this repository, but from the central one, https://github.com/kubernetes/kubernetes, in the **staging/src/k8s.io/api** directory, and the sources are synchronized from the **kubernetes** repository to the **api** repository.

To import packages of the API Library into the Go sources, you will need to use the **k8s.io/api** prefix—for example:

```
import "k8s.io/api/core/v1"
```

The packages into the API Library follow the **Group-Version-Resource** structure of the API. When you want to use structures for a given resource, you need to import the package related to the *group* and *version* of the resource by using this pattern:

```
import "k8s.io/api/<group>/<version>"
```

Content of a Package

Let's examine the files included in a package—for example, the **k8s.io/api/apps/v1** package.

types.go

This file can be considered the main file of the package because it defines all the *Kind* structures and other related substructures. It also defines all the types and constants for enumeration fields found in these structures. As an example, consider the **Deployment** *Kind*; the **Deployment** structure is first defined as follows:

```
type Deployment struct {
    metav1.TypeMeta
    metav1.ObjectMeta
    Spec        DeploymentSpec
    Status      DeploymentStatus
}
```

Then, the related substructures, **DeploymentSpec** and **DeploymentStatus,** are defined using this:

```
type DeploymentSpec struct {
```

```
    Replicas        *int32
    Selector        *metav1.LabelSelector
    Template        v1.PodTemplateSpec
    Strategy        DeploymentStrategy
    [...]
}

type DeploymentStatus struct {
    ObservedGeneration      int64
    Replicas                int32
    [...]
    Conditions              []DeploymentCondition
}
```

Then, continue in the same way for every structure used as a type in a previous structure.

The **DeploymentConditionType** type, used in the **DeploymentCondition** structure (not represented here), is defined, along with the possible values for this enumeration:

```
type DeploymentConditionType string

const (
    DeploymentAvailable DeploymentConditionType = "Available"
    DeploymentProgressing DeploymentConditionType = "Progressing"
    DeploymentReplicaFailure DeploymentConditionType = "ReplicaFailure"
)
```

You can see that every *Kind* embeds two structures: **metav1.TypeMeta** and **metav1.ObjectMeta**. It is mandatory for them to be recognized by the API Machinery. The **TypeMeta** structure contains information about the GVK of the *Kind*, and the **ObjectMeta** contains metadata for the *Kind*, like its name.

register.go

This file defines the group and version related to this package and the list of *Kinds* in this group and version. The public variable, **SchemeGroupVersion**, can be used when you need to specify the group and version of a resource from this group-version.

It also declares a function, **AddToScheme**, that can be used to add the group, version, and *Kinds* to a *Scheme*. The *Scheme* is an abstraction used in the API Machinery to create a mapping between Go structures and **Group-Version-Kinds**. This will be discussed further in Chapter 5, The API Machinery.

doc.go

This file and the following ones contain advanced information that you will not need to comprehend to start writing your first Kubernetes resources in Go, but they will help you understand how to declare new resources with Custom Resource Definitions in the next chapters.

The **doc.go** file contains the following instructions to generate files:

```
// +k8s:deepcopy-gen=package
// +k8s:protobuf-gen=package
// +k8s:openapi-gen=true
```

The first instruction is used by the **deepcopy-gen** generator to generate the **zz_generated.deepcopy.go** file. The second instruction is used by the **go-to-protobuf** generator to generate these files: **generated.pb.go** and **generated.proto**. The third instruction is used by the **genswaggertypedocs** generator to generate the **types_swagger_doc_generated.go** file.

generated.pb.go and generated.proto

These files are generated by the **go-to-protobuf** generator. They are used by the API Machinery when serializing the data to and from the Protobuf format.

types_swagger_doc_generated.go

This file is generated by the **genswaggertypedocs** generator. It is used during the generation of the complete **swagger** definition of the Kubernetes API.

zz_generated.deepcopy.go

This file is generated by the **deepcopy-gen** generator. It contains the generated definition of the **DeepCopyObject** method for each type defined in the package. This method is necessary for the structures to implement the **runtime.Object** interface, which is defined in the API Machinery Library, and the API Machinery expects that all *Kind* structures will implement this **runtime.Object** interface.

The interface is defined in this file as follows:

```
type Object interface {
    GetObjectKind() schema.ObjectKind
    DeepCopyObject() Object
}
```

The other necessary method, **GetObjectKind**, is automatically added to structures that embed the **TypeMeta** structure—this is the case for all *Kind* structures. The **TypeMeta** structure has the method that is defined as follows:

```
func (obj *TypeMeta) GetObjectKind() schema.ObjectKind {
  return obj
}
```

Specific Content in core/v1

The **core/v1** package defines, in addition to defining the structures for the Core resources, utility methods for specific types that can be useful when you incorporate these types into your code.

ObjectReference

An **ObjectReference** can be used to refer to any object in a unique way. The structure is defined as follows:

```
type ObjectReference struct {
    APIVersion          string
    Kind                string
    Namespace           string
```

```
    Name                string
    UID                 types.UID
    ResourceVersion     string
    FieldPath           string
}
```

Three methods are defined for this type:

- `SetGroupVersionKind(gvk schema.GroupVersionKind)` – this method will set the fields **APIVersion** and **Kind** based on the values of the **GroupVersionKind** value passed as a parameter.

- `GroupVersionKind() schema.GroupVersionKind` – this method will return a **GroupVersionKind** value based on the fields **APIVersion** and **Kind** of the **ObjectReference**.

- `GetObjectKind() schema.ObjectKind` – this method will cast the **ObjectReference** object as an **ObjectKind**. The two previous methods implement this **ObjectKind** interface. Because the **DeepCopyObject** method on **ObjectReference** also is defined, the **ObjectReference** will respect the **runtime.Object** interface.

ResourceList

The **ResourceList** type is defined as a map, the keys of which are **ResourceName**, and values are **Quantity**. This is used in various Kubernetes resources to define the **limits** and **requests** of **resources**.

In YAML, an example of usage is when you are defining the **requests** and **limits** of **resources** for a container, as follows:

```
apiVersion: v1
kind: Pod
metadata:
  name: mypod
spec:
  containers:
  - name: runtime
    resources:
```

```
    requests:
      memory: "64Mi"
      cpu: "250m"
    limits:
      memory: "128Mi"
      cpu: "500m"
```

In Go, you can write the **requests** part as:

```
requests := corev1.ResourceList{
    corev1.ResourceMemory:
        *resource.NewQuantity(64*1024*1024, resource.BinarySI),
    corev1.ResourceCPU:
        *resource.NewMilliQuantity(250, resource.DecimalSI),
}
```

The next chapter describes, in more detail, how to define quantities using the **resource.Quantity** type. The following methods exist for the **ResourceList** type:

- `Cpu() *resource.Quantity` – returns the quantity for the CPU key of the map, in decimal format (1, 250 m, etc.)

- `Memory() *resource.Quantity` – returns the quantity for the **Memory** key of the map, in binary format (512 Ki, 64 Mi, etc.)

- `Storage() *resource.Quantity` – returns the quantity for the **Storage** key of the map, in binary format (512 Mi, 1 Gi, etc.)

- `Pods() *resource.Quantity` – returns the quantity for the **Pods** key of the map, in decimal format (1, 10, etc.)

- `StorageEphemeral() *resource.Quantity` – returns the quantity for the **StorageEphemeral** key in the map, in binary format (512 Mi, 1 Gi, etc.)

For each of these methods, if the key is not defined in the map, a **Quantity** with a **Zero** value will be returned.

Another method, internally used by the previous ones, could be employed to get quantities in nonstandard format:

- Name(name ResourceName, defaultFormat resource.Format) *resource.Quantity – this returns the quantity for the *Name* key, in *defaultFormat* format.

  The defined enumeration values for the ResourceName type are ResourceCPU, ResourceMemory, ResourceStorage, ResourceEphemeralStorage, and ResourcePods.

Taint

The **Taint** resource is meant to be applied to Nodes to ensure that pods that do not tolerate these taints are not scheduled to these nodes. The **Taint** structure is defined as follows:

```
type Taint struct {
    Key          string
    Value        string
    Effect       TaintEffect
    TimeAdded    *metav1.Time
}
```

The **TaintEffect** enumeration can get the following values:

```
TaintEffectNoSchedule         = "NoSchedule"
TaintEffectPreferNoSchedule   = "PreferNoSchedule"
TaintEffectNoExecute          = "NoExecute"
```

The well-known **Taint** keys, used by the control-plane under special conditions, are defined as follows in this package:

```
TaintNodeNotReady
    = "node.kubernetes.io/not-ready"
TaintNodeUnreachable
    = "node.kubernetes.io/unreachable"
TaintNodeUnschedulable
    = "node.kubernetes.io/unschedulable"
TaintNodeMemoryPressure
    = "node.kubernetes.io/memory-pressure"
TaintNodeDiskPressure
```

```
                    = "node.kubernetes.io/disk-pressure"
TaintNodeNetworkUnavailable
    ="node.kubernetes.io/network-unavailable"
TaintNodePIDPressure
    = "node.kubernetes.io/pid-pressure"
TaintNodeOutOfService
    = "node.kubernetes.io/out-of-service"
```

The following two methods are defined on a **Taint**:

- `MatchTaint(taintToMatch *Taint) bool` – this method will return true if the two taints have the same **key** and **effect** values.

- `ToString() string` – this method will return a **string** representation of the **Taint** in this format: **<key>=<value>:<effect>**, **<key>=<value>:**, **<key>:<effect>**, or **<key>**.

Toleration

The **Toleration** resource is intended to be applied to Pods to make it tolerate taints in specific nodes. The **Toleration** structure is defined as follows:

```
type Toleration struct {
    Key                 string
    Operator            TolerationOperator
    Value               string
    Effect              TaintEffect
    TolerationSeconds   *int64
}
```

The **TolerationOperator** enumeration can get the following values:

```
TolerationOpExists    = "Exists"
TolerationOpEqual     = "Equal"
```

The **TaintEffect** enumeration can get these values:

```
TaintEffectNoSchedule           = "NoSchedule"
TaintEffectPreferNoSchedule     = "PreferNoSchedule"
TaintEffectNoExecute            = "NoExecute"
```

The following two methods are defined on a **Toleration** structure:

- `MatchToleration(tolerationToMatch *Toleration) bool` – this method returns true if the two tolerations have the same values for Key, Operator, Value, and Effect.

- `ToleratesTaint(taint *Taint) bool` – this method returns true if the toleration tolerates the **Taint**. The rules for a toleration to tolerate a taint are as follows:

  - **Effect**: For an empty **Toleration** effect, all Taint effects will match; otherwise, Toleration and Taint effects must match.

  - **Operator**: If **TolerationOperator** is **Exists**, all Taint values will match; otherwise, **TolerationOperator** is **Equal** and Toleration and Taint values must match.

  - **Key**: For an empty Toleration Key, **TolerationOperator** must be **Exists**, and all Taint keys (with any value) will match; otherwise, Toleration and Taint keys must match.

Well-Known Labels

The control-plane adds labels on nodes; well-known keys that are used and their usage can be found in the file **well_known_labels.go** of the **core/v1** package. The following are the most well-known.

The kubelet running on the node populates these labels:

```
LabelOSStable       = "kubernetes.io/os"
LabelArchStable     = "kubernetes.io/arch"
LabelHostname       = "kubernetes.io/hostname"
```

When the node is running on a cloud provider, these labels can be set, representing the instance type of the (virtual) machine, its zone, and its region:

```
LabelInstanceTypeStable
    = "node.kubernetes.io/instance-type"
LabelTopologyZone
```

```
    = "topology.kubernetes.io/zone"
LabelTopologyRegion
    = "topology.kubernetes.io/region"
```

Writing Kubernetes Resources in Go

You will need to write Kubernetes resources in Go to create or update resources into the cluster, either using an HTTP request or, more generally, using the client-go library. The client-go library is discussed in a future chapter; but for now, let's focus on writing the resources in Go.

To create or update a resource, you will need to create the structure for the *Kind* associated with the resource. For example, to create a *deployment*, you will need to create a **Deployment** kind; and for this, initiate a **Deployment** structure, which is defined in the **apps/v1** package of the API Library.

Importing the Package

Before you can work with the structure, you need to import the package that defines this structure. As was seen at the beginning of the chapter, the pattern for the package name is **k8s.io/api/<group>/<version>**. The last part of the path is a version number, but you should not confuse it with a version number of a Go module.

The difference is that when you are importing a specific version of a Go module (e.g., **k8s.io/klog/v2**), you will use the part before the version as a prefix to access symbols of the package, without defining any aliases. The reason is that in the library, the **v2** directory does not exist but represents a branch name, and the files going into the package start with the line **package klog**, not **package v2**.

On the contrary, when working with the Kubernetes API Library, the version number is the real name of a package in it, and the files into this package really start with **package v1**.

If you do not define an alias for the import, you would have to use the version name to use symbols from this package. But the version number alone is not meaningful when reading the code, and if you include several packages from the same file, you would end up with several **v1** package names, which is not possible.

The convention is to define an alias with the group name or, if you want to work with several versions of a same group, or if you want to make it clearer that the alias refers to an API group/version, you can create an alias with the group/version:

```
import (
    corev1 "k8s.io/api/core/v1"
    appsv1 "k8s.io/api/apps/v1"
)
```

You can now instantiate a **Deployment** structure:

```
myDep := appsv1.Deployment{}
```

To compile your program, you will need to fetch the library. For this, use:

```
$ go get k8s.io/api@latest
```

Or, if you want to use a specific version of the Kubernetes API (e.g., Kubernetes 1.23) use:

```
$ go get k8s.io/api@v0.23
```

All structures related to *Kinds* first embed two generic structures: **TypeMeta** and **ObjectMeta**. Both are declared in the **/pkg/apis/meta/v1** package of the API machinery library.

The TypeMeta Fields

The **TypeMeta** structure is defined as follows:

```
type TypeMeta struct {
    Kind            string
    APIVersion      string
}
```

You generally will not have to set values for these fields yourself because the API Machinery infers these values from the type of the structure by maintaining a *Scheme*— that is, a mapping between Group-Version-Kinds and Go structures. Note that the **APIVersion** value is another way to write the Group-Version as a single field that contains **<group>/<version>** (or only **v1** for the legacy core group).

The ObjectMeta Fields

The **ObjectMeta** structure is defined as follows (deprecated fields as well as internal fields have been removed):

```
Type ObjectMeta {
    Name                string
    GenerateName        string
    Namespace           string
    UID                 types.UID
    ResourceVersion     string
    Generation          int64
    Labels              map[string]string
    Annotations         map[string]string
    OwnerReferences     []OwnerReference
    [...]
}
```

The package **/pkg/apis/meta/v1** of the API Machinery Library defines Getters and Setters for fields of this structure. As the **ObjectMeta** is embedded in the resource structures, you can use these methods in the resources objects themselves.

Name

The most important information of this structure is the name of the resource. You can either use the **Name** field to specify the exact name of the resource or use the **GenerateName** field to request that the Kubernetes API selects a unique name for you; it is built by adding a suffix to the **GenerateName** value to make it unique.

You can use the methods **GetName() string** and **SetName(name string)** on a resource object to access the **Name** field of its embedded **ObjectMeta**, for example:

```
configmap := corev1.ConfigMap{}
configmap.SetName("config")
```

Namespace

Namespaced resources need to be placed into a specific namespace. You might think that you need to indicate this namespace in the **Namespace** field but, when you create or update a resource, you will define the namespace on which to place the resource as part of the request path. Chapter 2 has shown that the request to create a pod in the **project1** namespace is:

```
$ curl $HOST/api/v1/namespaces/project1/pods
```

If you specify a namespace in the **Pod** structure different from **project1**, you will get an error: *"the namespace of the provided object does not match the namespace sent on the request."* For these reasons, when creating a resource, it is not necessary to set the **Namespace** field.

UID, ResourceVersion, and Generation

The **UID** is a unique identifier across past, present and future resources in a cluster. It is set by the control plane and is never updated during the lifetime of a resource. It must be used to reference a resource, rather than its kind, name, and namespace, which could describe various resources across time.

The **ResourceVersion** is an opaque value representing the version of the resource. The **ResourceVersion** changes every time a resource is updated.

This **ResourceVersion** is used for Optimistic concurrency control: if you get a specific version of a resource from the Kubernetes API, modify it then send it back to the API to update it; the API will check that the **ResourceVersion** of the resource you are sending back is the last one. If another process modified the resource in the meantime, the **ResourceVersion** will have been modified, and your request will be rejected; in this case, it is your responsibility to read the new version and update it again. This is different from a Pessimist concurrency control where you would need to acquire a lock before reading the resource and release it after updating it.

The **Generation** is a sequence number that can be used by the resource's controller to indicate the version of the desired state (the **Spec**). It will be updated only when the **Spec** part of the resource is updated, not the other parts (labels, annotations, status). The controller generally uses an **ObservedGeneration** field in the **Status** part to indicate which generation was processed last and is reflected in the status.

Labels and Annotations

Labels and annotations are defined in Go as a map in which the keys and values are strings.

Even if labels and annotations have very different usage, they can be populated the same way. We will discuss in the present section how to populate the **labels** field, but this is also applicable to annotations.

If you know the keys and values you want to add as labels, the simplest way to write the labels' field is to directly write the map, for example:

```
mylabels := map[string]string{
    "app.kubernetes.io/component": "my-component",
    "app.kubernetes.io/name":      "a-name",
}
```

You can also add labels to an existing map, for example:

```
mylabels["app.kubernetes.io/part-of"] = "my-app"
```

If you need to build the labels field from dynamic values, the **labels** package provided in the API Machinery Library provides a **Set** type that may be helpful.

```
import "k8s.io/apimachinery/pkg/labels"
```

```
mylabels := labels.Set{}
```

Functions and methods are provided to manipulate this type:

- The function **ConvertSelectorToLabelsMap** transforms a selector string into a Set.

- The function **Conflicts** checks that two Sets do not have conflicting labels. Conflicting labels are labels that have the same key but different values.

- The function **Merge** will merge two Sets into a single Set. If there are conflicting labels between the two sets, the label in the second set will be used in the resulting Set,

- The function **Equals** checks that the two **Sets** have the same keys and values.

- The method **Has** indicates whether a **Set** contains a key.

- The method **Get** returns the value for a given key in the **Set**, or an empty string if the key is not defined in the **Set**.

71

You can instantiate a **Set** with values, and you can populate it with individual values the same as you do with a map:

```
mySet := labels.Set{
    "app.kubernetes.io/component": "my-component",
    "app.kubernetes.io/name":      "a-name",
}
mySet["app.kubernetes.io/part-of"] = "my-app"
```

You can use the following methods to access the labels and annotations of a resource:

- `GetLabels() map[string]string`

- `SetLabels(labels map[string]string)`

- `GetAnnotations() map[string]string`

- `SetAnnotations(annotations map[string]string)`

OwnerReferences

An **OwnerReference** is set on a Kubernetes resource when you want to indicate that this resource is owned by another one, and you want this resource to be collected by the garbage collector when the owner does not exist anymore.

This is used widely when developing controllers and operators. A controller or operator creates some resources to implement the specifications described by another resource, and it places an **OwnerReference** into the created resources, pointing to the resource giving the specifications.

For example, the Deployment controller creates **ReplicaSet** resources based on specifications found in a Deployment resource. When you delete the Deployment, the associated **ReplicaSet** resources are deleted by the garbage collector without any intervention from the controller.

The **OwnerReference** type is defined as follows:

```
type OwnerReference struct {
    APIVersion      string
    Kind            string
    Name            string
    UID             types.UID
```

```
    Controller          *bool
    BlockOwnerDeletion  *bool
}
```

To know the **UID** of the object to reference, you need to get the object from the Kubernetes API, using a *get* (or *list*) request.

Setting APIVersion and Kind

Using the **Client-go** Library (Chapter 4 shows how to use it), the **APIVersion** and **Kind** will not be set; you will need to set them on the referenced object before copying it, or set it directly into the **ownerReference**:

```
import (
        corev1 "k8s.io/api/core/v1"
        metav1 "k8s.io/apimachinery/pkg/apis/meta/v1"
)

// Get the object to reference
pod, err := clientset.CoreV1().Pods(myns).
    Get(context.TODO(), mypodname, metav1.GetOptions{})
If err != nil {
    return err
}

// Solution 1: set the APIVersion and Kind of the Pod
// then copy all information from the pod

pod.SetGroupVersionKind(
    corev1.SchemeGroupVersion.WithKind("Pod"),
)
ownerRef := metav1.OwnerReference{
    APIVersion: pod.APIVersion,
    Kind:       pod.Kind,
    Name:       pod.GetName(),
    UID:        pod.GetUID(),
}

// Solution 2: Copy name and uid from pod
```

// then set APIVersion and Kind on the OwnerReference

```
ownerRef := metav1.OwnerReference{
    Name: pod.GetName(),
    UID:  pod.GetUID(),
}
ownerRef.APIVersion, ownerRef.Kind =
    corev1.SchemeGroupVersion.WithKind("Pod").
        ToAPIVersionAndKind()
```

The **APIVersion** contains the same information as the **Group** and **Version**. You can get the information from the **SchemeGroupVersion** variable of type **schema.GroupVersion**, which is defined in the package of the API library related to the resource (here **k8s.io/api/core/v1** for the **Pod** resource). You can then add the **Kind** to create a **schema.GroupVersionKind**.

For the first solution, you can use the method **SetGroupVersionKind** on the referenced object to set the **APIVersion** and **Kind** from the **GroupVersionKind**. For the second solution, use the **ToAPIVersionAndKind** method on the **GroupVersionKind** to get the corresponding **APIVersion** and **Kind** values before moving them to the **OwnerReference**.

Chapter 5 describes the **API Machinery** Library and all the types and methods related to **Group**, **Version**, and **Kind**s. The **OwnerReference** structure also contains two optional boolean fields: **Controller** and **BlockOwnerDeletion**.

Setting Controller

The **Controller** field indicates whether the referenced object is the managing Controller (or Operator). A controller, or operator, must set this value to true on the owned resource to indicate that it is managing this owned resource.

The Kubernetes API will refuse to add two **OwnerReference**s with the **Controller** set to true on the same resource. This way, it is not possible that a resource is managed by two different controllers.

Note that this is different from being owned by various resources. A resource can have different owners; and in this case, the resource will be deleted when all its owners have been deleted, independent of which owner is the **Controller**, if any.

This uniqueness of controllers is useful for those that can "adopt" resources. For example, a **ReplicaSet** can adopt an existing pod that matches the selectors of the

ReplicaSet, but only if the **Pod** is not already controlled by another **ReplicaSet** or another controller.

The value of this field is a pointer to a boolean value. You can either declare a boolean value and affect its address when setting the **Controller** field, or use the **BoolPtr** function from the **Kubernetes Utils** Library:

```
// Solution 1: declare a value and use its address
controller := true
ownerRef.Controller = &controller
```

```
// Solution 2: use the BoolPtr function
import (
    "k8s.io/utils/pointer"
)

ownerRef.Controller = pointer.BoolPtr(true)
```

Setting BlockOwnerDeletion

The **OwnerReference** is useful for a controller or other process to not have to take care about deletion of owned resources: when the owner is deleted, the owned will be deleted by the Kubernetes Garbage Collector.

This behavior is configurable. When using the **Delete** operation on a resource, you can use the **Propagation Policy** option:

- **Orphan**: To indicate to the Kubernetes API to orphan the owned resources, so they will not be deleted by the garbage collector.

- **Background**: To indicate to the Kubernetes API to return from the DELETE operation immediately after the owner resource is deleted, and not wait for owned resources to be deleted by the garbage collector.

- **Foreground**: To indicate to the Kubernetes API to return from the DELETE operation after the owner and **the owned resources with BlockOwnerDeletion set to true** are deleted. The Kubernetes API will not wait for other owned resources to be deleted.

So, if you are writing a controller or another process that needs to wait for all the owned resources to be deleted, the process will need to set the **BlockOwnerDeletion** field to **true** on all the owned resources and to use the Foreground propagation policy when deleting the owner resource.

Spec and Status

After the common Type and Metadata, resource definitions are generally composed of two parts: the **Spec** and the **Status**.

Note that it is not true for all resources. For example, the core **ConfigMap** and **Secret** resources, to name a couple, do not contain **Spec** and **Status** parts. More generally, resources containing configuration data, which are not managed by any controller, do not contain these fields.

The **Spec** is the part that the user will define, which indicates the desired state by the user. The **Spec** will be read by the *Controller* managing this resource, which will create, update, or delete resources on the cluster according to the **Spec**, and retrieve the status of its operations into the **Status** part of the resource. This process used by a controller to read the **Spec**, apply to the cluster and retrieve the **Status** is called the *Reconcile Loop*.

Comparison with Writing YAML Manifests

When you write a Kubernetes manifest to be used with kubectl:

- The manifest starts with **apiVersion** and **kind**.

- The metadata field contains all the metadata for the resource.

- The **Spec** and **Status** fields (or others) follow.

When you write a Kubernetes structure in Go, the following occur:

- The type of the structure determines the **apiVersion** and **Kind**; there is no need to specify them.

- The metadata can be defined either by embedding the **metav1. ObjectMeta** structure, or by using *metadata setters* on the resource.

- The **Spec** and **Status** fields (or others) follow, using their own Go structures or other types.

As an example, here are the ways to define a **Pod** with a YAML manifest vs. Go. In YAML:

```
apiVersion: v1
kind: Pod
metadata:
  name: nginx
  labels:
  - component: my-component,
spec:
  containers:
  - image: nginx
    name: nginx
```

In Go, when you are using setters for metadata:

```
pod := corev1.Pod{
    Spec: corev1.PodSpec{
        Containers: []corev1.Container{
          {
              Name:  "runtime",
              Image: "nginx",
          },
        },
    },
}
pod.SetName("my-pod")
pod.SetLabels(map[string]string{
     "component": "my-component",
})
```

Or, in Go, when you are embedding the **metav1.ObjectMeta** structure into the **Pod** structure:

```
pod2 := corev1.Pod{
    ObjectMeta: metav1.ObjectMeta{
        Name: "nginx",
        Labels: map[string]string{
            "component": "mycomponent",
        },
    },
```

```
    Spec: corev1.PodSpec{
        Containers: []corev1.Container{
            {
                    Name:  "runtime",
                    Image: "nginx",
            },
        },
    },
}
```

A Complete Example

This complete example uses the concepts learned up to this point to create a **Pod** on the cluster using a *POST* request.

❶ Build a **Pod** object using a Go structure, as has been shown earlier in this chapter

❷ Serialize the **Pod** object in JSON using a serializer (see Chapter 5 for more about this)

❸ Build an HTTP *POST* request with the body that contains the **Pod** to create, serialized in JSON

❹ Call the Kubernetes API with the request built

❺ Get the body from the response

❻ Depending on the response status code:

If the request returns a 2xx status code:

❼ Deserialize the response body as a **Pod** Go structure

❽ Display the created **Pod** object as JSON for information;

otherwise:

❾ Deserialize the response body as a **Status** Go structure

❿ Display the **Status** object as JSON for information:

```go
package main

import (
  "bytes"
  "encoding/json"
  "fmt"
  "io"
  "net/http"

  corev1 "k8s.io/api/core/v1"
  metav1 "k8s.io/apimachinery/pkg/apis/meta/v1"
  "k8s.io/apimachinery/pkg/runtime"
  "k8s.io/apimachinery/pkg/runtime/schema"
  "k8s.io/apimachinery/pkg/runtime/serializer/json"
)

func createPod() error {
  pod := createPodObject() ❶

  serializer := getJSONSerializer()
  postBody, err := serializePodObject(serializer, pod) ❷
  if err != nil {
    return err
  }

  reqCreate, err := buildPostRequest(postBody) ❸
  if err != nil {
    return err
  }

  client := &http.Client{}
  resp, err := client.Do(reqCreate) ❹
  if err != nil {
    return err
  }
  defer resp.Body.Close()
```

```go
  body, err := io.ReadAll(resp.Body) ❺
  if err != nil {
    return err
  }

  if resp.StatusCode < 300 { ❻
    createdPod, err := deserializePodBody(serializer, body) ❼
    if err != nil {
      return err
    }
    json, err := json.MarshalIndent(createdPod, "", "  ")
    if err != nil {
      return err
    }
    fmt.Printf("%s\n", json) ❽
  } else {
    status, err := deserializeStatusBody(serializer, body) ❾
    if err != nil {
      return err
    }
    json, err := json.MarshalIndent(status, "", "  ")
    if err != nil {
      return err
    }
    fmt.Printf("%s\n", json) ❿
  }
  return nil
}

func createPodObject() *corev1.Pod { ❶
    pod := corev1.Pod{
        Spec: corev1.PodSpec{
            Containers: []corev1.Container{
                {
                    Name:  "runtime",
                    Image: "nginx",
```

```
                },
            },
        },
    }

    pod.SetName("my-pod")
    pod.SetLabels(map[string]string{
        "app.kubernetes.io/component": "my-component",
        "app.kubernetes.io/name":        "a-name",
    })
    return &pod
}

func serializePodObject( ❷
    serializer runtime.Serializer,
    pod *corev1.Pod,
) (
    io.Reader,
    error,
) {
    var buf bytes.Buffer
    err := serializer.Encode(pod, &buf)
    if err != nil {
        return nil, err
    }
    return &buf, nil
}

func buildPostRequest( ❸
    body io.Reader,
) (
    *http.Request,
    error,
) {
    reqCreate, err := http.NewRequest(
        "POST",
```

```go
        "http://127.0.0.1:8001/api/v1/namespaces/default/pods",
        body,
    )
    if err != nil {
        return nil, err
    }
    reqCreate.Header.Add(
"Accept",
"application/json",
)
    reqCreate.Header.Add(
"Content-Type",
"application/json",
)
    return reqCreate, nil
}

func deserializePodBody( ❼
    serializer runtime.Serializer,
    body []byte,
) (
    *corev1.Pod,
    error,
) {
    var result corev1.Pod
    _, _, err := serializer.Decode(body, nil, & result)
    if err != nil {
        return nil, err
    }
    return &result, nil

}

func deserializeStatusBody( ❾
    serializer runtime.Serializer,
    body []byte,
) (
```

```go
    *metav1.Status,
    error,
) {
    var status metav1.Status
    _, _, err := serializer.Decode(body, nil, & status)
    if err != nil {
        return nil, err
    }
    return & status, nil
}

func getJSONSerializer() runtime.Serializer {
    scheme := runtime.NewScheme()
    scheme.AddKnownTypes(
        schema.GroupVersion{
            Group:   "",
            Version: "v1",
        },
        &corev1.Pod{},
        &metav1.Status{},
    )
    return json.NewSerializerWithOptions(
        json.SimpleMetaFactory{},
        nil,
        scheme,
        json.SerializerOptions{},
    )
}
```

Conclusion

In this chapter, you have discovered a first library to work with Kubernetes in Go—the API Library. It is essentially a collection of Go structures to declare Kubernetes resources. The chapter also has explored the definition of the metadata fields common to all resources, defined in the API Machinery Library.

At the end of the chapter, there is an example of a program for building a **Pod** definition using the API Library and then creating this **Pod** in the cluster by calling the API Server using an HTTP request.

The next chapters explores other fundamental libraries—the API Machinery and the Client-go—with which you will no longer need to build HTTP requests.

CHAPTER 4

Using Common Types

The previous chapter describes how to define a Kubernetes resource using Go structures. Particularly, it explains the content of packages of the Kubernetes API Library, and the common fields of every resource associated with a Kubernetes *Kind*.

This chapter examines common types that can be used in various places when defining Kubernetes resources.

Pointers

Optional values in Go structures generally are declared as a pointer to a value. Thus, if you do not want to specify the optional value, you just need to keep it as a nil pointer, and if you need to specify a value, you have to create the value and pass its reference.

The **pointer** package of the **Kubernetes Utils** library defines utility functions to declare such optional values.

```
import (
    "k8s.io/utils/pointer"
)
```

Getting the Reference of a Value

The **Int**, **Int32**, **Int64**, **Bool**, **String**, **Float32**, **Float64**, and **Duration** functions accept a parameter of the same type and return a pointer to the value passed as parameter. For example, the **Int32** function is defined as follows:

```
func Int32(i int32) *int32 {
    return &i
}
```

Then, you can use it this way:

© Philippe Martin 2023
P. Martin, *Kubernetes Programming with Go*, https://doi.org/10.1007/978-1-4842-9026-2_4

```
spec := appsv1.DeploymentSpec{
    Replicas: pointer.Int32(3),
    [...]
}
```

Dereferencing a Pointer

The other way you can get the value referenced by the pointer, or a default value if the pointer is **nil**.

The **IntDeref**, **Int32Deref**, **Int64Deref**, **BoolDeref**, **StringDeref**, **Float32Deref**, **Float64Deref**, and **DurationDeref** functions accept a pointer and a default value as a parameter of the same type, and it returns the referenced value if the pointer is not nil, or the default value otherwise. For example, the **Int32Deref** function is defined as follows:

```
func Int32Deref(ptr *int32, def int32) int32 {
    if ptr != nil {
        return *ptr
    }
    return def
}
```

Then, you can use it this way:

```
replicas := pointer.Int32Deref(spec.Replicas, 1)
```

Comparing Two Referenced Values

It can be useful to compare two pointer values, considering that they are equal if they are both nil, or if they reference two equal values.

The **Int32Equal**, **Int64Equal**, **BoolEqual**, **StringEqual**, **Float32Equal**, **Float64Equal**, and **DurationEqual** functions accept two pointers of the same type, and return true if the two pointers are nil, or if they reference equal values. For example, the **Int32Equal** function is defined as follows:

```
func Int32Equal(a, b *int32) bool {
    if (a == nil) != (b == nil) {
        return false
```

```
    }
    if a == nil {
        return true
    }
    return *a == *b
}
```

Then, you can use it this way:

```
eq := pointer.Int32Equal(
    spec1.Replicas,
    spec2.Replicas,
)
```

Note that to test the equality of an optional value, also considering its default value, you should instead use the following:

```
isOne := pointer.Int32Deref(spec.Replicas, 1) == 1
```

Quantities

Quantity is a fixed-point representation of a number and is used to define quantities of resources to allocate (i.e., memory, cpu, etc.). The smallest value the **Quantity** can represent is one nano (10^{-9}).

Internally, a **Quantity** is represented either by an **Integer** (on 64 bits) and a **Scale**, or, if the **int64** is not large enough to support it, by an **inf.Dec** value (as defined by the package at `https://github.com/go-inf/inf`).

```
import (
    "k8s.io/apimachinery/pkg/api/resource"
)
```

Parsing a String as Quantity

A first way to define a **Quantity** is to parse its value from a string by using one of the following functions:

- `func MustParse(str string) Quantity` – parses a quantity from the `string`, or panics if the string does not represent a quantity. It is to be used when you are applying a hard-coded value that you know is valid.

- `func ParseQuantity(str string) (Quantity, error)` – parses a quantity from the `string` or return an error if the string does not represent a quantity. It is to be used when you are not sure the value is valid.

The **Quantity** can be written using a sign, a digit number, and a suffix. The sign and suffix are optional. The suffix can be either a binary, a decimal, or a decimal exponent.

The defined binary suffixes are Ki (2^{10}), Mi (2^{20}), Gi (2^{30}), Ti (2^{40}), Pi (2^{50}), and Ei (2^{60}). The defined decimal suffixes are n (10^{-9}), u (10^{-6}), m (10^{-3}), "" (10^{0}), k (10^{3}), M (10^{6}), G (10^{9}), T(10^{12}), P(10^{15}), and E(10^{18}). The decimal exponent suffix is written with an **e** or **E** sign followed by the decimal exponent—for example, **E2** to represent 10^{2}.

The suffix format (either binary, decimal, or exponent decimal) is saved in the **Quantity** and is used when serializing the quantity.

Using these functions, the way the **Quantity** is represented internally (either a scaled integer or an **inf.Dec**) will be decided depending on whether the parsed value can be represented as a scaled integer or not.

Using an inf.Dec as a Quantity

Use the following to use an **inf.Dec** as a **Quantity**:

- `func NewDecimalQuantity(b inf.Dec, format Format) *Quantity` – declares a **Quantity** by giving an **inf.Dec** value, and by indicating with which suffix format you want it to be serialized.

- `func (q *Quantity) ToDec() *Quantity` – forces a **Quantity**— previously defined by parsing a string or using a new function to initialize it—to be stored as an **inf.Dec**.

- `func (q *Quantity) AsDec() *inf.Dec` – gets a representation of the **Quantity** as **inf.Dec** without modifying the internal representation.

Using a Scaled Integer as a Quantity

Use the following to use a scaled integer as a **Quantity**:

- `func NewScaledQuantity(value int64, scale Scale)` `*Quantity` – declares a **Quantity** by giving an `int64` value and a scale. The format of the suffix will be the decimal format.

- `func (q *Quantity) SetScaled(value int64, scale Scale)` – overrides a **Quantity** value with a scaled integer. The format of the suffix will remain unchanged.

- `func (q *Quantity) ScaledValue(scale Scale) int64` – gets a representation of the **Quantity** as an integer, considering the given scale, without modifying the internal representation.

- `func NewQuantity(value int64, format Format) *Quantity` – declares a **Quantity** by giving an `int64` value, the scale being fixed to **0**, and a suffix format is to be used during serialization.

- `func (q *Quantity) Set(value int64)` – overrides a **Quantity** value with an integer and a scale fixed to **0**. The format of the suffix will remain unchanged.

- `func (q *Quantity) Value() int64` – gets a representation of the **Quantity** as an integer with a scale to **0**, without modifying the internal representation.

- `func NewMilliQuantity(value int64, format Format)` `*Quantity` – declares a **Quantity** by giving an `int64` value, the scale being fixed to **−3** and a suffix format to be used during serialization.

- `func (q *Quantity) SetMilli(value int64)` – overrides a **Quantity** value with an integer and a scale fixed to **−3**. The format of the suffix will remain unchanged.

- `func (q *Quantity) MilliValue() int64` – gets a representation of the **Quantity** as an integer with a scale to **−3** without modifying the internal representation.

Operations on Quantities

The following are the ways to make operations on the **Quantity**:

- `func (q *Quantity) Add(y Quantity)` – adds the **y** Quantity to the **q** Quantity.

- `func (q *Quantity) Sub(y Quantity)` – subtracts the **y** Quantity from the **q** Quantity.

- `func (q *Quantity) Cmp(y Quantity) int` – compares the **q** and **y** quantities. Return **0** if both quantities are equal, **1** if **q** is greater than **y**, and **−1** if **q** is less than **y**.

- `func (q *Quantity) CmpInt64(y int64) int` – compares **q** Quantity with the **y** integer. Return **0** if both quantities are equal, **1** if **q** is greater than **y**, and **−1** if **q** is less than **y**.

- `func (q *Quantity) Neg()` – makes **q** the negative value of itself.

- `func (q Quantity) Equal(v Quantity) bool` – tests to see whether **q** and **v** quantities are equal.

IntOrString

Some fields of Kubernetes resources accept either an integer value or a string value. For example, a port can be defined with the port number or a IANA service name (as defined in `https://www.iana.org/assignments/service-names-port-numbers/service-names-port-numbers.xhtml`).

Another example is fields that can accept either an integer or a percentage.

```
import (
    "k8s.io/apimachinery/pkg/util/intstr"
)
```

The **IntOrString** structure is defined as follows:

```
type IntOrString struct {
    Type    Type
    IntVal int32
```

```
    StrVal string
}
```

The **Type** can be either **Int** or **String**.

Because all the fields of the structure are public, you can create a value or extract information from it by accessing its fields directly. For convenience, these functions are useful for creating and manipulating **IntOrString** values:

- `func FromInt(val int) IntOrString` – declares an **IntOrString** containing an integer value.

- `func FromString(val string) IntOrString` – declares an **IntOrString** containing a string value.

- `func Parse(val string) IntOrString` – declares an **IntOrString**, trying first to extract an integer from the string before storing it as a string.

- `func (intstr *IntOrString) String() string` – returns the **IntOrString** value as a string, converting it using **Itoa** if the value is stored as an integer.

- `func (intstr *IntOrString) IntValue() int` – returns the **IntOrString** value as an integer. If stored as a string, return its converted value using **Atoi** or **0** if parsing fails.

- `func ValueOrDefault(intOrPercent *IntOrString, defaultValue IntOrString) *IntOrString` – returns the **intOrPercent** value if not nil, or the **defaultValue.**

- `func GetScaledValueFromIntOrPercent(intOrPercent *IntOrString, total int, roundUp bool) (int, error)` – this function can be used for **IntOrString** values expected to contain either an integer or a percentage. If the value is an integer, it is returned as is.

If the value is a string representing a percentage (a number followed by a **%** sign), the function returns the percentage of the **total** value, rounding the result up or down depending on **roundUp**. If the string is not parseable as a percentage, the function returns an error.

Time

The **Time** type defined in the API Machinery Library is used for all fields of Kubernetes resources declaring a time. It is a wrapper around the Go **time.Time** type, and it provides factories wrapping the **time.Time** factories.

```
import (
    metav1 "k8s.io/apimachinery/pkg/apis/meta/v1"
)
```

Factory Methods

The available factory methods are the following:

- `func NewTime(time time.Time) Time` – returns a **metav1.Time** value wrapping that is the provided **time.Time** value.

- `func Date(year int, month time.Month, day, hour, min, sec, nsec int, loc *time.Location) Time` – returns a **metav1.Time** value based on the various elements of the time (e.g., year, month, day, hour, minutes, seconds, nanoseconds, location). It is a wrapper around the **time.Date** function.

- `func Now() Time` – returns a **metav1.Time** value containing the current local time. It is a wrapper around the **time.Now** function.

- `func Unix(sec int64, nsec int64) Time` – returns a **metav1.Time** value corresponding to the given Unix time expressed in seconds and nanoseconds. It is a wrapper around the **time.Unix** function.

Operations on Time

Use the following to define the **Time** operations:

- `func (t *Time) DeepCopyInto(out *Time)` – returns a copy of the **metav1.Time** value.

- `func (t *Time) IsZero() bool` – returns true if the **metav1.Time** value represents the zero time instant, January 1, year 1, 00:00:00 UTC. It is a wrapper around the **time.IsZero** method.

- `func (t *Time) Before(u *Time) bool` – returns true if the **metav1.Time** instant **t** is before **u**. It is a wrapper around the **time. Before** method.

- `func (t *Time) Equal(u *Time) bool` – returns true if the **metav1.Time** instant **t** is equal to **u**. It is a wrapper around the **time. Equal** method.

- `func (t Time) Rfc3339Copy() Time` – returns a copy of the **metav1. Time t** value, removing its nanosecond precision.

Conclusion

This chapter covered common types used when defining Kubernetes resources in Go. Pointer values are used to specify optional values, quantities are used to specify memory and CPU quantities, the **IntOrString** type is used for values writeable either as integers or strings (e.g., ports that can be defined either by number or by name), and Time—a serializable type wrapping the Go **Time** type.

CHAPTER 5

The API Machinery

The previous chapters explored how the Kubernetes API works at the HTTP level. They also explored the Kubernetes API Library, which defines the resources served by the Kubenretes API in Go.

This chapter explores the Kubernetes API Machinery Library, which provides utilities for working with API objects that follow the Kubernetes API object conventions. These conventions include:

- The API objects embed a common metadata structure, **TypeMeta**, containing two fields: **APIVersion** and **Kind**.

- The API objects are provided in a separate package.

- The API objects are versioned.

- Conversion functions are provided to convert between versions.

The API Machinery will provide the following utilities:

- A **Scheme** abstraction, used to:

  - Register the API objects as Group-Version-Kinds

  - Convert between API Objects of different versions

  - Serialize/deserialize API Objects

- A **RESTMapper**, mapping between API Objects (based on embedded **APIVersion** and **Kind**) and resource names (in the REST sense).

This chapter details the functions provided by the API Machinery.

© Philippe Martin 2023
P. Martin, *Kubernetes Programming with Go*, https://doi.org/10.1007/978-1-4842-9026-2_5

The Schema Package

The **schema** package of the **API Machinery** Library defines useful structures and functions to work with Group, Versions, Kinds, and Resources.

```
import (
    "k8s.io/apimachinery/pkg/runtime/schema"
)
```

The structures **GroupVersionResource**, **GroupVersionKind**, **GroupVersion**, **GroupResource**, and **GroupKind** are defined, with methods to pass from one to another.

Also, functions to convert between **GroupVersionKind** and **(apiVersion, kind)** are provided: **ToAPIVersionAndKind** and **FromAPIVersionAndKind**.

api machinery Schema

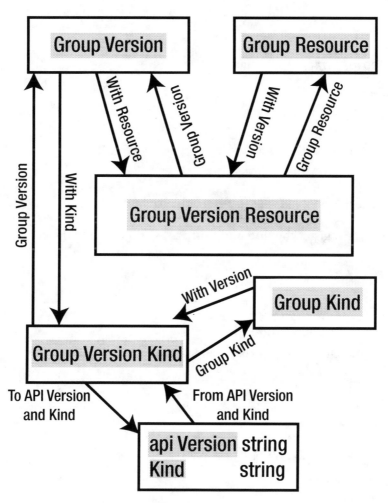

Figure 5-1. *GVK and GVR related structures and methods*

Scheme

A **Scheme** is an abstraction used to register the API objects as **Group-Version-Kinds**, convert between API Objects of various versions, and serialize/deserialize API Objects. The **Scheme** is a structure provided by the API Machinery in the **runtime** package. All the fields of this structure are unexported.

Initialization

The **Scheme** structure can be initialized with the **NewScheme** function:

```
import (
    "k8s.io/apimachinery/pkg/runtime"
)

Scheme := runtime.NewScheme()
```

After the structure is initialized, you can register new API objects with the **AddKnownTypes** method as follows:

```
func (s *Scheme) AddKnownTypes(gv schema.GroupVersion, types ...Object)
```

For example, to register the **Pod** and **ConfigMap** objects into the **core/v1** group, you could use:

```
import (
    corev1 "k8s.io/api/core/v1"
    "k8s.io/apimachinery/pkg/runtime"
    "k8s.io/apimachinery/pkg/runtime/schema"
)

Scheme := runtime.NewScheme()

func init() {
    Scheme.AddKnownTypes(
        schema.GroupVersion{
            Group:   "",
            Version: "v1",
        },
        &corev1.Pod{},
        &corev1.ConfigMap{},
    )
}
```

By doing this, the API Machinery will be able to know that the **Group-Version-Kind** *core-v1-Pod* to be used when executing requests related to *pods* must be the **corev1. Pod** structure, and the *core-v1-ConfigMap* to be used when executing requests related to *configmaps* must be the **corev1.ConfigMap** structure.

It has been shown that the API objects can be versioned. You can register a same kind for various versions this way—for example, use the following to add the **v1** and **v1beta1** versions of the **Deployment** object:

```
import (
    appsv1 "k8s.io/api/apps/v1"
    appsv1beta1 "k8s.io/api/apps/v1beta1"
    "k8s.io/apimachinery/pkg/runtime"
    "k8s.io/apimachinery/pkg/runtime/schema"
)

Scheme := runtime.NewScheme()

func init() {
   Scheme.AddKnownTypes(
      schema.GroupVersion{
         Group:   "apps",
         Version: "v1",
      },
      &appsv1.Deployment{},
   )
   Scheme.AddKnownTypes(
      schema.GroupVersion{
         Group:   "apps",
         Version: "v1beta1",
      },
      &appsv1beta1.Deployment{},
   )
}
```

It is advisable to initialize the **Scheme** structure and to add known types to it at the very beginning of the execution—for example, using the **init** functions.

Mapping

After initialization, you can use various methods on the structure to map between Goup-Version-Kinds and Go **Types**:

- KnownTypes(gv schema.GroupVersion) map[string]reflect. Type – gets all the Go types registered for a specific **Group-Version**—here **apps/v1**:

```
types := Scheme.KnownTypes(schema.GroupVersion{
    Group:   "apps",
    Version: "v1",
})
```

```
-> ["Deployment": appsv1.Deployment]
```

- VersionsForGroupKind(gk schema.GroupKind) []schema. GroupVersion – gets all the **Group-Versions** registered for a specific *Kind*—here the **Deployment**:

```
groupVersions := Scheme.VersionsForGroupKind(
schema.GroupKind{
        Group: "apps",
        Kind:  "Deployment",
})
```

```
-> ["apps/v1" "apps/v1beta1"]
```

- ObjectKinds(obj Object) ([]schema.GroupVersionKind, bool, error) – gets all the possible Group-Version-Kinds for a given object—here an **appsv1.Deployment**:

```
gvks, notVersioned, err := Scheme.ObjectKinds(&appsv1.
Deployment{})
```

```
-> ["apps/v1 Deployment"]
```

- New(kind schema.GroupVersionKind) (Object, error) – builds an object, given a Group-Version-Kind:

```
obj, err := Scheme.New(schema.GroupVersionKind{
    Group:   "apps",
    Version: "v1",
    Kind:    "Deployment",
})
```

- This method returns a value of type **runtime.Object**, which is an interface implemented by all the API objects. The concrete type of the value will be the object mapping the Group-Version-Kind—here **appsv1.Deployment**.

Conversion

The **Scheme** structure registers *Kind*s by Group-Version. By providing to the **Scheme** conversion functions between kinds of the same Group and different Versions, it is then possible to convert between any kinds of the same Group.

It is possible to define conversion functions of two levels: *conversion functions* and *generated conversion functions*. Conversion functions are functions written by hand, when generated conversion functions are generated using the **conversion-gen** tool.

When converting between two versions, the conversion function, if it exists, will take priority over the generated conversion function.

Adding Conversion Functions

These two methods add a conversion function between **a** and **b**, which are two objects of types belonging to the same Group.

```
AddConversionFunc(
    a, b interface{},
    fn conversion.ConversionFunc,
) error

AddGeneratedConversionFunc(
    a, b interface{},
    fn conversion.ConversionFunc,
) error
```

The **a** and **b** values must be pointers to structures and can be nil pointers. The signature of the conversion function is defined as follows:

```
type ConversionFunc func(
    a, b interface{},
    scope Scope,
) error
```

Here is an example, to add a conversion function between **apps/v1** and **apps/ v1beta1** deployments:

```
Scheme.AddConversionFunc(
    (*appsv1.Deployment)(nil),
    (*appsv1beta1.Deployment)(nil),
    func(a, b interface{}, scope conversion.Scope) error{
        v1deploy := a.(*appsv1.Deployment)
        v1beta1deploy := b.(*appsv1beta1.Deployment)
        // make conversion here
        return nil
    })
```

As for registering known types to the scheme, the recommendation is to register conversion functions at the very beginning of the execution—for example, using **init** functions.

Converting

Once conversion functions have been registered, it is possible to convert between two versions of the same kind with the **Convert** function.

```
Convert(in, out interface{}, context interface{}) error
```

This example defines a **v1.Deployment**, then converts it to the **v1beta1** version:

```
v1deployment := appsv1.Deployment{
    [...]
}
v1deployment.SetName("myname")

var v1beta1Deployment appsv1beta1.Deployment
scheme.Convert(&v1deployment, &v1beta1Deployment, nil)
```

Serialization

Packages of the API Machinery Library provide serializers for various formats: JSON, YAML, and Protobuf. These serializers implement the **Serializer** interface, which embeds the **Encoder** and **Decoder** interfaces. First, you can see how to instantiate serializers for different formats, then how to use them to encode and decode API objects.

JSON and YAML Serializer

The **json** package provides a serializer for both JSON and YAML formats.

```
import (
    "k8s.io/apimachinery/pkg/runtime/serializer/json"
)
```

The **NewSerializerWithOptions** function is used to create a new serializer.

```
NewSerializerWithOptions(
    meta      MetaFactory,
    creater   runtime.ObjectCreater,
    typer     runtime.ObjectTyper,
    options   SerializerOptions,
) *Serializer
```

The options give the possibility to choose between a JSON and a YAML serializer (**Yaml** field) to choose a human-readable output for a JSON output (**Pretty** field) and to check for duplicate fields in JSON and YAML (**Strict** fields).

```
type SerializerOptions struct {
    Yaml      bool
    Pretty    bool
    Strict    bool
}
```

The **Scheme** can be used for **creator** and **typer** because it implements these two interfaces, and the **SimpleMetaFactory** structure can be used as **meta**.

```
serializer := jsonserializer.NewSerializerWithOptions(
    jsonserializer.SimpleMetaFactory{},
    Scheme,
```

```
    Scheme,
    jsonserializer.SerializerOptions{
        Yaml: false, // or true for YAML serializer
        Pretty: true, // or false for one-line JSON
        Strict: false, // or true to check duplicates
    },
)
```

Protobuf Serializer

The **protobuf** package provides a serializer for a Protobuf format.

```
import (
    "k8s.io/apimachinery/pkg/runtime/serializer/protobuf"
)
```

The **NewSerializer** function is used to create a new serializer.

```
NewSerializer(
    creater      runtime.ObjectCreater,
    typer        runtime.ObjectTyper,
) *Serializer
```

The **Scheme** can be used for **creator** and **typer** because it implements these two interfaces.

```
serializer := protobuf.NewSerializer(Scheme, Scheme)
```

Encoding and Decoding

The various serializers implement the **Serializer** interface, which embeds the **Decoder** and **Encoder** interfaces, defining the **Encode** and **Decode** methods.

- Encode(obj Object, w io.Writer) error – the **Encode** function takes an API object as a parameter, encodes the object, and writes the result using the writer.

- Decode(

```
        data []byte,
        defaults *schema.GroupVersionKind,
        into Object,
    ) (
        Object,
        *schema.GroupVersionKind,
        error,
    )
```

- this function takes an array of bytes as a parameter and tries to decode its content. If the content to decode does not specify **apiVersion** and *Kind*, the default **GroupVersionKind** (GVK) will be used.

The result will be placed in the **into** object if not nil and if the concrete type of **into** matches the content GVK (either the initial one, or the **defaults** one). In any case, the result will be returned as an Object, and the GVK applied to it will be returned as a **GroupVersionKind** structure.

RESTMapper

The API Machinery provides a concept of RESTMapper, used to map between REST resources and *Kind*s.

```
import (
    "k8s.io/apimachinery/pkg/api/meta"
)
```

The **RESTMapping** type provides the result of a mapping using the **RESTMapper**:

```
type RESTMapping struct {
    Resource            schema.GroupVersionResource
    GroupVersionKind    schema.GroupVersionKind
    Scope               RESTScope
}
```

As Chapter 1 discussed, a GVR (Group-Version-Resource, or **Resource** for short) is used to build the path to which to make a request. For example, to get the list of deployments in all namespaces, you will use the path **/apis/apps/v1/deployments**, where **apps** is the Group, **v1** is the Version, and **deployments** is the (plural) **Resource** name. So, a resource managed by an API can be uniquely identified by its GVR.

When making requests to this path, generally you want to exchange data, either in the request to create or update a resource, or in the response to get or list resources. The format of this exchanged data is called the *Kind* (or **GroupVersionKind**), associated with the resource.

The **RESTMapping** structure brings together a **Resource** and its associated **GroupVersionKind**. The API machinery provides a **RESTMapper** interface, and a default implementation, **DefaultRESTMapper**.

```
type RESTMapper interface {

    RESTMapping(gk schema.GroupKind, versions ...string)
          (*RESTMapping, error)

    RESTMappings(gk schema.GroupKind, versions ...string)
          ([]*RESTMapping, error)

    KindFor(resource schema.GroupVersionResource)
          (schema.GroupVersionKind, error)

    KindsFor(resource schema.GroupVersionResource)
          ([]schema.GroupVersionKind, error)

    ResourceFor(input schema.GroupVersionResource)
          (schema.GroupVersionResource, error)

    ResourcesFor(input schema.GroupVersionResource)
          ([]schema.GroupVersionResource, error)

    ResourceSingularizer(resource string)
          (singular string, err error)
}
```

Kind to Resource

The **RESTMapping** and **RESTMappings** methods return an element or an array of **RESTMapping** structures as a result, given a **Group** and **Kind**. An optional list of versions indicates the preferred versions.

The **RESTMappings** method returns all matches, the **RESTMapping** method returns a single match or an error if there are multiple matches. The resulting **RESTMapping** elements will contain the fully qualified **Kind** (including the version) and the fully qualified **Resource**.

To sum up, these methods are used to map a **Kind** to a **Resource**.

Resource to Kind

The **KindFor** and **KindsFor** methods return an element or an array of **GroupVersionKind**, given a *partial* Group-Version-Resource. Partial means that you can omit the group, the version, or both. The resource name can be the singular or the plural name of the resource.

The **KindsFor** method returns all matches, the **KindFor** method returns a single match or an error if there are multiple matches.

To sum up, these methods are used to map a **Resource** to a **Kind**.

Finding Resources

The **ResourceFor** and **ResourcesFor** methods return an element or an array of **GroupVersionResource**, given a *partial* Group-Version-Resource. Partial means that you can omit the group, the version, or both. The resource name can be the singular or the plural name of the resource.

The **ResourcesFor** method returns all matches, the **ResourceFor** method returns a single match or an error if there are multiple matches.

To sum up, these methods are used to find fully qualified resources based on a singular or plural resource name.

The DefaultRESTMapper Implementation

The API Machinery provides a default implementation of a **RESTMapper**.

- ```
  NewDefaultRESTMapper(
      defaultGroupVersions []schema.GroupVersion,
  ) *DefaultRESTMapper
  ```
  ```

- this factory method is used to build a new **DefaultRESTMapper**, and accepts a list of default Group-Versions, which will be used to find Resources or Kinds when the provided GVR is partial.

- `Add(kind schema.GroupVersionKind, scope RESTScope)` – this method is used to add a mapping between a **Kind** and a **Resource**. The resource name will be guessed from the Kind, by getting the lowercase word, and by pluralizing it (adding "es" to words ending with "s," replacing terminal "y" with "ies" to words ending with "y," and adding "s" to other words).

- ```
  AddSpecific(
      kind schema.GroupVersionKind,
      plural, singular schema.GroupVersionResource,
      scope RESTScope)
  ```

  - this method is used to add a mapping between a **Kind** and a **Resource**, by giving the singular and plural names explicitly.

After creating a **DefaultRESTMapper** instance, you can use it as a **RESTMapper** by calling the methods defined in the interface of the same name.

Conclusion

This chapter has explored the API Machinery, introducing the **Scheme** abstraction used to serialize resources between Go and JSON or YAML, and to convert resources between several versions. The chapter also covered the **RESTMapper** interface to help map between resources and kinds.

The next chapter covers the Client-go Library, a high-level one used by developers to call the Kubernetes API without needing to work with HTTP calls.
  ```

CHAPTER 6

The Client-go Library

The previous chapters explored the *Kubernetes API Library*, a collection of Go structures to work with the objects of the Kubernetes API, and the *API Machinery Library*, which provides utilities for working with the API objects that follow the Kubernetes API object conventions. Specifically, you have seen that the API Machinery provides *Scheme* and *RESTMapper* abstractions.

This chapter explores the *Client-go Library*, which is a high-level library that can be used by developers to interact with the Kubernetes API using the Go language. The Client-go Library brings together the Kubernetes API and the API Machinery libraries, providing a *Scheme* preconfigured with Kubernetes API's objects and a *RESTMapper* implementation for the Kubernetes API. It also provides a set of clients to use to execute operations on the resources of the Kubernetes API in a simple way.

To use this library, you will need to import packages from it with the prefix **k8s.io/client-go**. For example, to use the package **kubernetes**, let's use the following:

```
import (
    "k8s.io/client-go/kubernetes"
)
```

You also need to download a version of the Client-go Library. For this you can employ the **go get** command to obtain the version you want to use:

```
$ go get k8s.io/client-go@v0.24.4
```

The version of the Client-go Library is aligned with the version of Kubernetes—version 0.24.4 corresponds to version 1.24.4 of the server.

Kubernetes is backward-compatible so you can use older versions of Client-go with newer versions of clusters, but you may well want to get a recent version to be able to use a current feature, because only bug fixes are backported to previous client-go releases, not new features.

P. Martin, *Kubernetes Programming with Go*, https://doi.org/10.1007/978-1-4842-9026-2_6

Connecting to the Cluster

The first step before connecting to the Kubernetes API Server is to have the configuration connect to it—that is, the address of the server, its credentials, the connection parameters, and so on.

The **rest** package provides a **rest.Config** structure, which contains all the configuration information necessary for an application to connect to a *REST* API Server.

In-cluster Configuration

By default, a container running on a Kubernetes Pod contains all the information needed to connect to the API Server:

- A *token* and the *root certificate*, provided by the **ServiceAccount** used for the Pod, are available in this directory: **/var/run/secrets/ kubernetes.io/serviceaccount/**.

  Note that it is possible to disable this behavior by setting **automountServiceAccountToken: false** in the **ServiceAccount** used by the Pod, or in the specifications of the Pod directly

- The environment variables, **KUBERNETES_SERVICE_HOST** and **KUBERNETES_SERVICE_PORT**, defined in the container environment, added by kubelet, define the host and port to which to contact the API Server.

When an application is dedicated to run inside a Pod's container, you can use the following function to create an appropriate **rest.Config** structure, leveraging the information just described:

```
import "k8s.io/client-go/rest"

func InClusterConfig() (*Config, error)
```

Out-of-Cluster Configuration

Kubernetes tools generally rely on the **kubeconfig** file—that is, a file that contains connection configuration for one or several Kubernetes clusters.

You can build a **rest.Config** structure based on the content of this **kubeconfig** file by using one of the following functions from the **clientcmd** package.

From kubeconfig in Memory

The **RESTConfigFromKubeConfig** function can be used to build a **rest.Config** structure from the content of a **kubeconfig** file as an array of bytes.

```
func RESTConfigFromKubeConfig(
    configBytes []byte,
) (*rest.Config, error)
```

If the **kubeconfig** file contains several *contexts*, the current context will be used, and the other contexts will be ignored. For example, you can read the content of a **kubeconfig** file first, then use the following function:

```
import "k8s.io/client-go/tools/clientcmd"

configBytes, err := os.ReadFile(
    "/home/user/.kube/config",
)
if err != nil {
    return err
}
config, err := clientcmd.RESTConfigFromKubeConfig(
    configBytes,
)
if err != nil {
    return err
}
```

From a kubeconfig on Disk

The **BuildConfigFromFlags** function can be used to build a **rest.Config** structure either from the URL of the API Server, or based on a **kubeconfig** file given its path, or both.

```
func BuildConfigFromFlags(
    masterUrl,
```

```
    kubeconfigPath string,
) (*rest.Config, error)
```

The following code allows you to get a **rest.Config** structure:

```
import "k8s.io/client-go/tools/clientcmd"

config, err := clientcmd.BuildConfigFromFlags(
    "",
    "/home/user/.kube/config",
)
```

The following code gets the configuration from the **kubeconfig**, and overrides the URL of the API Server:

```
config, err := clientcmd.BuildConfigFromFlags(
    "https://192.168.1.10:6443",
    "/home/user/.kube/config",
)
```

From a Personalized kubeconfig

The previous functions use an **api.Config** structure internally, representing the data in the **kubeconfig** file (not to be confused with the **rest.Config** structure that contains the parameters for the *REST* HTTP connection).

If you need to manipulate this intermediary data, you can use the **BuildConfigFromKubeconfigGetter** function accepting a **kubeconfigGetter** function as an argument, which itself will return an **api.Config** structure.

```
BuildConfigFromKubeconfigGetter(
    masterUrl string,
    kubeconfigGetter KubeconfigGetter,
) (*rest.Config, error)

type KubeconfigGetter
    func() (*api.Config, error)
```

For example, the following code will load the **kubeconfig** file with the **clientcmd.Load** or **clientcmd.LoadFromFile** functions from the **kubeconfigGetter** function:

```
import (
    "k8s.io/client-go/tools/clientcmd"
    "k8s.io/client-go/tools/clientcmd/api"
)

config, err :=
clientcmd.BuildConfigFromKubeconfigGetter(
    "",
    func() (*api.Config, error) {
        apiConfig, err := clientcmd.LoadFromFile(
            "/home/user/.kube/config",
        )
        if err != nil {
            return nil, nil
        }
        // TODO: manipulate apiConfig
        return apiConfig, nil
    },
)
```

From Several kubeconfig Files

The kubectl tool uses by default the **$HOME/.kube/config kubeconfig** file, and you can
specify another **kubeconfig** file path using the **KUBECONFIG** environment variable.

More than that, you can specify a list of **kubeconfig** file paths in this
environment variable, and the **kubeconfig** files will be *merged* into just one
before being used. You can obtain the same behavior with this function:
NewNonInteractiveDeferredLoadingClientConfig.

```
func NewNonInteractiveDeferredLoadingClientConfig(
    loader ClientConfigLoader,
    overrides *ConfigOverrides,
) ClientConfig
```

The type **clientcmd.ClientConfigLoadingRules** implements the
ClientConfigLoader interface, and you can get a value for this type using the following
function:

113

```
func NewDefaultClientConfigLoadingRules()
 *ClientConfigLoadingRules
```

This function will get the value of the **KUBECONFIG** environment variable, if it exists, to obtain the list of **kubeconfig** files to merge, or will fallback on using the default **kubeconfig** file located in **$HOME/.kube/config**.

Using the following code to create the **rest.Config** structure, your program will have the same behavior as **kubectl**, as previously described:

```
import (
    "k8s.io/client-go/tools/clientcmd"
)

config, err :=
clientcmd.NewNonInteractiveDeferredLoadingClientConfig(
    clientcmd.NewDefaultClientConfigLoadingRules(),
    nil,
).ClientConfig()
```

Overriding kubeconfig with CLI Flags

It has been shown that the second parameter of this function, **NewNonInteractiveDeferredLoadingClientConfig**, is a **ConfigOverrides** structure. This structure contains values to override some fields of the result of merging the **kubeconfig** files.

You can set specific values in this structure yourself, or, if you are creating a CLI using the *spf13/pflag library* (i.e., **github.com/spf13/pflag**), you can use the following code to automatically declare default flags for your CLI and bind them to the **ConfigOverrides** structure:

```
import (
    "github.com/spf13/pflag"
    "k8s.io/client-go/tools/clientcmd"
)

var (
    flags pflag.FlagSet
    overrides clientcmd.ConfigOverrides
    of = clientcmd.RecommendedConfigOverrideFlags("")
)
```

```
clientcmd.BindOverrideFlags(&overrides, &flags, of)
flags.Parse(os.Args[1:])

config, err :=
clientcmd.NewNonInteractiveDeferredLoadingClientConfig(
    clientcmd.NewDefaultClientConfigLoadingRules(),
    &overrides,
).ClientConfig()
```

Note that you can declare a prefix for the added flags when calling the function **RecommendedConfigOverrideFlags**.

Getting a Clientset

The Kubernetes package provides functions to create a clientset of the type **kubernetes. Clientset**.

- `func NewForConfig(c *rest.Config) (*Clientset, error)` – The **NewForConfig** function returns a **Clientset**, using the provided **rest. Config** built with one of the methods seen in the previous section.

- `func NewForConfigOrDie(c *rest.Config) *Clientset` – this function is like the previous one, but panics in case of error, instead of returning the error. This function can be used with a hard-coded config for which you will want to assert its validity.

- ```
  NewForConfigAndClient(
      c *rest.Config,
      httpClient *http.Client,
  ) (*Clientset, error)
  ```

  – this **NewForConfigAndClient** function returns a **Clientset**, using the provided **rest.Config**, and the provided **http.Client**.

  The previous function **NewForConfig** uses a default HTTP Client built with the function **rest.HTTPClientFor**. If you want to personalize the HTTP Client before building the **Clientset**, you can use this function instead.
  ```

Using the Clientset

The **kubernetes.Clientset** type implements the interface **kubernetes.Interface**, defined as follows:

```
type Interface interface {
    Discovery() discovery.DiscoveryInterface
    [...]
    AppsV1()           appsv1.AppsV1Interface
    AppsV1beta1()      appsv1beta1.AppsV1beta1Interface
    AppsV1beta2()      appsv1beta2.AppsV1beta2Interface
    [...]
    CoreV1()            corev1.CoreV1Interface
    [...]
}
```

The first method **Discovery()** gives access to an interface that provides methods to discover the groups, versions, and resources available in the cluster, as well as preferred versions for resources. This interface also provides access to the server version and the **OpenAP**I v2 and v3 definitions. This is examined in detail in the Discovery client section.

Apart from the **Discovery()** method, the **kubernetes.Interface** is composed of a series of methods, one for each Group/Version defined by the Kubernetes API. When you see the definition of this interface, it is possible to understand that the **Clientset** is a set of clients, and each client is dedicated to its own Group/Version.

Each method returns a value that implements an interface specific to the Group/Version. For example, the **CoreV1()** method of **kubernetes.Interface** returns a value, implementing the interface **corev1.CoreV1Interface**, defined as follows:

```
type CoreV1Interface interface {
    RESTClient() rest.Interface
    ComponentStatusesGetter
    ConfigMapsGetter
    EndpointsGetter
    [...]
}
```

The first method in this **CoreV1Interface** interface is **RESTClient() rest.Interface**, which is a method used to get a *REST* client for the specific Group/Version. This low-level client will be used internally by the Group/Version client, and you can use this *REST* client to build requests not provided natively by the other methods of this interface: **CoreV1Interface**.

The interface **rest.Interface** implemented by the *REST* client is defined as follows:

```
type Interface interface {
    GetRateLimiter()            flowcontrol.RateLimiter
    Verb(verb string)           *Request
    Post()                      *Request
    Put()                       *Request
    Patch(pt types.PatchType)   *Request
    Get()                       *Request
    Delete()                    *Request
    APIVersion()                schema.GroupVersion
}
```

As you can see, this interface provides a series of methods—**Verb**, **Post**, **Put**, **Patch**, **Get**, and **Delete**—that return a **Request** object with a specific HTTP **Verb**. This is examined further in the "How to Use These **Request** Objects to Complete Operations" section.

The other methods in the **CoreV1Interface** are used to get specific methods for each Resource of the Group/Version. For example, the **ConfigMapsGetter** embedded interface is defined as follows:

```
type ConfigMapsGetter interface {
    ConfigMaps(namespace string) ConfigMapInterface
}
```

Then, the interface **ConfigMapInterface** is returned by the method **ConfigMaps** and is defined as follows:

```
type ConfigMapInterface interface {
    Create(
```

```
        ctx context.Context,
        configMap *v1.ConfigMap,
        opts metav1.CreateOptions,
    ) (*v1.ConfigMap, error)
    Update(
        ctx context.Context,
        configMap *v1.ConfigMap,
        opts metav1.UpdateOptions,
    ) (*v1.ConfigMap, error)
    Delete(
        ctx context.Context,
        name string,
        opts metav1.DeleteOptions,
    ) error
    [...]
}
```

You can see that this interface provides a series of methods, one for each *Kubernetes API Verb*.

Each method related to an operation takes as a parameter an Option structure, named after the name of the operation: **CreateOptions**, **UpdateOptions**, **DeleteOptions**, and so on. These structures, and the related constants, are defined in this package: **k8s.io/apimachinery/pkg/apis/meta/v1**.

Finally, to make an operation on a resource of a Group-Version, you can chain the calls following this pattern for namespaced resources, where **namespace** can be the empty string to indicate a cluster-wide operation:

```
clientset.
    GroupVersion().
    NamespacedResource(namespace).
    Operation(ctx, options)
```

Then, the following is the pattern for non-namespaced resources:

```
clientset.
    GroupVersion().
    NonNamespacedResource().
```

```
Operation(ctx, options)
```

For example, use the following to *List* the *Pods* of the *core/v1* Group/Version in namespace **project1**:

```
podList, err := clientset.
    CoreV1().
    Pods("project1").
    List(ctx, metav1.ListOptions{})
```

To get the *list* of *pods* in *all* namespaces, you need to specify an empty namespace name:

```
podList, err := clientset.
    CoreV1().
    Pods("").
    List(ctx, metav1.ListOptions{})
```

To get the list of nodes (which are non-namespaced resources) use this:

```
nodesList, err := clientset.
    CoreV1().
    Nodes().
    List(ctx, metav1.ListOptions{})
```

The following sections describe in detail the various operations using the *Pod* resource. You can apply the same examples by removing the namespace parameter when working with non-namespaced resources.

Examining the Requests

If you want to know which *HTTP* requests are executed when calling client-go methods, you can enable logging for your program. The Client-go Library uses the **klog** library (https://github.com/kubernetes/klog), and you can enable the log flags for your command with the following code:

```
import (
    "flag"
```

```
    "k8s.io/klog/v2"
)

func main() {
    klog.InitFlags(nil)
    flag.Parse()
    [...]
}
```

Now, you can run your program with the flag -v <level>—for example, -v 6 to get the URL called for every request. You can find more detail about the defined log levels in Table 2-1.

Creating a Resource

To create a new resource in the cluster, you first need to declare this resource in memory using the dedicated *Kind* structure, then use the **Create** method for the resource you want to create. For example, use the following to create a **Pod** named **nginx-pod** in the **project1** namespace:

```
wantedPod := corev1.Pod{
    Spec: corev1.PodSpec{
        Containers: []corev1.Container{
            {
                Name:  "nginx",
                Image: "nginx",
            },
        },
    },
}
wantedPod.SetName("nginx-pod")

createdPod, err := clientset.
    CoreV1().
    Pods("project1").
    Create(ctx, &wantedPod, v1.CreateOptions{})
```

The various options used to declare the **CreateOptions** structure, when creating a resource, are:

- `DryRun` – this indicates which operations on the API server-side should be executed. The only available value is `metav1.DryRunAll`, indicating execution of all the operations except persisting the resource to storage.

  Using this option, you can get, as result of the command, the exact object that would have been created in the cluster without really creating it, and check whether an error would occur during this creation.

- `FieldManager` – this indicates the name of the field manager for this operation. This information will be used for future server-side Apply operations.

- `FieldValidation` – this indicates how the server should react when duplicate or unknown fields are present in the structure. The following are the possible values:

  - `metav1.FieldValidationIgnore` to ignore all duplicate or unknown fields

  - `metav1.FieldValidationWarn` to warn when duplicate or unknown fields are present

  - `metav1.FieldValidationStrict` to fail when duplicate or unknown fields are present

  Note that using this method, you will not be able to define duplicate or unknown fields because you are using a structure to define the object.

In case of error, you can test its type with the functions defined in the package **k8s. io/apimachinery/pkg/api/errors**. All the possible errors are defined in section "Errors and Statuses", and here are the possible errors specific to the **Create** operation:

- `IsAlreadyExists` – this function indicates whether the request failed because a resource with the same name already exists in the cluster:

  ```
  if errors.IsAlreadyExists(err) {
  ```

```
        // ...
    }
```

- `IsNotFound` – this function indicates whether the namespace you specified in the request does not exist.

- `IsInvalid` – this function indicates whether the data passed into the structure is invalid.

Getting Information About a Resource

To get information about a specific resource in the cluster, you can use the **Get** method for the resource you want to get information from. For example, to get information about the pod named **nginx-pod** in the **project1** namespace:

```
pod, err := clientset.
    CoreV1().
    Pods("project1").
    Get(ctx, "nginx-pod", metav1.GetOptions{})
```

The various options to declare it into the **GetOptions** structure, when getting information about a resource are:

- `ResourceVersion` – to request a version of the resource not older than the specified version.

  If **ResourceVersion** is "0," indicates to return any version of the resource. You will generally receive the latest version of the resource, but this is not guaranteed; receiving an older version can happen on high availability clusters due to partitioning or stale cache.

  If the option is not set, you are guaranteed to receive the most recent version of the resource.

The possible error specific to the **Get** operation is:

- `IsNotFound` – this function indicates that the namespace you specified in the request does not exist, or that the resource with the specified name does not exist.

Getting List of Resources

To get a list of resources in the cluster, you can use the **List** method for the resource you want to list. For example, use the following to list the pods in the **project1** namespace:

```
podList, err := clientset.
    CoreV1().
    Pods("project1").
    List(ctx, metav1.ListOptions{})
```

Or, to get the list of pods in all namespaces, use:

```
podList, err := clientset.
    CoreV1().
    Pods("").
    List(ctx, metav1.ListOptions{})
```

The various options to declare into the **ListOptions** structure, when listing resources are the following:

- `LabelSelector, FieldSelector` – this is used to filter the list by label or by field. These options are detailed in the "Filtering the Result of a List" section.

- `Watch, AllowWatchBookmarks` – this is used to run a Watch operation. These options are detailed in the "Watching Resources" section.

- `ResourceVersion, ResourceVersionMatch` – this indicates which version of the List of resources you want to obtain.

  Note that, when receiving a response of a **List** operation, a **ResourceVersion** value is indicated for the List element itself, as well as **ResourceVersion** values for each element of the list. The **ResourceVersion** to indicate in the Options refers to the **ResourceVersion** of the List.

  For a **List** operation without pagination (you can refer to the "Paginating Results" and "Watching Resources" sections for the behavior of these options in other circumstances):

- When **ResourceVersionMatch** is not set, the behavior is the same as for a **Get** operation:

  ResourceVersion indicates that you should return a list that is not older than the specified version.

  If **ResourceVersion** is "0," this indicates that it is necessary to return to any version of the list. You generally will receive the latest version of it, but this is not guaranteed; receiving an older version can happen on high-availability clusters because of a partitioning or a stale cache.

  If the option is not set, you are guaranteed to receive the most recent version of the list.

- When ResourceVersionMatch is set to **metav1. ResourceVersionMatchExact**, the ResourceVersion value indicates the exact version of the list you want to obtain.

  Setting **ResourceVersion** to "0," or not defining it, is invalid.

- When ResourceVersionMatch is set to metav1. ResourceVersionMatchNotOlderThan, ResourceVersion indicates you will obtain a list that is not older than the specified version.

  If **ResourceVersion** is "0," this indicates a return any version of the list. You generally will receive the latest version of the list, but this is not guaranteed; receiving an older version can happen on high-availability clusters because of a partitioning or a stale cache.

  Not defining **ResourceVersion** is invalid.

- `TimeoutSeconds` – this limits the duration of the request to the indicated number of seconds.

- `Limit, Continue` – this is used for paginating the result of the list. These options are detailed in Chapter 2's "Paginating Results" section.

The following are the possible errors specific to the **List** operation:

- `IsResourceExpired` – this function indicates that the specified **ResourceVersion** with a **ResourceVersionMatch,** set to **metav1. ResourceVersionMatchExact**, is expired.

Note that, if you specify a nonexisting namespace for a **List** operation, you will not receive a **NotFound** error.

Filtering the Result of a List

As described in Chapter 2's "Filtering the Result of a List" section, it is possible to filter the result of a **List** operation with labels selectors and field selectors. This section shows how to use the **fields** and **labels** packages of the API Machinery Library to create a string applicable to the **LabelSelector** and **FieldSelector** options.

Setting LabelSelector Using the Labels Package

Here is the necessary import information to use the **labels** package from the API Machinery Library.

```
import (
    "k8s.io/apimachinery/pkg/labels"
)
```

The package provides several methods for building and validating a **LabelsSelector** string: using Requirements, parsing a **labelSelector** string, or using a set of key-value pairs.

Using Requirements

You first need to create a **labels.Selector** object using the following code:

```
labelsSelector := labels.NewSelector()
```

Then, you can create **Requirement** objects using the **labels.NewRequirement** function:

```
func NewRequirement(
    key string,
    op selection.Operator,
```

```
    vals []string,
    opts ...field.PathOption,
) (*Requirement, error)
```

Constants for the possible values of **op** are defined in the **selection** package (i.e., **k8s.io/apimachinery/pkg/selection**). The number of values in the **vals** array of strings depends on the operation:

- `selection.In; selection.NotIn` – the value attached to **key** must equal one of (In)/must not equal one of (NotIn) the values defined of **vals**.

  vals must be non-empty.

- `selection.Equals; selection.DoubleEquals; selection.NotEquals` – the value attached to **key** must equal (**Equals**, **DoubleEquals**) or must not equal (**NotEquals**) the value defined in **vals**.

  vals must contain a single value.

- `selection.Exists; selection.DoesNotExist` – the **key** must be defined (**Exists**) or must not be defined (**DoesNotExist**).

  vals must be empty.

- `selection.Gt; selection.Lt` – the value attached to a **key** must be greater than (**Gt**) or less than (**Lt**) the value defined in **vals**.

  vals must contain a single value, representing an integer.

For example, to require that the value of the key **mykey** equals **value1**, you can declare a **Requirement** with:

```
req1, err := labels.NewRequirement(
    "mykey",
    selection.Equals,
    []string{"value1"},
)
```

After defining the **Requirement**, you can add the requirements to the selector using the **Add** method on the selector:

```
labelsSelector = labelsSelector.Add(*req1, *req2)
```

Finally, you can obtain the String to be passed for the **LabelSelector** option with:

```
s := labelsSelector.String()
```

Parsing a LabelSelector String

If you already have a string describing the label selector, you can check its validity
with the **Parse** function. The **Parse** function will validate the string and return a
LabelSelector object. You can use the **String** method on this **LabelSelector** object to
obtain the string as validated by the **Parse** function.

As an example, the following code will parse, validate, and return the canonical form
of the label selector, "**mykey = value1, count < 5**":

```
selector, err := labels.Parse(
    "mykey = value1, count < 5",
)
if err != nil {
    return err
}
s := selector.String()
// s = "mykey=value1,count<5"
```

Using a Set of Key-value Pairs

The function **ValidatedSelectorFromSet** can be used when you only want to use the
Equal operation, for one or several requirements:

```
func ValidatedSelectorFromSet(
    ls Set
) (Selector, error)
```

In this case, the **Set** will define the set of key-value pairs you want to check for
equality.

As an example, the following code will declare a label selector that requires the key,
key1, to equal **value1** and the key, **key2**, to equal **value2**:

```
set := labels.Set{
```

```
        "key1": "value1",
        "key2": "value2",
}

selector, err = labels.ValidatedSelectorFromSet(set)
s = selector.String()
// s = "key1=value1,key2=value2"
```

Setting Fieldselector Using the Fields Package

Here is the necessary code to use to import the **fields** package from the API Machinery Library.

```
import (
        "k8s.io/apimachinery/pkg/fields"
)
```

The package provides several methods for building and validating a FieldSelector string: assembling one term selectors, parsing a **fieldSelector** string, or using a set of key-value pairs.

Assembling One Term Selectors

You can create one term selectors with the functions **OneTermEqualSelector** and **OneTermNotEqualSelector**, then assemble the selectors to build a complete field selector with the function **AndSelectors**.

```
func OneTermEqualSelector(
        k, v string,
) Selector

func OneTermNotEqualSelector(
        k, v string,
) Selector

func AndSelectors(
        selectors ...Selector,
) Selector
```

For example, this code builds a field selector with an **Equal** condition on the field **status.Phase** and a **NotEqual** condition on the field **spec.restartPolicy**:

```
fselector = fields.AndSelectors(
    fields.OneTermEqualSelector(
        "status.Phase",
        "Running",
    ),
    fields.OneTermNotEqualSelector(
        "spec.restartPolicy",
        "Always",
    ),
)
fs = fselector.String()
```

Parsing a FieldSelector String

If you already have a string describing the field selector, you can check its validity with the **ParseSelector** or **ParseSelectorOrDie** functions. The **ParseSelector** function will validate the string and return a **fields.Selector** object. You can use the **String** method on this **fields.Selector** object to obtain the string, as validated by the **ParseSelector** function.

As an example, this code will parse, validate, and return the canonical form of the field selector "**status.Phase** = **Running, spec.restartPolicy** != **Always**":

```
selector, err := fields.ParseSelector(
    "status.Phase=Running, spec.restartPolicy!=Always",
)
if err != nil {
    return err
}
s := selector.String()
// s = "spec.restartPolicy!=Always,status.Phase=Running"
```

Using a Set of Key-Value Pairs

The function **SelectorFromSet** can be used when you want to use only the **Equal** operation, for one or several single selectors.

```
func SelectorFromSet(ls Set) Selector
```

In this case, the **Set** will define the set of key-value pairs you want to check for equality.

As an example, the following code will declare a field selector that requires the key, **key1**, to equal **value1** and the key, **key2**, to equal **value2**:

```
set := fields.Set{
    "field1": "value1",
    "field2": "value2",
}

selector = fields.SelectorFromSet(set)
s = selector.String()
// s = "key1=value1,key2=value2"
```

Deleting a Resource

To delete a resource from the cluster, you can use the **Delete** method for the resource you want to delete. For example, to delete a Pod named **nginx-pod** from the **project1** namespace use:

```
err = clientset.
    CoreV1().
    Pods("project1").
    Delete(ctx, "nginx-pod", metav1.DeleteOptions{})
```

Note that it is not guaranteed that the resource is deleted when the operation terminates. The **Delete** operation will not effectively delete the resource, but mark the resource to be deleted (by setting the field **.metadata.deletionTimestamp)**, and the deletion will happen asynchronously.

The different options, to declare into the **DeleteOptions** structure, when deleting a resource are:

- DryRun – this indicates which operations on the API server-side should be executed. The only available value is **metav1.DryRunAll**, indicating that it is to execute all the operations except (the operation of) persisting the resource to storage. Using this option, you can get the result of the command, without really deleting the resource, and check whether an error would occur during this deletion.

- GracePeriodSeconds – this value is useful when deleting pods only. This indicates the duration in seconds before the pod should be deleted.

  The value must be a pointer to a non-negative integer. The value zero indicates delete immediately. If this value is nil, the default grace period for the pod will be used, as indicated in the **TerminationGracePeriodSeconds** field of the pod specification.

  You can use the **metav1.NewDeleteOptions** function to create a **DeleteOptions** structure with the **GracePeriodSeconds** defined:

```
err = clientset.
    CoreV1().
    Pods("project1").
    Delete(ctx,
        "nginx-pod",
        *metav1.NewDeleteOptions(5),
    )
```

- Preconditions – When you delete an object, you may want to be sure to delete the expected one. The **Preconditions** field lets you indicate which resource you expect to delete, either by:

  ○ Indicating the UID, so if the expected resource is deleted and another resource is created with the same name, the deletion will fail, producing a **Conflict** error. You can use the **metav1.NewPreconditionDeleteOptions** function to create a **DeleteOptions** structure with the UID of the **Preconditions** set:

  ```
  uid := createdPod.GetUID()
  ```

```
err = clientset.

    CoreV1().

    Pods("project1").

    Delete(ctx,

        "nginx-pod",

        *metav1.NewPreconditionDeleteOptions(

            string(uid),

        ),

    )

if errors.IsConflict(err) {

    [...]

}
```

      o   Indicating the **ResourceVersion**, so if the resource is updated in the meantime, the deletion will fail, with a Conflict error. You can use the **metav1.NewRVDeletionPrecondition** function to create a DeleteOptions structure with the ResourceVersion of the Preconditions set:

```
rv := createdPod.GetResourceVersion()
err = clientset.
    CoreV1().
    Pods("project1").
    Delete(ctx,
        "nginx-pod",
        *metav1.NewRVDeletionPrecondition(
            rv,
        ),
    )
if errors.IsConflict(err) {
    [...]
}
```

- OrphanDependents – this field is deprecated in favor of **PropagationPolicy**. PropagationPolicy – this indicates whether and how garbage collection will be performed. See also Chapter 3's "OwnerReferences" section. The acceptable values are:

  - metav1.DeletePropagationOrphan – to indicate to the Kubernetes API to orphan the resources owned by the resource you are deleting, so they will not be deleted by the garbage collector.

  - metav1.DeletePropagationBackground – to indicate to the Kubernetes API to return from the **Delete** operation immediately after the owner resource is marked for deletion, not to wait for owned resources to be deleted by the garbage collector.

  - metav1.DeletePropagationForeground – to indicate to the Kubernetes API to return from the **Delete** operation after the owner and the **owned resources** with **BlockOwnerDeletion** set to **true** are deleted. The Kubernetes API will not wait for other owned resources to be deleted.

The following are the possible errors specific to the **Delete** operation:

- IsNotFound – this function indicates that the resource or the namespace you specified in the request does not exist.

- IsConflict – this function indicates that the request failed because a precondition is not respected (either UID or **ResourceVersion**)

Deleting a Collection of Resources

To delete a collection of resources from the cluster, you can use the **DeleteCollection** method for the resource you want to delete. For example, to delete a collection of Pods from the **project1** namespace:

```
err = clientset.
    CoreV1().
    Pods("project1").
    DeleteCollection(
        ctx,
```

```
        metav1.DeleteOptions{},
        metav1.ListOptions{},
    )
```

Two sets of options must be provided to the function:

- The **DeleteOptions**, indicating the options for the **Delete** operation on each object, as described in the "Deleting a Resource" section.

- The **ListOptions**, refining the collection of resources to delete, as described in the "Getting List of Resources" section.

Updating a Resource

To update a resource in the cluster, you can use the **Update** method for the resource you want to update. For example, use the following to update a Deployment in the **project1** namespace:

```
updatedDep, err := clientset.
    AppsV1().
    Deployments("project1").
    Update(
        ctx,
        myDep,
        metav1.UpdateOptions{},
    )
```

The various options, to declare into the **UpdateOptions** structure when updating a resource, are the same as the options in **CreateOptions** described in the "Creating a Resource" section.

The possible errors specific to the **Update** operation are:

- IsInvalid – this function indicates that the data passed into the structure is invalid.

- IsConflict – this function indicates that the **ResourceVersion** incorporated into the structure (here **myDep**) is a version older than the one in the cluster. More information is available to in Chapter 2's "Updating a Resource Managing Conflicts" section.

Using a Strategic Merge Patch to Update a Resource

You have seen in Chapter 2's "Using a Strategic Merge Patch to Update a Resource" section how patching a resource with a strategic merge patch works. To sum up, you need to:

- Use the **Patch** operation

- Specify a specific value for the content-type header

- Pass into the body the only fields you want to modify

Using the Client-go Library, you can use the **Patch** method for the resource you want to patch.

```
Patch(
    ctx context.Context,
    name string,
    pt types.PatchType,
    data []byte,
    opts metav1.PatchOptions,
    subresources ...string,
    ) (result *v1.Deployment, err error)
```

The **patch** type indicates whether you want to use a **StrategicMerge** patch (**types. StrategicMergePatchType**) or a merge patch (**types.MergePatchType**). These constants are defined in the **k8s.io/apimachinery/pkg/types** package.

The data field contains the patch you want to apply to the resource. You could write this patch data directly, like was done in Chapter 2, or you can use the following functions of the *controller-runtime library* to help you build this patch. This library is explored in more depth in Chapter 10).

```
import "sigs.k8s.io/controller-runtime/pkg/client"
```

```
func StrategicMergeFrom(
    obj Object,
    opts ...MergeFromOption,
) Patch
```

The **StrategicMergeFrom** function accepts a first parameter of **type Object**, representing any Kubernetes object. You will pass by this parameter the object you want to patch, before any change.

The function then accepts a series of options. The only accepted option at this time is the **client.MergeFromWithOptimisticLock{}** value. This value asks the library to add the **ResourceVersion** to the patch data, so the server will be able to check whether the resource version you want to update is the last one.

After you have created a **Patch** object by using the **StrategicMergeFrom** function, you can create a deep copy of the object you want to patch, then modify it. Then, when you are done updating the object, you can build the data for the patch with the dedicated **Data** method of the **Patch** object.

As an example, to build patch data for a Deployment, containing the **ResourceVersion** for optimistic lock, you can use the following code (**createdDep** is a **Deployment** structure that reflects a Deployment created in the cluster):

```
patch := client.StrategicMergeFrom(
    createdDep,
    pkgclient.MergeFromWithOptimisticLock{},
)

updatedDep := createdDep.DeepCopy()
updatedDep.Spec.Replicas = pointer.Int32(2)

patchData, err := patch.Data(updatedDep)
// patchData = []byte(`{
//    "metadata":{"resourceVersion":"4807923"},
//    "spec":{"replicas":2}
// }`)

patchedDep, err := clientset.
    AppsV1().Deployments("project1").Patch(
        ctx,
        "dep1",
        patch.Type(),
        patchData,
        metav1.PatchOptions{},
    )
```

Note that the **MergeFrom** and **MergeFromWithOptions** functions are also available, if you prefer to execute a *Merge Patch* instead.

The **Type** method of the **Patch** object can be used to retrieve the patch type, instead of using the constants in the **type** package. You can pass **PatchOptions** when calling the patch operation. The possible options are:

- DryRun – this indicates which operations on the API server -side should be executed. The only available value is **metav1.DryRunAll**, indicating execution of all the operations except persisting the resource to storage.

- Force – this option can be used only for *Apply* patch requests and must be unset when working with *StrategicMergePatch* or *MergePatch* requests.

- FieldManager – this indicates the name of the field manager for this operation. This information will be used for future server-side *Apply* operations. This option is optional for *StrategicMergePatch* or *MergePatch* requests.

- FieldValidation – this indicates how the server should react when duplicate or unknown fields are present in the structure. The following are the possible values:

  - metav1.FieldValidationIgnore – to ignore all duplicate or unknown fields

  - metav1.FieldValidationWarn – to warn when duplicate or unknown fields are present

  - metav1.FieldValidationStrict – to fail when duplicate or unknown fields are present

Note that the **Patch** operation accepts a **subresources** parameter. This parameter can be used to patch a subresource of the resource on which the **Patch** method is applied. For example, to patch the Status of a Deployment, you can use the value **"status"** for the subresources parameter.

The possible errors specific to the **MergePatch** operation are:

- IsInvalid – this function indicates whether the data passed as a patch is invalid.

- IsConflict – this function indicates whether the **ResourceVersion** incorporated into the patch (if you are using the Optimistic lock when building the patch data) is a version older than the one in the cluster. More information is available in Chapter 2's "Updating a Resource Managing Conflicts" section.

Applying Resources Server-side with Patch

Chapter 2's "Applying Resources Server-side" section described how a Server-side Apply patch works. To sum up, wee need to:

- Use the **Patch** operation

- Specify a specific value for the content-type header

- Pass into the body the only fields you want to modify

- Provide a **fieldManager** name

Using the Client-go Library, you can use the **Patch** method for the resource you want to patch. Note that you also can use the **Apply** method; see the next section, "Applying Resources Server-side with Apply."

```
Patch(
    ctx context.Context,
    name string,
    pt types.PatchType,
    data []byte,
    opts metav1.PatchOptions,
    subresources ...string,
) (result *v1.Deployment, err error)
```

The **Patch** type indicates the type of patch, **types.ApplyPatchType** in this case, defined in the **k8s.io/apimachinery/pkg/types** package.

The **data** field contains the patch you want to apply to the resource. You can use the **client.Apply** value to build this data. This value implements the **client.Patch** interface, providing the **Type** and **Data** methods.

Note that you need to set the **APIVersion** and **Kind** fields in the structure of the resource you want to patch. Also note that this **Apply** operation also can be used to create the resource.

The **Patch** operation accepts a **subresources** parameter. This parameter can be used to patch a subresource of the resource on which the **Patch** method is applied. For example, to patch the **Status** of a Deployment, you can use the value **"status"** for the subresources parameter.

```
import "sigs.k8s.io/controller-runtime/pkg/client"

wantedDep := appsv1.Deployment{
    Spec: appsv1.DeploymentSpec{
        Replicas: pointer.Int32(1),
    [...]
}
wantedDep.SetName("dep1")

wantedDep.APIVersion, wantedDep.Kind =
    appsv1.SchemeGroupVersion.
        WithKind("Deployment").
        ToAPIVersionAndKind()

patch := client.Apply
patchData, err := patch.Data(&wantedDep)

patchedDep, err := clientset.
    AppsV1().Deployments("project1").Patch(
        ctx,
        "dep1",
        patch.Type(),
        patchData,
        metav1.PatchOptions{
        FieldManager: "my-program",
    },
    )
```

You can pass **PatchOptions** when calling the **Patch** operation. The following are the possible options:

- DryRun – this indicates which operations on the API Server-side should be executed. The only available value is **metav1.DryRunAll**, indicating the execution of all the operations except persisting the resource to storage.

- Force – this option indicates *force Apply* requests. It means the field manager for this request will acquire conflicting fields owned by other field managers.

- FieldManager – this indicates the name of the field manager for this operation. This option is mandatory for *Apply Patch* requests.

- FieldValidation – this indicates how the server should react when duplicate or unknown fields are present in the structure. The possible values are:

    - metav1.FieldValidationIgnore – to ignore all duplicate or unknown fields

    - metav1.FieldValidationWarn – to warn when duplicate or unknown fields are present

    - metav1.FieldValidationStrict – to fail when duplicate or unknown fields are present

The following are the possible errors specific to the **ApplyPatch** operation:

- IsInvalid – this function indicates whether the data passed as a patch is invalid.

- IsConflict – this function indicates whether some fields modified by the patch are in conflict because they are owned by another field manager. To resolve this conflict, you can use the **Force** option so that these fields will be acquired by the field manager of this operation.

Server-side Apply Using Apply Configurations

The previous section has shown how to execute a server-side *Apply* operation by using the **Patch** method. The disadvantage is that the data must be passed in JSON format, which can be error-prone.

Starting with Version 1.21, the Client-go **Clientset** provides an **Apply** method to execute the server-side *Apply* operation using typed structures. The following is the signature for the **Apply** method:

```
Apply(
    ctx context.Context,
    deployment *acappsv1.DeploymentApplyConfiguration,
    opts metav1.ApplyOptions,
) (result *v1.Deployment, err error)
```

The **ApplyOptions** structure defines the following options:

- DryRun – this indicates which operations on the API Server-side should be executed. The only available value is **metav1.DryRunAll**, indicating execution of all the operations except persisting the resource to storage.

- Force – this caller will reacquire the conflicting fields owned by other managers.

- FieldManager – this is the name of the *manager* making the **Apply** operation. This value is required.

This signature of **Apply** is like the signatures of the **Create** or **Update** operations, except that a **DeploymentApplyConfiguration** object is expected, instead of a **Deployment** object.

As seen in Chapter 2's "Applying Resources Server-side" section, the **Apply** operation permits several *managers* to work on the same resource, each manager owning a set of values in the resource specification.

For this reason, the data passed for the operation will not define all the fields, but only the fields the *manager* is *responsible for*. Some of the fields are required in the structures of resource definitions; it is not possible to use these structures for the **Apply** operation.

The Client-go Library introduces new structures, named *Apply Configurations*, in the **applyconfigurations** directory of the library, with all fields being optional, using pointers. This directory contains generated source code for all native resources of the Kubernetes API, with the same structure of it. For example, to access the structures needed to define the data for applying a **Deployment** from the **apps/v1** group, you need to import the following package:

```
import (
    acappsv1 "k8s.io/client-go/applyconfigurations/apps/v1"
)
```

Note that, for the same reason as you want to define an alias for packages imported from the Kubernetes API Library (because most packages are named **v1**), you will want to use aliases when importing these packages. This book uses the same system as the API Library, prefixing the alias with **ac** to indicate it comes from the **applyconfigurations** directory.

Two possibilities are offered by the Client-go to build an **ApplyConfiguration**: from scratch or from an existing resource.

Building an ApplyConfiguration from Scratch

The first way to build an **ApplyConfiguration** is to build it from scratch. You first need to initialize the structure with the mandatory fields: kind, apiVersion, name, and namespace (if the resource is namespaced); this is done with a helper function that is provided by the related package. For example, for a `Deployment` resource:

```
deploy1Config := acappsv1.Deployment(
    "deploy1",
    "default",
)
```

The implementation of this function uses the following:

```
func Deployment(
    name string,
    namespace string,
) *DeploymentApplyConfiguration {
    b := &DeploymentApplyConfiguration{}
    b.WithName(name)
    b.WithNamespace(namespace)
    b.WithKind("Deployment")
    b.WithAPIVersion("apps/v1")
    return b
}
```

Then, you can specify the fields you want to manage. Helper functions in the form With*Field*() are provided to establish specific fields. For example, if your program is responsible only for setting the number of replicas for the deployment, the code will be:

```
deploy1Config.WithSpec(acappsv1.DeploymentSpec())
deploy1Config.Spec.WithReplicas(2)
```

Finally, you can call the **Apply** method. The complete code is the following:

```
import (
    acappsv1 "k8s.io/client-go/applyconfigurations/apps/v1"
)

deploy1Config := acappsv1.Deployment(
    "deploy1",
    "default",
)
deploy1Config.WithSpec(acappsv1.DeploymentSpec())
deploy1Config.Spec.WithReplicas(2)

result, err := clientset.AppsV1().
    Deployments("default").Apply(
        ctx,
        deploy1Config,
        metav1.ApplyOptions{
            FieldManager: "my-manager",
            Force:        true,
        },
    )
```

Building an ApplyConfiguration from an Existing Resource

The second way to build an **ApplyConfiguration** is to start from an existing resource in the cluster. Sometimes a program is not able to build the entire **Apply Configuration** in one place. For example, imagine your program is responsible for defining a container with a specific image for a Deployment in one place and also is responsible for setting the number of replicas in another place.

If the program defines the container and its image first, it will be marked as the owner of the container and its image. Then, if the program builds an **ApplyConfiguration** and sets only the number of replicas, without specifying the container and its image, the server-side **Apply** operation will try to delete the container. This is because the program designated the owner of this container, but it does not specify it anymore in the **ApplyConfiguration**.

A possibility would be to use diverse manager names for the various parts of the program. If you want to keep a single manager name, however, the packages in the **applyconfigurations** directory provide an **Extract*Resource*()** helper function to assist you in this case.

These functions will get as parameter a resource read from the cluster (with a **Get** or a **List** operation) and will build an **ApplyConfiguration** containing only the fields owned by the specified **fieldManager**. For example, the signature for the **ExtractDeployment** helper function is:

```
ExtractDeployment(
    deployment *apiappsv1.Deployment,
    fieldManager string,
) (*DeploymentApplyConfiguration, error)
```

The first steps are to read the deployment from the cluster, then extract the **ApplyConfiguration** from it. At this point, it will contain all the fields managed by the program (container and its image and the replicas). Then, you can specify the only fields you want to modify—that is, the replicas for in this example:

```
gotDeploy1, err := clientset.AppsV1().
    Deployments("default").Get(
        ctx,
        "deploy1",
    metav1.GetOptions{},
    )
if err != nil {
    return err
}
deploy1Config, err := acappsv1.ExtractDeployment(
    gotDeploy1,
    "my-manager",
)
```

```
if err != nil {
    return err
}
If deploy1Config.Spec == nil {
    deploy1Config.WithSpec(acappsv1.DeploymentSpec())
}
deploy1Config.Spec.WithReplicas(2)
result, err := clientset.AppsV1().
    Deployments("default").Apply(
        ctx,
        deploy1Config,
        metav1.ApplyOptions{
            FieldManager: "my-manager",
            Force:        true,
        },
    )
```

Watching Resources

Chapter 2's "Watching Resources" section describes how the Kubernetes API can *watch* resources. Using the Client-go Library, you can use the **Watch** method for the resource you want to watch.

```
Watch(
    ctx context.Context,
    opts metav1.ListOptions,
) (watch.Interface, error)
```

This **Watch** method returns an object that implements the interface **watch.Interface** and providing the following methods:

```
import "k8s.io/apimachinery/pkg/watch"

type Interface interface {
    ResultChan() <-chan Event
    Stop()
}
```

The **ResultChan** method returns a Go channel (which you can only read) on which you will be able to receive all the events.

The **Stop** method will stop the **Watch** operation and close the channel that was received using **ResultChan**.

The **watch.Event** object, received using the channel, is defined as follows:

```
type Event struct {
    Type EventType
    Object runtime.Object
}
```

The **Type** field can get the values described earlier in Chapter 2's Table 2-2, and you can find constants for these various values in the **watch** package: **watch.Added**, **watch. Modified**, **watch.Deleted**, **watch.Bookmark**, and **watch.Error**.

The **Object** field implements the **runtime.Object** interface, and its concrete type can be different depending on the value of the **Type**.

For a **Type**, other than **Error**, the concrete type of the Object will be the type of the resource you are watching (e.g., the **Deployment** type if you are watching for *deployments*).

For the **Error** type, the concrete type generally will be **metav1.Status**, but it could be any other type, depending on the resource you are watching. As an example, here is a code for watching Deployments:

```
import "k8s.io/apimachinery/pkg/watch"

watcher, err := clientset.AppsV1().
    Deployments("project1").
    Watch(
        ctx,
        metav1.ListOptions{},
    )
if err != nil {
    return err
}

for ev := range watcher.ResultChan() {
    switch v := ev.Object.(type) {
    case *appsv1.Deployment:
```

```
        fmt.Printf("%s %s\n", ev.Type, v.GetName())
    case *metav1.Status:
        fmt.Printf("%s\n", v.Status)
        watcher.Stop()
    }
}
```

The various options to be declared into the **ListOptions** structure, when watching resources, are the following:

- `LabelSelector, FieldSelector` – this is used to filter the elements watched by label or by field. These options are detailed in the "Filtering the Result of a List" section.

- `Watch, AllowWatchBookmarks` – the **Watch** option indicates that a *Watch* operation is running. This option is set automatically when executing the **Watch** method; you do not have to set it explicitly.

  The **AllowWatchBookmarks** option asks the server to return *Bookmarks* regularly. The use of bookmarks is described in Chapter 2's, "Allowing Bookmarks to Efficiently Restart a *Watch* Request" section.

- `ResourceVersion, ResourceVersionMatch` – this indicates at which version of the **List** of resources you want to start the **Watch** operation.

  Note that, when receiving a response of a **List** operation, a **ResourceVersion** value is indicated for the list element itself, as well as *ResourceVersion* values for each element of the list. The **ResourceVersion** to indicate in the Options refers to the **ResourceVersion** of the list.

  The **ResourceVersionMatch** option is not used for **Watch** operations. For a **Watch** operations do the following:

  ○ When **ResourceVersion** is not set, the API will start the **Watch** operation at the most recent list of resources. The channel first receives ADDED events to declare the initial state of the resource, followed by other events when changes occur on the cluster.

- ° When **ResourceVersion** is set to a specific version, the API will start the **Watch** operation at the specified version of the list of resources. The channel will **not** receive ADDED events to declare the initial state of the resource, but only events when changes occur on the cluster after this version (which can be events that occurred between the specified version and the time you run the **Watch** operation).

  A use case is to watch for the deletion of a specific resource. For this, you can:

  1. List the resources, including the one you want to delete, and save the **ResourceVersion** of the received List.

  2. Execute a **Delete** operation on the resource (the deletion being asynchronous, the resource probably will not be deleted when the operation terminates).

  3. Start a **Watch** operation by specifying the **ResourceVersion** received in Step 1. Even if the deletion occurs between Steps 2 and 3, you are guaranteed to receive the **DELETED** event.

- ° When ResourceVersion is set to "0," the API will start the **Watch** operation at **any** list of resources. The channel first receives ADDED events to declare the initial state of the resource, followed by other events when changes occur on the cluster after this initial state.

  You have to take special care when using this semantic because the **Watch** operation will generally start with the most recent version; however, starting with an older version is possible.

- • `TimeoutSeconds` – this limits the duration of the request to the indicated number of seconds.

- • `Limit, Continue` – this is used for paginating the result of a **List** operation. These options are not supported for a **Watch** operation.

Note that, if you specify a nonexisting namespace for a **Watch** operation, you will not receive a *NotFound* error.

Also note that, if you specify an expired **ResourceVersion**, you will not receive an error when calling the **Watch** method, but will get an ERROR event containing a **metav1. Status** object indicating a **Reason** with a value **metav1.StatusReasonExpired**.

The **metav1.Status** is the base object used to build the errors returned by calls using the Clientset. You will be able to learn more in the "Errors and Statuses" section.

Errors and Statuses

As Chapter 1 has shown, the Kubernetes API defines *Kinds* for exchanging data with the caller. For the moment, you should consider that *Kinds* are related to the resources, either the *Kind* having the singular name of the resource (e.g., **Pod**), or the *Kind* for a list of resources (e.g., **PodList**). When an API operation returns neither a resource nor a list or resources, it uses a common *Kind*, **metav1.Status**, to indicate the status of the operation.

Definition of the metav1.Status Structure

The **metav1.Status** structure is defined as follows:

```
type Status struct {
    Status      string
    Message     string
    Reason      StatusReason
    Details     *StatusDetails
    Code        int32
}
```

- Status – this indicates the status of the operation and is either **metav1.StatusSuccess** or **metav1.StatusFailure**.

- Message – this is a free form human-readable description of the status of the operation.

- Code – this indicates the HTTP status code returned for the operation.

- Reason – this indicates why the operation is in the **Failure** status. A **Reason** is related to a given HTTP status code. The defined **Reasons** are:

  ○ `StatusReasonBadRequest` (400) – this request itself is invalid. This is different from **StatusReasonInvalid**, which indicates that the API call could possibly succeed, but the data was invalid. A request replying **StatusReasonBadRequest** can never succeed, whatever the data.

  ○ `StatusReasonUnauthorized` (401) – the authorization credentials are missing, incomplete, or invalid.

  ○ `StatusReasonForbidden` (403) – the authorization credentials are valid, but the operation on the resource is forbidden for these credentials.

  ○ `StatusReasonNotFound` (404) – the requested resource or resources cannot be found.

  ○ `StatusReasonMethodNotAllowed` (405) – the operation requested in the resource is not allowed because it id not implemented. A request replying **StatusReasonMethodNotAllowed** can never succeed, whatever the data.

  ○ `StatusReasonNotAcceptable` (406) – none of the Accept types indicated in the Accept header by the client is possible. A request replying **StatusReasonNotAcceptable** can never succeed, whatever the data.

  ○ `StatusReasonAlreadyExists` (409) – the resource being created already exists.

  ○ `StatusReasonConflict` (409) – the request cannot be completed because of a conflict—for example, because the operation tries to update a resource with an older resource version, or because a precondition in a **Delete** operation is not respected.

  ○ `StatusReasonGone` (410) – an item is no longer available.

- StatusReasonExpired (410) – the content has expired and is no longer available—for example, when executing a **List** or **Watch** operation with an expired resource version.

- StatusReasonRequestEntityTooLarge (413) – the request entity is too large.

- StatusReasonUnsupportedMediaType (415) – the content type indicated in the Content-Type header is not supported for this resource. A request replying **StatusReasonUnsupportedMediaType** can never succeed, whatever the data.

- StatusReasonInvalid (422) – the data sent for a **Create** or **Update** operation is invalid. The **Causes** field enumerates the invalid fields of the data.

- StatusReasonTooManyRequests (429) – the client should wait at least the number of seconds specified in the field **RetryAfterSeconds** of the **Details** field before performing an action again.

- StatusReasonUnknown (500) – the server did not indicate any reason for the failure.

- StatusReasonServerTimeout (500) – the server can be reached and understand the request, but cannot complete the action in a reasonable time. The client should retry the request after the number of seconds specified in the field **RetryAfterSeconds** of the **Details** field.

- StatusReasonInternalError (500) – an internal error occurred; it is unexpected and the outcome of the call is unknown.

- StatusReasonServiceUnavailable (503) – the request was valid, but the requested service is unavailable at this time. Retrying the request after some time might succeed.

- StatusReasonTimeout (504) – the operation cannot be completed within the time specified by the timeout in the request. If the field **RetryAfterSeconds** of the **Details** field is specified, the

151

client should wait this number of seconds before performing the action again.

- Details – these can contain more details about the reason, depending on the **Reason** field.

The type **StatusDetails** of the **Details** field is defined as follows:

```
type StatusDetails struct {
    Name string
    Group string
    Kind string
    UID types.UID
    Causes []StatusCause
    RetryAfterSeconds int32
}
```

The **Name**, **Group**, **Kind**, and **UID** fields indicate, if specified, which resource is impacted by the failure.

The **RetryAfterSeconds** field, if specified, indicates how many seconds the client should wait before performing an operation again.

The **Causes** field enumerates the causes of the failure. When performing a **Create** or **Update** operation resulting in a failure with a **StatusReasonInvalid** reason, the **Causes** field enumerates the invalid fields and the type of error for each field.

The **StatusCause** type of the **Causes** field is defined as follows:

```
type StatusCause struct {
    Type        CauseType
    Message     string
    Field       string
}
```

Error Returned by Clientset Operations

This chapter earlier contained a description of the various operations provided by the Clientset that the operations generally return an **error**, and that you can use functions from the **errors** package to test the cause of the error—for example, with the function **IsAlreadyExists**.

The concrete type of these errors is **errors.StatusError**, defined as:

```
type StatusError struct {
    ErrStatus metav1.Status
}
```

It can be seen that this type includes only the **metav1.Status** structure that has been explored earlier in this section. Functions are provided for this **StatusError** type to access the underlying **Status**.

- `Is<ReasonValue>(err error) bool` – one for each **Reason** value enumerated earlier in this section, indicating whether the error is of a particular status.

- `FromObject(obj runtime.Object) error` – When you are receiving a **metav1.Status** during a **Watch** operation, you can build a **StatusError** object using this function.

- `(e *StatusError) Status() metav1.Status` – returns the underlying Status.

- `ReasonForError(err error) metav1.StatusReason` – returns the **Reason** of the underlying Status.

- `HasStatusCause(err error, name metav1.CauseType) bool` – this indicates whether an error declares a specific cause with the given **CauseType**.

- `StatusCause(err error, name metav1.CseType) (metav1.StatusCause, bool)` – returns the cause for the given **causeType** if it exists, or false otherwise.

- `SuggestsClientDelay(err error) (int, bool)` – this indicates whether the error indicates a value in the **RetryAfterSeconds** field of the **Status** and the value itself.

RESTClient

Earlier in this chapter in the "Using the Clientset" section, you can get a *REST* client for each group/version of the Kubernetes API. For example, the following code returns the REST client for the **Core/v1** group:

```
restClient := clientset.CoreV1().RESTClient()
```

The **restClient** object implements the interface **rest.Interface**, defined as:

```
type Interface interface {
    GetRateLimiter()             flowcontrol.RateLimiter
    Verb(verb string)            *Request
    Post()                       *Request
    Put()                        *Request
    Patch(pt types.PatchType)    *Request
    Get()                        *Request
    Delete()                     *Request
    APIVersion()                  schema.GroupVersion
}
```

In this interface, you can see the generic method, **Verb**, and the helper methods **Post**, **Put**, **Patch**, **Get**, and **Delete** returning a **Request** object.

Building the Request

The **Request** structure contains only private fields, and it provides methods to personalize the Request. As shown in Chapter 1, the form of the path for a Kubernetes resource or subresource (some segments may be absent depending on the operation and resource) is the following:

/apis/<group>/<version>
    /namespaces/<namesapce_name>
        /<resource>
            /<resource_name>
                /<subresource>

The following methods can be used to build this path. Note that the **<group>** and **<version>** segments are fixed, as the REST client is specific to a group and version.

- `Namespace(namespace string) *Request;`
  `NamespaceIfScoped(namespace string, scoped bool)`
  `*Request` – these indicate the namespace of the resource to query.
  NamespaceIfScoped will add the namespace part only if the request
  is marked as scoped.

- `Resource(resource string) *Request` – this indicates the resource
  to query.

- `Name(resourceName string) *Request` – this indicates the name of
  the resource to query.

- `SubResource(subresources ...string) *Request` – this indicates
  the subresource of the resource to query.

- `Prefix(segments ...string) *Request; Suffix(segments`
  `...string) *Request` – add segments to the beginning or end
  of the request path. The prefix segments will be added before the
  "namespace" segment. The suffix segments will be added after the
  subresource segment. New calls to these methods will add prefixes
  and suffixes to the existing ones.

- `AbsPath(segments ...string) *Request` – resets the prefix with the
  provided segments.

The following methods complete the request with query parameters, body, and
headers:

- `Param(paramName, s string) *Request` – adds a query parameter
  with the provided name and value.

- `VersionedParams(`

    `obj runtime.Object,`

    `codec runtime.ParameterCodec,`

  `) *Request`

  Adds a series of parameters, extracted from the object **obj**. The
  concrete type of **obj** is generally one of the structures **ListOptions**,
  GetOptions, **DeleteOptions**, **CreateOptions**, **PatchOptions**,
  ApplyOptions, **UpdateOptions,** or **TableOptions**.

The **codec** is generally the parameter codec provided by the **scheme** package of the client-go library: **scheme.ParameterCodec**.

```
SpecificallyVersionedParams(

    obj runtime.Object,

    codec runtime.ParameterCodec,

    version schema.GroupVersion,

) *Request
```

With VersionedParams, the object will be encoded using the group and version of the REST Client. With SpecificallyVersionedParams, you can indicate a specific group and version.

- `SetHeader(key string, values ...string) *Request` – sets values for the specified header for the request. If the header with this key is already defined, it will be overwritten.

- `Body(obj interface{}) *Request` – sets the body content of the request, based on **obj**. The **obj** can be of different type:

  - `string` – the file with the given name will be read and its content used as body

  - `[]byte` – the data will be used for the body

  - `io.Reader` – the data read from the reader will be used for the body

  - `runtime.Object` – the object will be marshaled and the result used for the body. The Content-Type header will be set to indicate in which type the object is marshaled (json, yaml, etc.).

Other methods can be used to configure the technical properties of the request:

- `BackOff(manager BackoffManager) *Request` – sets a Backoff manager for the request. The default backoff manager is a **rest. NoBackoff** manager provided by the **rest** package, which won't wait before to execute a new request after a failing request.

The **rest** package provides another backoff manager, **rest. URLBackoff**, which will wait before to retry a new request on a server which replied previously with a 5xx error.

You can build and use a **rest.URLBackoff** object with:

```
request.BackOff(&rest.URLBackoff{
    Backoff: flowcontrol.NewBackOffWithJitter(
        1*time.Second,
        30*time.Second,
        0.1,
    ),
})
```

If you get continuous 5xx errors calling the Kubernetes API, the RESTClient will add exponential delays between the requests, here 1 second, then 2 seconds, then 4 seconds, and so on, capping the delays to 30 seconds, and adding a jitter of maximum 10% to delays, until the server replies with a non-5xx status.

If you do not want to add jitter:

```
request.BackOff(&rest.URLBackoff{
    Backoff: flowcontrol.NewBackOff(
        1*time.Second,
        30*time.Second,
    ),
})
```

Note that, instead of using this code to declare an exponential backoff for each requests, you can declare the environment variables **KUBE_ CLIENT_BACKOFF_BASE=1** and **KUBE_CLIENT_BACKOFF_ DURATION=30** to have a similar behavior (without adding jitter) when running programs using the client-go library for all requests.

The parameter accepted by **BackOff()** being an interface, you can write your own BackOff manager, by implementing the **rest. BackoffManager** interface:

```go
type BackoffManager interface {
    UpdateBackoff(
        actualUrl *url.URL,
        err error,
        responseCode int,
    )
    CalculateBackoff(
        actualUrl *url.URL,
    ) time.Duration
    Sleep(d time.Duration)
}
```

For example, to implement a linear backoff on 5xx errors (working when calling only one host):

```go
type MyLinearBackOff struct {
    next time.Duration
}

func (o *MyLinearBackOff) UpdateBackoff(
    actualUrl *url.URL,
    err error,
    responseCode int,
) {
    if responseCode > 499 {
        o.next += 1 * time.Second
        return
    }
    o.next = 0
}

func (o *MyLinearBackOff) CalculateBackoff(
    actualUrl *url.URL,
) time.Duration {
    return o.next
}

func (o *MyLinearBackOff) Sleep(
```

```
    d time.Duration,
) {
    time.Sleep(d)
}
```

- `Throttle(limiter flowcontrol.RateLimiter) *Request` – throttling will limit the number of requests per second the RESTClient can execute.

  By default, a *Token Bucket Rate Limiter* is used, with a QPS of 5 queries/second and a Burst of 10.

  This means that the RESTClient can make a maximum of 5 requests per second, plus a bonus (bucket) of 10 requests that it can use at any time. The bucket can be refilled at the rate of QPS, in this case the bucket is refilled with 5 tokens per second, the maximal size of the bucket remaining 10.

  You can build and use a **flowcontrol.tokenBucketRateLimiter** object with:

```
request.Throttle(
    flowcontrol.NewTokenBucketRateLimiter(5.0, 10),
)
```

  In this example, a Token Bucket Rate Limiter with a rate of 5.0 queries/second (QPS) and a burst of 10 will be used for the Request.

  Note that you can obtain the same behavior for all requests by setting the QPS and Burst of the Config used to create the RESTClient.

  The default Rate Limiter for a Request is inherited from the Config used to create the clientset. You can change the Rate Limiter for all the requests by setting the Rate Limiter in the Config.

- `MaxRetries(maxRetries int) *Request` – this indicates the number of retries the RESTClient will perform when the Request receives a response with a **Retry-After** header and a **429** status code (*Too Many Requests*).

The default value is 10, meaning that the Request will be performed a maximum of 11 times before to return with an error.

- `Timeout(d time.Duration) *Request` – this indicates the number of seconds the RESTClient will wait for a response to the Request before returning an error. The default Timeout for a Request is inherited from the HTTPClient used to build the clientset.

- `WarningHandler(handler WarningHandler) *Request` – the API server can return Warnings for a Request using a specific header (the "Warning" header). By default, the warnings with be logged, and the **rest** package provides several built-in implementations of handlers:

  - **WarningLogger{}** logs warnings (the default)

  - **NoWarning{}** suppresses warnings

  - **NewWarningWriter()** writes warnings to the provided writer. Options can be specified:

  - **Deduplicate** – true to write a given warning only once

  - **Color** – true to write warning in Yellow color

You can write your own implementation of a **WarningHandler** by implementing this interface:

```
type WarningHandler interface {
    HandleWarningHeader(
        code int,
        agent string,
        text string,
    )
}
```

Note that you can set a default **Warning Handler** for all the requests from all clients by calling the following global function:

```
rest.SetDefaultWarningHandler(l WarningHandler)
```

Executing the Request

Once the Request is built, we can execute it. The following methods on a **Request** object can be used:

- `Do(ctx context.Context) Result` – this executes the Request and return a Result object. We will see in the next section how to exploit this Result object.

- `Watch(ctx context.Context) (watch.Interface, error)` – this executes a **Watch** operation on the requested location, and returns an object implementing the interface **watch.Interface**, used to receive events. You can see the section "Watching Resources" of this chapter to see how to use the returned object.

- `Stream(ctx context.Context) (io.ReadCloser, error)` – this executes the Request and Stream the result body through a ReadCloser.

- `DoRaw(ctx context.Context) ([]byte, error)` – this executes the Request and return the result as an array of bytes.

Exploiting the Result

When you execute the **Do()** method on a Request, the method returns a Result object.
The Result structure does not have any public field. The following methods can be used to get information about the result:

- `Into(obj runtime.Object) error` – this decodes and stores the content of the result body into the object, if possible. The concrete type of the object passed as parameter must match the kind defined in the body. Also return the error executing the request.

- `Error() error` – this returns the error executing the request. This method is useful when executing a request returning no body content.

- `Get() (runtime.Object, error)` – this decodes and returns the content of the result body as an object. The concrete type of the returned object will match the kind defined in the body. Also return the error executing the request.

- `Raw() ([]byte, error)` – this returns the body as an array of bytes, and the error executing the request.

- `StatusCode(statusCode *int) Result` – this stores the status code into the passed parameter, and return the Result, so the method can be chained.

- `WasCreated(wasCreated *bool) Result` – this stores a value indicating if the resource requested to be created has been created successfully, and return the Result, so the method can be chained.

- `Warnings() []net.WarningHeader` – this returns the list of Warnings contained in the Result.

Getting Result as a Table

You have seen in Chapter 2's "Getting Result as a Table" section that it is possible to get the result of a *List* request as a list of columns and rows so as to display the information in a tabular representation. For this, you have to make a List operation and specify a specific **Accept** header.

Here is the code to list the pods of the **project1** namespace, in a tabular representation, using the RESTClient:

```
import (
    metav1 "k8s.io/apimachinery/pkg/apis/meta/v1"
)

restClient := clientset.CoreV1().RESTClient()        ❶
req := restClient.Get().
    Namespace("project1").                    ❷
    Resource("pods").                         ❸
    SetHeader(                                ❹
    "Accept",
    fmt.Sprintf(
        "application/json;as=Table;v=%s;g=%s",
        metav1.SchemeGroupVersion.Version,
```

```
        metav1.GroupName
    ))

var result metav1.Table          ❺
err = req.Do(ctx).               ❻
    Into(&result)                ❼
if err != nil {
    return err
}

for _, colDef := range result.ColumnDefinitions {      ❽
    // display header
}

for _, row := range result.Rows {          ❾
    for _, cell := range row.Cells {          ❿
        // display cell
    }
}
```

❶ Get the RESTClient for the **core/v1** group

❷ Indicate the namespace from which to list the resources (here **project1**)

❸ Indicate the resources to list (here **pods**)

❹ Set the required header to get the result as tabular information

❺ Prepare a variable of type **metav1.Table** to store the result of the request

❻ Execute the request

❼ Store the result in the **metav1.Table** object

❽ Range over the definitions of the columns returned to display the table header

❾ Range over the rows of the table returned to display the row of data containing information about a specific pod

❿ Range over the cells of the row to display them

Discovery Client

The Kubernetes API provides endpoints to discover the resources served by the API. **kubectl** is using these endpoints to display the result of the command **kubectl api-resources** (Figure 6-1).

```
$ kubectl api-resources
NAME                              SHORTNAMES       APIVERSION                        NAMESPACED   KIND
bindings                                           v1                                true         Binding
componentstatuses                 cs               v1                                false        ComponentStatus
configmaps                        cm               v1                                true         ConfigMap
endpoints                         ep               v1                                true         Endpoints
events                            ev               v1                                true         Event
limitranges                       limits           v1                                true         LimitRange
namespaces                        ns               v1                                false        Namespace
nodes                             no               v1                                false        Node
persistentvolumeclaims            pvc              v1                                true         PersistentVolumeClaim
persistentvolumes                 pv               v1                                false        PersistentVolume
pods                              po               v1                                true         Pod
podtemplates                                       v1                                true         PodTemplate
replicationcontrollers            rc               v1                                true         ReplicationController
resourcequotas                    quota            v1                                true         ResourceQuota
secrets                                            v1                                true         Secret
serviceaccounts                   sa               v1                                true         ServiceAccount
services                          svc              v1                                true         Service
mutatingwebhookconfigurations                      admissionregistration.k8s.io/v1   false        MutatingWebhookConfiguration
validatingwebhookconfigurations                    admissionregistration.k8s.io/v1   false        ValidatingWebhookConfiguration
customresourcedefinitions         crd,crds         apiextensions.k8s.io/v1           false        CustomResourceDefinition
apiservices                                        apiregistration.k8s.io/v1         false        APIService
controllerrevisions                                apps/v1                           true         ControllerRevision
daemonsets                        ds               apps/v1                           true         DaemonSet
deployments                       deploy           apps/v1                           true         Deployment
replicasets                       rs               apps/v1                           true         ReplicaSet
statefulsets                      sts              apps/v1                           true         StatefulSet
applications                      app,apps         argoproj.io/v1alpha1              true         Application
applicationsets                   appset,appsets   argoproj.io/v1alpha1              true         ApplicationSet
```

Figure 6-1. *kubectl api-resources*

The client can be obtained either by calling the **Discovery()** method on a **Clientset** (see how to obtain a Clientset in Chapter 6's "Getting a Clientset" section), or by using functions provided by the **discovery** package.

```
import "k8s.io/client-go/discovery"
```

All these function, expect a **rest.Config**, as a parameter. You can see in Chapter 6's "Connecting to the Cluster" section how to get such a **rest.Config** object.

```
NewDiscoveryClientForConfig(
    c *rest.Config,
) (*DiscoveryClient, error)
```

– this returns a DiscoveryClient, using the provided **rest.Config**

- ```
  NewDiscoveryClientForConfigOrDie(

  c *rest.Config,

  ) *DiscoveryClient
  ```

  Similar to the previous one, but panics in case of error, instead of returning the error. This function can be used with a hard-coded config whose we want to assert the validity.

- ```
  NewDiscoveryClientForConfigAndClient(

      c *rest.Config,

      httpClient *http.Client,

  ) (*DiscoveryClient, error)
  ```

  – this returns a DiscoveryClient, using the provided **rest.Config**, and the provided **httpClient**.

  The previous function **NewDiscoveryClientForConfig** uses a default HTTP Client built with the function **rest.HTTPClientFor**. If you want to personalize the HTTP Client before building the **DiscoveryClient**, you can use this function instead.

RESTMapper

You have seen in Chapter 5's "RESTMapper" section that the API Machinery provides a concept of RESTMapper, used to map between REST Resources and Kubernetes Kinds.

The API Machinery also provides a default implementation of the RESTMapper, the **DefaultRESTMapper**, for which the group/version/kinds must be added manually.

The Client-go Library provides several implementations of a RESTMapper, taking advantage of the Discovery client to provide the list of group/version/kinds and resources.

PriorityRESTMapper

The **PriorityRESTMapper** is gets all the groups served by the Kubernetes API, with the help of the Discovery client, and takes care about the multiple versions that could be part of given groups and the preferred version for each group, to return the preferred version.

A **restmapper.PriorityRESTMapper** object is obtained by calling the function **restmapper.NewDiscoveryRESTMapper**:

```
import "k8s.io/client-go/restmapper"

func NewDiscoveryRESTMapper(
    groupResources []*APIGroupResources,
) meta.RESTMapper
```

The **groupResources** parameter can be built with the function **restmapper. GetAPIGroupResources**:

```
func GetAPIGroupResources(
    cl discovery.DiscoveryInterface,
) ([]*APIGroupResources, error)
```

Here is the code necessary to build a **PriorityRESTMapper**:

```
import "k8s.io/client-go/restmapper"

discoveryClient := clientset.Discovery()

apiGroupResources, err :=
    restmapper.GetAPIGroupResources(
        discoveryClient,
    )
if err != nil {
    return err
}

restMapper := restmapper.NewDiscoveryRESTMapper(
    apiGroupResources,
)
```

You can now use the RESTMapper as defined in Chapter 5's "RESTMapper" section.

DeferredDiscoveryRESTMapper

The **DeferredDiscoveryRESTMapper** uses a **PriorityRESTMapper** internally, but will wait for the first request to initialize the RESTMapper.

```
func NewDeferredDiscoveryRESTMapper(
    cl discovery.CachedDiscoveryInterface,
) *DeferredDiscoveryRESTMapper
```

The function **NewDeferredDiscoveryRESTMapper** is used to build such a RESTMapper, and it gets an object which implements the the **discovery. CachedDiscoveryInterface** to get a Cached Discovery Client.

The Client-go Library provides an implementation for this interface, which is returned by the function **memory.NewMemCacheClient**.

```
func NewMemCacheClient(
    delegate discovery.DiscoveryInterface,
) discovery.CachedDiscoveryInterface
```

Here is the code necessary to build a **DeferredDiscoveryRESTMapper**:

```
import "k8s.io/client-go/restmapper"

discoveryClient := clientset.Discovery()

defRestMapper :=
    restmapper.NewDeferredDiscoveryRESTMapper(
        memory.NewMemCacheClient(discoveryClient),
    )
```

You can now use the RESTMapper as defined in Chapter 5's "RESTMapper" section.

Conclusion

In this chapter, you have seen how to connect to a cluster and how to obtain a Clientset. It is a set of clients, one for each Group-Version, with which you can execute operations on resources (get, list, create, etc.).

You also have covered the REST client, internally used by the Clientset, and that the developer can use to build more specific requests. Finally, the chapter covered the Discovery client, used to discover the resources served by the Kubernetes API in a dynamic way.

The next chapter covers how to test applications written with the Client-go Library, using the fake implementations of the clients provided by it.

CHAPTER 7

Testing Applications Using Client-go

The Client-go Library provides a number of clients that can act with the Kubernetes API.

- The **kubernetes.Clientset** provides a set of clients, one for each group/version of the API, to execute Kubernetes operations on resources (Create, Update, Delete, etc.).

- The **rest.RESTClient** provides a client to perform REST operations on resources (Get, Post, Delete, etc.).

- The **discovery.DiscoveryClient** provides a client to discover the resources served by the API.

All these clients implement interfaces that are defined by the Client-go Library: **kubernetes.Interface**, **rest.Interface**, and **discovery.DiscoveryInterface**.

In addition, the Client-go Library provides *fake* implementations of these interfaces to help you write unit tests for your functions. These *fake* implementations are defined in **fake** packages, each located inside the directory of the *real* implementation: **kubernetes/fake**, **rest/fake**, and **discovery/fake**.

The **testing** directory contains common tools that are used by *fake* clients—for example, an object tracker or a system to track invocations. You will learn about these tools during this chapter.

To be able to test your functions using these clients, the functions need to define a parameter to pass the client implementation, and the type of the parameter must be the interface, not the concrete type. For example:

```
func CreatePod(
    ctx context.Context,
    clientset kubernetes.Interface,
```

© Philippe Martin 2023
P. Martin, *Kubernetes Programming with Go*, https://doi.org/10.1007/978-1-4842-9026-2_7

```
    name string,
    namespace string,
    image string,
) (pod *corev1.Pod, error)
```

This way, you will create the client outside of the function, and simply use any implementation inside the function.

For the real code, you will create the client, as defined in Chapter 6. For the tests, you will substitute the client using the helper functions from the *fake* packages.

Fake Clientset

The following function is used to create a *fake* Clientset:

```
import "k8s.io/client-go/kubernetes/fake"

func NewSimpleClientset(
    objects ...runtime.Object,
) *Clientset
```

The *fake* Clientset is backed by an object tracker that processes *create, update,* and *delete* operations without any validation or mutation, and it returns the objects in response to *get* and *list* operations.

You can pass as parameters a list of Kubernetes objects, which will be added to the Clientset's object tracker. For example, use the following to create a *fake* Clientset and to call the **CreatePod** function defined earlier:

```
import "k8s.io/client-go/kubernetes/fake"

clientset := fake.NewSimpleClientset()
pod, err := CreatePod(
    context.Background(),
    clientset,
    aName,
    aNs,
    anImage,
)
```

During the test, after you call the function that is being tested (in this case, **CreatePod**), you have several ways to verify that the function has done what you expected. Let's consider this implementation of the **CreatePod** function:

```go
func CreatePod(
    ctx context.Context,
    clientset kubernetes.Interface,
    name string,
    namespace string,
    image string,
) (pod *corev1.Pod, err error) {

    podToCreate := corev1.Pod{
        Spec: corev1.PodSpec{
            Containers: []corev1.Container{
                {
                    Name:  "runtime",
                    Image: image,
                },
            },
        },
    }
    podToCreate.SetName(name)

    return clientset.CoreV1().
    Pods(namespace).
    Create(
        ctx,
        &podToCreate,
        metav1.CreateOptions{},
    )
}
```

Checking the Result of the Function

When calling the **CreatePod** function with the *fake* Clientset, the actual Kubernetes API will not be called, the resource will not be generated in the **etcd** database, and no validation and mutation will be performed on the resource. Instead, the resource will be stored as-is in an in-memory storage, with only minimal transformation.

In this example, the only transformation between the **podToCreate** passed to the **Create** function and the pod returned by the **Create** function is the namespace, which is passed through the call into the **Pods(namespace)** and is added to the returned **Pod**.

To test that the value returned by the **CreatePod** function is what you expected, you can write the following test:

```go
func TestCreatePod(t *testing.T) {
    var (
        name      = "a-name"
        namespace = "a-namespace"
        image     = "an-image"

        wantPod = &corev1.Pod{
            ObjectMeta: v1.ObjectMeta{
                Name:      "a-name",
                Namespace: "a-namespace",
            },
            Spec: corev1.PodSpec{
                Containers: []corev1.Container{
                    {
                        Name:  "runtime",
                        Image: "an-image",
                    },
                },
            },
        }
    )

    clientset := fake.NewSimpleClientset()
    gotPod, err := CreatePod(
        context.Background(),
        clientset,
        name,
        namespace,
        image,
```

```
    )
    if err != nil {
        t.Errorf("err = %v, want nil", err)
    }
    if !reflect.DeepEqual(gotPod, wantPod) {
        t.Errorf("CreatePod() = %v, want %v",
            gotPod,
            wantPod,
        )
    }
}
```

This test will assert that—given a name, a namespace, and an image—the result of the function will be **wantPod**, when no validation or mutation occurs in the **Pod**.

It is not possible to use this test to understand what would happen with a *real* client because the result would be different—that is, the *real* client, and the underlying API, would mutate the object to add default values, and so on.

Reacting to Actions

The *fake* Clientset stores the resources as-is without any validation or mutation. During the tests, you may want to simulate the changes done to resources by the various controllers. For this, the fake *clientset* provides methods to add *Reactors. Reactors* are functions that are executed when specific operations are done on specific resources.

The type of Reactor function for all operations, except **Watch and Proxy**, is defined as follows:

```
type ReactionFunc func(
    action Action,
) (handled bool, ret runtime.Object, err error)
```

The type of Reactor function for the **Watch** operation is defined as follows:

```
type WatchReactionFunc func(
    action Action,
) (handled bool, ret watch.Interface, err error)
```

The type of Reactor function for the **Proxy** operation is defined as follows:

```
type ProxyReactionFunc func(
    action Action,
) (
handled bool,
    ret restclient.ResponseWrapper,
    err error
)
```

The **Fake** field of the *fake* Clientset maintains several lists of **Reaction** functions: **ReactionChain**, **WatchReactionChain**, and **ProxyReactionChain**.

Every time an operation on a resource is invoked, the reactors are executed in chain-like fashion. The first reactor returning a *true* **handled** value will terminate the chain immediately, and the following reactors will not be called.

You can register new **Reaction** functions by calling the following methods on the **Fake** field of the *fake* Clientset:

- AddReactor(

    verb, resource string,

    reaction ReactionFunc,

)

- PrependReactor(

    verb, resource string,

    reaction ReactionFunc,

)

- AddWatchReactor(

    resource string,

    reaction WatchReactionFunc,

)

- PrependWatchReactor(

    resource string,

```
reaction WatchReactionFunc,
)
```

- AddProxyReactor(

```
resource string,

reaction ProxyReactionFunc,

)
```

- PrependProxyReactor(

```
resource string,

reaction ProxyReactionFunc,

)
```

The **verb** and **resource** values are used to indicate the operations for which the reactor will be invoked.

You can specify a value of `"*"` for both parameters, to indicate that the reactor must be executed for the operations of any **verb** and/or on any **resource**. Note that the **Reactor** function gets the **action** as a parameter; it is possible for the **Reactor** to do additional filtering on the invoked operation using this **action** parameter.

When the *fake* Clientset is created, a **Reactor** is added for both chains: **ReactionChain** and **WatchReactionChain**. These reactors contain the code for the *fake* Clientset to use the object tracker, which was discussed earlier. As a result of these reactors, for example, when you invoke a **Create** operation using the *fake* Clientset, the resource will be attached to an in-memory database, and a subsequent invocation of a **Get** operation on this resource will return the previously saved resource.

If you do not want to use this default behavior, you can redefine the chains, **ReactionChain** and/or **WatchReactionChain**, to be empty chains. Note that these default reactors always return a *true* **handled** value; if you add reactors using **AddReactor** or **AddWatchReactor** when the default reactor is still at the beginning of the list of reactors, they will never be requested.

If you want to get some validation or some mutation on the passed resource, you can precede reactors using **PrependReactor** or **PrependWatchReactor**, so they can:

- Return early with a *true* **handled** value and a specific value for the object to be returned (and the default **Reactor** will not be called).

- Mutate the object to return and return a *false* **handled** value. The
  mutated object will be the source object for the next reactors.

As an example, use the following code to mutate the created pods to add them a
value for their **NodeName** field:

```go
import (
    "context"

    corev1 "k8s.io/api/core/v1"
    "k8s.io/client-go/kubernetes/fake"
    "k8s.io/apimachinery/pkg/runtime"
    ktesting "k8s.io/client-go/testing"
)

clientset := fake.NewSimpleClientset()

clientset.Fake.PrependReactor("create", "pods", func(
    action ktesting.Action,
) (handled bool, ret runtime.Object, err error) {
    act := action.(ktesting.CreateAction)
    ret = act.GetObject()
    pod := ret.(*corev1.Pod)
    pod.Spec.NodeName = "node1"
    return false, pod, nil
})

pod, _ := CreatePod(
    context.Background(),
    clientset,
    name,
    namespace,
    image,
)
```

Checking the Actions

If you are using the *mock* system provided by the Go team (github.com/golang/mock), you may want to *mock* the calls to the Client-go Library in a similar way. The *mock* system helps you verify that specific functions were called during the execution of the tested code, with specific parameters and returning specific values.

Following this principle, to assess the **CreatePod** function, you may want to check that the **Create** function of the Clientset was called, with specific parameters. For this, the *fake* Clientset registers all the *Actions* done on it, and you can access these *Actions* to check they are match what you expected.

After executing the code to assess, you can access the *Actions* with the following call:

```
actions := clientset.Actions()
```

This call returns a list of objects that implements the following *Action* interface:

```
type Action interface {
    GetNamespace() string
    GetVerb() string
    GetResource() schema.GroupVersionResource
    Matches(verb, resource string) bool
    [...]
}
```

In Chapter 6's "Using the Clientset" section, you saw that the pattern to execute an action on a resource is (the namespace is omitted for non-namespaced resources) the following:

```
clientset.
    GroupVersion().
    Resource(namespace).
    Operation(ctx, options)
```

- **GetNamespace()** – this method on the *Action* returns the **namespace** specified in the call.

- **GetVerb()** – this method on the *Action* returns the **Operation** used in the call.

- **GetResource()** – this method on the *Action* returns a GVR built from the **GroupVersion** and **Resource** used in the call.

- **Matches(verb, resource string)** – this checks that the *verb* and *resource* match the **Operation** and **Resource** used in the call.

Using these four methods, you can check that the actions made on the Clientset are what you expected.

After you have checked the Verb of the *Action*, you can cast it to one of the interfaces related to the **Verb: GetAction, ListAction, CreateAction, UpdateAction, DeleteAction, DeleteCollectionAction, PatchAction, WatchAction, ProxyGetAction,** and **GenericAction**.

These interfaces provide more methods to get information specific to the **Operation**.

- **GetAction interface** – defined as:

```
type GetAction interface {
    Action
    GetName() string
}
```

As seen in Chapter 6's "Getting Information About a Resource" section, the signature of the method to execute the **Get** operation is:

```
Get(ctx context.Context, name string, opts metav1.GetOptions)
```

– this **GetName()** method from the **GetAction** interface will return the *name* passed as parameter to the **Get** method.

- **ListAction interface** – defined as:

```
type ListAction interface {
    Action
    GetListRestrictions() ListRestrictions
}

type ListRestrictions struct {

    Labels labels.Selector
    Fields fields.Selector
}
```

As seen in Chapter 6's "Getting List of Resources" section, the signature of the method to execute the **List** operation is:

List(ctx context.Context, opts metav1.ListOptions) – With ListOptions defined as:

```
type ListOptions struct {
    LabelSelector string
    FieldSelector string
    [...]
}
```

The **GetListRestrictions()** method from the *ListAction* interface will return the *LabelSelector* and *FieldSelector* passed as parameters through the **ListOptions** structure to the **List** method.

- **CreateAction interface** – defined as:

```
type CreateAction interface {
    Action
    GetObject() runtime.Object
}
```

As seen in Chapter 6's "Creating a Resource" section, the signature of the method to execute the **Create** operation is (here for *Pods*) the following:

Create(ctx context.Context, pod *v1.Pod, opts metav1. CreateOptions)

– this **GetObject()** method from the *CreateAction* interface will return the *object* (here *pod*) passed as parameter to the **Create** method

- **UpdateAction interface** – defined as:

```
type UpdateAction interface {
    Action
    GetObject() runtime.Object
}
```

As seen in Chapter 6's "Updating a Resource" section, the signature of the method to execute the **Update** operation is (here for *Pods*):

```
Update(ctx context.Context, pod *v1.Pod, opts metav1.
UpdateOptions).
```

– this **GetObject()** method from the UpdateAction interface will return the *object* (here *pod*) passed as parameter to the **Update** method.

- **DeleteAction interface** – the code follows:

```
type DeleteAction interface {
    Action
    GetName() string
    GetDeleteOptions() metav1.DeleteOptions
}
```

As seen in Chapter 6's "Deleting a Resource" section, the signature of the method to execute the **Delete** operation is as follows:

```
Delete(ctx context.Context, name string, opts metav1.
DeleteOptions)
```

– this **GetName()** method from the *DeleteAtion* interface will return the *name* passed as parameter to the **Delete** method.

The **GetDeleteOptions()**

– method from the *DeleteAtion* interface will return the *opts* passed as parameter to the **Delete** method.

- **DeleteCollectionAction interface** – defined as:

```
type DeleteCollectionAction interface {
    Action
    GetListRestrictions() ListRestrictions
}

type ListRestrictions struct {

    Labels labels.Selector
    Fields fields.Selector
}
```

As seen in Chapter 6's "Deleting a Collection of Resources" section, the signature of the method to execute the DeleteCollection operation is:

DeleteCollection(ctx context.Context, opts metav1. DeleteOptions, listOpts metav1.ListOptions) – with ListOptions defined as:

```
type ListOptions struct {
    LabelSelector string
    FieldSelector string
    [...]
}
```

The **GetListRestrictions()** method from the DeleteCollectionAction interface will return the *LabelSelector* and *FieldSelector* passed as parameters through the ListOptions structure to the **DeleteCollection** method.

- **PatchAction interface** – defined as:

```
type PatchAction interface {
    Action
    GetName() string
    GetPatchType() types.PatchType
    GetPatch() []byte
}
```

As seen in Chapter 6's "Using a Sstrategic Merge Patch to Update a Resource" and "Applying Resources Server-side" sections, the signature of the method to execute the **Patch** operation is:

```
Patch(
    ctx context.Context,
    name string,
    pt types.PatchType,
    data []byte,
    opts metav1.PatchOptions,
    subresources ...string,
)
```

The **GetName()** method from the *PatchAction* interface will return the *name* passed as parameter to the **Patch** method.

The **GetPatchType()** method from the *PatchAction* interface will return the *pt* passed as parameter to the **Patch** method.

The **GetPatch()** method from the *PatchAction* interface will return the *data* passed as parameter to the **Patch** method.

- **WatchAction interface** – defined as:

```
type WatchAction interface {
    Action
    GetWatchRestrictions() WatchRestrictions
}

type WatchRestrictions struct {
    Labels          labels.Selector
    Fields          fields.Selector
    ResourceVersion string
}
```

As seen in Chapter 6's "Watching Resources" section, the signature of the method to execute the **Watch** operation is:

```
Watch(ctx context.Context, opts metav1.ListOptions)
```
– The **GetWatchRestrictions()** method from the *WatchAction* interface will return the *LabelSelector* and *FieldSelector* and *ResourceVersion* passed as parameters through the ListOptions structure to the **Watch** method.

As an example, here is how you can use **Action** and *CreateAction* interfaces and their methods to test the **CreatePod** function:

```
import (
    "context"
    "reflect"
    "testing"

    corev1 "k8s.io/api/core/v1"
```

```go
    metav1 "k8s.io/apimachinery/pkg/apis/meta/v1"
    "k8s.io/client-go/kubernetes/fake"
    ktesting "k8s.io/client-go/testing"
)

func TestCreatePodActions(t *testing.T) {
    var (
        name      = "a-name"
        namespace = "a-namespace"
        image     = "an-image"

        wantPod = &corev1.Pod{
            ObjectMeta: metav1.ObjectMeta{
                Name: "a-name",
            },
            Spec: corev1.PodSpec{
                Containers: []corev1.Container{
                    {
                        Name:  "runtime",
                        Image: "an-image",
                    },
                },
            },
        }

        wantActions = 1
    )

    clientset := fake.NewSimpleClientset()          ❶
    _, _ = CreatePod(                               ❷
        context.Background(),
        clientset,
        name,
        namespace,
        image,
    )

    actions := clientset.Actions()                  ❸
```

```
    if len(actions) != wantActions {                    ❹
        t.Errorf("# actions = %d, want %d",
            len(actions),
            wantActions,
        )
    }
    action := actions[0]                                ❺

    actionNamespace := action.GetNamespace()            ❻
    if actionNamespace != namespace {
        t.Errorf("action namespace = %s, want %s",
            actionNamespace,
            namespace,
        )
    }

    if !action.Matches("create", "pods") {              ❼
        t.Errorf("action verb = %s, want create",
            action.GetVerb(),
        )
        t.Errorf("action resource = %s, want pods",
            action.GetResource().Resource,
        )
    }

    createAction := action.(ktesting.CreateAction)      ❽
    obj := createAction.GetObject()                     ❾
    if !reflect.DeepEqual(obj, wantPod) {
        t.Errorf("create action object = %v, want %v",
            obj,
            wantPod,
        )
    }
}
```

❶ Create a *fake* Clientset

❷ Call the **CreatePod** function to test

❸ Get the actions done during the execution of the function

❹ Assert the number of actions

❺ Get the first and only action done during execution

❻ Assert the *namespace* value passed during the **Action**

❼ Assert the *Verb* and *Resource* used for the **Action**

❽ Cast the **Action** to the *CreateAction* interface

❾ Assert the object value passed during the *CreateAction*

Fake REST Client

A *fake* **RESTClient** structure is available in the **rest/fake** package of the Client-go Library. The structure is specified as follows:

```
import "k8s.io/client-go/rest/fake"

type RESTClient struct {
    NegotiatedSerializer runtime.NegotiatedSerializer
    GroupVersion         schema.GroupVersion
    VersionedAPIPath     string

    Err error
    Req *http.Request
    Client *http.Client
    Resp *http.Response
}
```

The **NegotiatedSerializer** field accepts a Codec. You will need to use the Codec provided by the Client-go Library to be able to encode and decode resources from the Kubernetes API.

A **RESTClient** from the **Client-go** Library is specific to a **Group** and **Version**. You can specify the Group and the Version using the **GroupVersion** field.

VersionedAPIPath can be employed to specify a prefix for the API path. The other fields are utilized to imitate the result of the request:

- If Err is not nil, this error will be returned immediately for any call using the **RESTClient**.

- Else, if **Client** is not nil, this *http.Client* is used to make the *HTTP* request for any call using the **RESTClient**.

- Else, Resp is returned as a response for any call using the **RESTClient**.

With the fields **Err** and **Resp**, you can hardcode the result of calls to the **RESTClient**, either to return a specific error or return a specific response.

Using the **Client** field, you can have some advanced code that will return a specific result depending on the request, or make some computation based on the request, and so on. As an example, here is a function that **getPods** from a specific namespace, using the **RESTClient**:

```
func getPods(
    ctx context.Context,
    restClient rest.Interface,
    ns string,
) ([]corev1.Pod, error) {
    result := corev1.PodList{}
    err := restClient.Get().
        Namespace(ns).
        Resource("pods").
        Do(ctx).
        Into(&result)
    if err != nil {
        return nil, err
    }
    return result.Items, nil
}
```

To call this function from your code, you want to provide a **RESTClient** from a Clientset—for example, using the following code:

```
restClient := clientset.CoreV1().RESTClient()
```

```
pods, err := getPods(
    context.Background(),
    restClient,
    "default",
)
```

To evaluate how the function behaves when it returns specific values, you should use the *fake* **RESTClient** instead. For example, to assert the result of the function when the **RESTClient** call returns an error, you can create this *fake* **RESTClient**:

```
import (
    "context"
    "errors"

    corev1 "k8s.io/api/core/v1"
    "k8s.io/client-go/kubernetes/scheme"
    "k8s.io/client-go/rest/fake"
)

restClient := &fake.RESTClient{
    GroupVersion:           corev1.SchemeGroupVersion,
    NegotiatedSerializer:   scheme.Codecs,

    Err: errors.New("an error from the rest client"),
}

pods, err := getPods(
    context.Background(),
    restClient,
    "default",
)
```

Another example, to assert the result of the function when the call returns a **NotFound** (404) status, you can define the following *fake* **RESTClient**:

```
import (
    "net/http"

    corev1 "k8s.io/api/core/v1"
    "k8s.io/client-go/kubernetes/scheme"
```

```
    "k8s.io/client-go/rest/fake"
)
restClient := &fake.RESTClient{
    GroupVersion:          corev1.SchemeGroupVersion,
    NegotiatedSerializer: scheme.Codecs,

    Err: nil,
    Resp: &http.Response{
        StatusCode: http.StatusNotFound,
    },
}
```

FakeDiscovery Client

A **FakeDiscovery** structure is specified in the **discovery/fake** package of the Client-go Library. The structure is defined as follows:

```
type FakeDiscovery struct {
    *testing.Fake
    FakedServerVersion *version.Info
}
```

An implementation of such a **FakeDiscovery** client is accessible from the *fake* Clientset:

```
import (
    "k8s.io/client-go/kubernetes/fake"
    fakediscovery "k8s.io/client-go/discovery/fake"
)

clientset := fake.NewSimpleClientset()
discoveryClient, ok :=
    clientset.Discovery().(*fakediscovery.FakeDiscovery)
if !ok {
    t.Fatalf("couldn't convert Discovery() to *FakeDiscovery")
}
```

Stubbing the ServerVersion

The **FakeDiscovery** structure provides a field **FakedServerVersion** that you can use to simulate the server version returned by the **ServerVersion()** method of the **discovery. DiscoveryInterface**. As an example, here is a function you should test, checking that the server version is at least a provided version:

```
func checkMinimalServerVersion(
    clientset kubernetes.Interface,
    minMinor int,
) (bool, error) {
    discoveryClient := clientset.Discovery()
    info, err := discoveryClient.ServerVersion()
    if err != nil {
        return false, err
    }
    major, err := strconv.Atoi(info.Major)
    if err != nil {
        return false, err
    }
    minor, err := strconv.Atoi(info.Minor)
    if err != nil {
        return false, err
    }

    return major == 1 && minor >= minMinor, nil
}
```

You can now assert the result of the function when the **Discovery** client returns a specific version, here **1.10**.

As an exercise, you can rewrite this test function by using a table-driven test instead so as to be able to test the result for various values of the server versions.

```
func Test_getServerVersion(t *testing.T) {
    client := fake.NewSimpleClientset()

    fakeDiscovery, ok := client.Discovery().(*fakediscovery.FakeDiscovery)
    if !ok {
```

```
        t.Fatalf("couldn't convert Discovery() to *FakeDiscovery")
    }

    fakeDiscovery.FakedServerVersion = &version.Info{
        Major: "1",
        Minor: "10",
    }

    res, err := checkMinimalServerVersion(client, 20)
    if res != true && err != nil {
        t.Error(err)
    }

}
```

Actions

The methods **ServerVersion**, **ServerGroups**, **ServerResourcesForGroupVersion**, and **ServerGroupsAndResources** of the *fake* **Discovery** client all use the concept of *Actions* used by the *fake* Clientset, as described in this chapter's "Reacting to Actions" and "Checking the Actions" sections.

To evaluate your functions' use of these methods, you can assert the actions done by the **Discovery** client, by adding reactors or by checking the actions executed. Note that the **Verb** and **Resource** used for these methods are:

- ServerVersion – **"get"**, **"version"**

- ServerGroups – **"get"**, **"group"**

- ServerResourcesForGroupVersion – **"get"**, **"resource"**

- ServerGroupsAndResources – **"get"**, **"group"** and **"get"**, **"resource"**

Mocking Resources

For the real implementation, the **ServerGroups**, **ServerResourcesForGroupVersion**, and **ServerGroupsAndResources** methods rely on groups and resources defined by the API server.

For the *fake* implementation, these methods rely on the **Resources** field of the **Fake** field of the *fake* Clientset. To mock the result of these methods with various values of groups and resources, you can fill this **Resources** field before calling these methods.

Conclusion

This chapter has shown how to use the *fake* implementations of the Clienset, REST client, and Discovery client; all are helpful to write unit tests for functions using the Client-go Library using the Client-go Library.

It closes the first part of this book, which covers libraries to work with the native Kubernetes resources. In the following chapters, you will learn how to extend the Kubernetes API by creating custom resources.

CHAPTER 8

Extending Kubernetes API with Custom Resources Definitions

In the first part of this book, you learned that the Kubernetes API is organized in groups. The groups contain one or more resources, each of them being versioned.

To work with the Kubernetes API in Go, there exist two fundamental libraries. The API Machinery Library[1] provides the tools to communicate with the API independently of the resources served by the API. The API Library[2] provides the definitions of the native Kubernetes resources provided with the Kubernetes API, to be used with the API Machinery.

The Client-go Library leverages the API Machinery and the API Library to provide an access to the Kubernetes API.

The Kubernetes API is extensible through its Custom Resource Definition (CRD) mechanism.

A **CustomResourceDefinition** is a specific Kubernetes resource, used to define new Kubernetes resources served by the API, in a dynamic way.

Defining new resources for Kubernetes is used to represent *Domain Specific Resources*, for example a Database, a CI/CD Job or a Certificate.

Combined with a custom controller, these custom resources can be implemented in the cluster by the controller.

Like other resources, you can get, list, create, delete, and update resources of this kind. The CRD resource is a non-namespaced resource.

---

[1] https://github.com/kubernetes/apimachinery

[2] https://github.com/kubernetes/api

© Philippe Martin 2023
P. Martin, *Kubernetes Programming with Go*, https://doi.org/10.1007/978-1-4842-9026-2_8

This CRD resource is defined in the **apiextensions.k8s.io/v1** group and version. The HTTP path to access the resource respects the standard format to access non-core and non-namespaced resources, **/apis/<group>/<version>/<plural_resource_name>**, and is **/apis/apiextensions.k8s.io/v1/customresourcedefinitions/**.

The Go definition of this resource is not declared in the API Library, like for other native resources, but in the **apiextensions-apiserver** library. To access the definitions from Go sources, you will need to use the following import:

```
import (
  "k8s.io/apiextensions-apiserver/pkg/apis/apiextensions/v1"
)
```

Performing Operations in Go

To perform operations on CRD resources using Go, you can use a clientset, similar to the clientset provided by the client-go library but included in the **apiextensions-apiserver** library.

To use this clientset, you will need to use the following import:

```
import (
  "k8s.io/apiextensions-apiserver/pkg/client/clientset/clientset"
)
```

You can use this CRD clientset the exact same way you use the Client-go Clientset. As an example, here is how you can list the CRDs declared into a cluster:

```
import (
    "context"
    "fmt"

    "k8s.io/apiextensions-apiserver/pkg/client/clientset/clientset"
    metav1 "k8s.io/apimachinery/pkg/apis/meta/v1"
)

// config is a standard rest.Config defined in client-go
```

```
clientset, err := clientset.NewForConfig(config)
if err != nil {
    return err
}
ctx := context.Background()
list, err := clientset.ApiextensionsV1().
    CustomResourceDefinitions().
    List(ctx, metav1.ListOptions{})
```

The CustomResourceDefinition in Detail

The definition of the CustomReourceDefinition Go structure is:

```
type CustomResourceDefinition struct {
    metav1.TypeMeta
    metav1.ObjectMeta

    Spec CustomResourceDefinitionSpec
    Status CustomResourceDefinitionStatus
}
```

Like any other Kubernetes resources, the CRD resource embeds the **TypeMeta** and **ObjectMeta** structures. The value of the **Name** in the **ObjectMeta** field must equal **<Spec.Names.Plural>** + *". "* + **<Spec.Group>**.

Like resources being managed by a Controller or Operator, the resource contains a **Spec** structure to define the desired state, and a **Status** structure to contain the status of the resource as described by the controller or operator.

```
type CustomResourceDefinitionSpec struct {
    Group              string
    Scope              ResourceScope
    Names              CustomResourceDefinitionNames
    Versions           []CustomResourceDefinitionVersion
    Conversion         *CustomResourceConversion
    PreserveUnknownFields bool
}
```

The **Group** field of the Spec indicates the name of the group in which the resource resides.

The **Scope** field indicates if the resource is namespaced or non-namespaced. The ResourceScope type contains two values: **ClusterScoped** and **NamespaceScoped**.

Naming the Resource

The **Names** field indicates the diverse names for the resource and associated information. This information will be used by the Discovery mechanism of the Kubernetes API, to be able to include CRDs in the results of discovery calls. The **CustomResourceDefinitionNames** type is defined as:

```
type CustomResourceDefinitionNames struct {
    Plural          string
    Singular        string
    ShortNames      []string
    Kind            string
    ListKind        string
    Categories      []string
}
```

Plural is the lowercase plural name of the resource, used in the URL to access the resource—for example, **pods**. This value is required.

Singular is the lowercase singular name of the resource. For example, **pod**. This value is optional, and if not specified, the lowercase value of the **Kind** field is used.

ShortNames is a list of lowercase short names for the resource, which can be used to invoke this resource in commands like **kubectl get <shortname>**. As an example, the **services** resource declares the **svc** shortname, so you can execute **kubectl get svc** instead of **kubectl get services**.

Kind is the **CamelCase** and singular name for the resource, used during resource serialization—for example, **Pod** or **ServiceAccount**. This value is required.

ListKind is the name used during the serialization of lists of this resource—for example, **PodList**. This value is optional, and if not specified, the Kind value suffixed with **List** is used.

Categories is a list of grouped resources the resource belongs to, which can be used by commands like **kubectl get <category>**. The **all** category is the best known one, but other categories exist (**api-extensions**), and you can define your own category names.

Definition of the Resource Versions

All the information provided up to this point is valid for all versions of the resource.

The **Versions** field contains version-specific information, as a list of definitions, one for each version of the resource. The type CustomResourceDefinitionVersion is defined as:

```
type CustomResourceDefinitionVersion struct {
    Name                      string
    Served                    bool
    Storage                   bool
    Deprecated                bool
    DeprecationWarning        *string
    Schema                    *CustomResourceValidation
    Subresources              *CustomResourceSubresources
    AdditionalPrinterColumns  []CustomResourceColumnDefinition
}
```

Name indicates the version name. Kubernetes resources use a standard format for versions: **v<number>[(alpha|beta)<number>]**, but you can use any format you want.

The **Served** boolean indicates whether this specific version must be served by the API Server. If not, the version is still defined and can be used as Storage (see the following), but the user cannot create or get resource instances in this specific version.

The **Storage** boolean indicates whether this specific version is the one used for persisting resources. Exactly one version must define this field to be true. You have seen in Chapter 5's "Conversion" section that Conversion functions exist between versions of the same resource. The user can create resources in any available version, the API Server will convert it into the version with **Storage=true** before to persist the data in **etcd**.

The **Deprecated** boolean indicates whether this specific version of the resource is deprecated. If true, the server will add a Warning header to responses for this version.

The **DeprecationWarning** is the warning message returned to the caller when **Deprecated** is true. If Deprecated is true and this field is nil, a default warning message is sent.

Schema describes the schema of this version of the resource. The schema is used to validate the data sent to the API when creating or updating resources. This field is optional. The schemas will be discussed in more detail in Section "Schema of the Resource".

Subresources defines the subresources that will be served for this version of the resource. This field is optional. The type of this field is defined as:

```
type CustomResourceSubresources struct {
    Status *CustomResourceSubresourceStatus
    Scale *CustomResourceSubresourceScale
}
```

- If **Status** is not nil, the "/status" sub-resource will be served.

- If **Scale** is not nil, the "/scale" sub-resource will be served.

AdditionalPrinterColumns is the list of additional columns to return when the Table output format is requested by the user. This field is optional. More information about the Table output format can be found in Chapter 2's, "Getting Result as Table" section. You will see how to define additional printer columns in the "Additional Printer Columns" section of this chapter.

Converting Between Versions

Conversion indicates how conversions between versions of this resource are handled. The type for this field is defined as follows:

```
type CustomResourceConversion struct {
    Strategy ConversionStrategyType
    Webhook *WebhookConversion
}
```

Strategy can get a value of **NoneConverter** or **WebhookConverter**. A NoneConverter value indicates to the API Server to change only the APIVersion field before it persists.

A **WebhookConverter** value indicates that the API Server is to call an external webhook to do the conversion. When this value is used, the **Webhook** field needs to contain all the information necessary for the API Server to call the webhook.

Schema of the Resource

The schema of a resource for a specific version is defined using the OpenAPI v3 schema format.[3] The complete description of this format is out of the scope of this book. Here is a short introduction that will help you define a schema for your resources.

A Custom resource will generally have a **Spec** section and a **Status** section. For this, you will have to declare a top-level schema of type **object**, and declare the fields with the **properties** property. In this example, the top-level schema will have Spec and Status properties. You can then describe each property recursively.

The **Spec** and **Status** fields will also be of type **object** and contain properties. The accepted data types are:

- string

- number

- integer

- boolean

- array

- object

Specific formats can be given for string and number types:

- **string**: date, date-time, byte, int-or-string

- **number**: float, double, int32, int64

In an object, the required fields are indicated using the **required** property.

You can declare that a property accepts only a set of values, using the **enum** property. To declare a map of values, you need to use the **object** type and specify the **additionalProperties** property. This property can accept a **true** value (to indicate that

---

[3] https://swagger.io/docs/specification/data-models/

the entries can have any type), or define the type of the entries of the map by giving a type as value:

```
type: object
additionalProperties:
  type: string
```

Or

```
type: object
additionalProperties:
  type: object
  properties:
    code:
      type: integer
    text:
      type: string
```

When declaring an array, you must define the type of the items of the array:

```
type: array
items:
  type: string
```

As an example, here is a schema for a custom resource containing three fields in Spec (**image**, **replicas**, and **port**), and a **state** field in Status.

```
schema:
  openAPIV3Schema:
    type: object
    properties:
      spec:
        type: object
        properties:
          image:
            type: string
          replicas:
            type: integer
          port:
```

```
        type: string
        format: int-or-string
    required: [image,replicas]
  status:
    type: object
    properties:
      state:
        type: string
        enum: [waiting,running]
```

Deploying a Custom Resource Definition

To deploy a new resource definition to the cluster, you need to execute a Create operation on a CRD object. You can either use the Clientset provided by the **apiextensions-apiserver** Library and write the resource definition in Go using the structures you have seen in previous sections, or you can create a YAML file and "apply" it using **kubectl**.

As an example, you will create a new resource named **myresources** in the group **mygroup.example.com**, and with a version **v1alpha1**, using the YAML format and **kubectl** to deploy it.

```
apiVersion: apiextensions.k8s.io/v1          ❶
kind: CustomResourceDefinition               ❷
metadata:
  name: myresources.mygroup.example.com      ❸
spec:
  group: mygroup.example.com                 ❹
  scope: Namespaced                          ❺
  names:
    plural: myresources                      ❻
    singular: myresource                     ❼
    shortNames:
    - my                                     ❽
    - myres
    kind: MyResource
```

```
    categories:
    - all                                    ⑨
  versions:
  - name: v1alpha1                           ⑩
    served: true
    storage: true
    schema:
      openAPIV3Schema:
        type: object                         ⑪
```

❶ The group and version of the CRD resource

❷ The kind of the CRD resource

❸ The complete name of the new resource, including its group

❹ The group the new resource belongs to

❺ The new resource can be created in specific namespaces

❻ The plural name of the new resource, used in the path to access this new resource

❼ The singular name of the resource, you can use **kubectl get myresource**

❽ Short names of the new resource, you can use **kubectl get my, kubectl get myres**

❾ Adds the resource to the category **all**; resources of this kind will appear when running **kubectl get all**

❿ **v1alpha1** version is the only version defined for the new resource

⑪ Defines the new resource schema as an object, with no field

Now, you can "apply" this resource using kubectl, using the following command:

$ kubectl apply -f myresource.yaml
```
customresourcedefinition.apiextensions.k8s.io/myresources.mygroup.example.
com created
```

From there, you can work with this new resource.

For example, you can get the list of resources cluster-wide or in a specific namespace, using HTTP requests (you will need to execute **kubectl proxy** from another terminal before running these commands):

$ curl
http://localhost:8001/apis/mygroup.example.com/v1alpha1/myresources
```
{"apiVersion":"mygroup.example.com/v1alpha1","items":[],"kind":"MyResourceL
ist","metadata":{"continue":"","resourceVersion":"186523407"}}
```

$ curl
http://localhost:8001/apis/mygroup.example.com/v1alpha1/namespaces/default/
myresources
```
{"apiVersion":"mygroup.example.com/v1alpha1","items":[],"kind":"MyResourceL
ist","metadata":{"continue":"","resourceVersion":"186524840"}}
```

Or, you can obtain these lists using kubectl:

$ kubectl get myresources
```
No resources found in default namespace.
```

You can define a new resource using the YAML format, and "apply" it to the cluster, using **kubectl**:

$ kubectl apply -f - <<EOF
```
apiVersion: mygroup.example.com/v1alpha1
kind: MyResource
metadata:
  name: myres1
```
EOF

$ kubectl get myresources
```
NAME      AGE
myres1    10s
```

Additional Printer Columns

You can see in the output of the previous **kubectl get myresources** command that the columns displayed are the *name* and *age* of the resources.

The **AdditionalPrinterColumns** field of the CRD spec is used to indicate which columns of the resource you want to be displayed in the output of **kubectl get <resource>**.

When no additional printer columns are defined, the *name* and *age* are returned by default. If you specify columns, they will be returned in addition to the *name*. If you want to keep the *age* when adding columns, you will need to add it explicitly.

For each additional column, you need to specify a name, a JSON path. and a type. The name will be used as a header for the column in the output, the JSON path is used by the API Server to get the value for this column from the resource data, and the type is an indication for kubectl to display this data.

As an example, here is the myresource CRD with some fields defined in the Spec and Status, and additional printer columns also are defined:

```
apiVersion: apiextensions.k8s.io/v1
kind: CustomResourceDefinition
metadata:
  name: myresources.mygroup.example.com
spec:
  group: mygroup.example.com
  scope: Namespaced
  names:
    plural: myresources
    singular: myresource
    shortNames:
    - my
    - myres
    kind: MyResource
    categories:
    - all
  versions:
  - name: v1alpha1
    served: true
```

```
      storage: true
      subresources:
        status: {}
      schema:
        openAPIV3Schema:
          type: object
          properties:
            spec:
              type: object
              properties:
                image:
                  type: string
                memory:
                  x-kubernetes-int-or-string: true
            status:
              type: object
              properties:
                state:
                  type: string
  additionalPrinterColumns:
    - name: image
      jsonPath: .spec.image
      type: string
    - name: memory
      jsonPath: .spec.memory
      type: string
    - name: age
      jsonPath: .metadata.creationTimestamp
      type: date
```

In this CRD, the schema indicates that the data for the resources will be an object containing two properties, **spec** and **status**. These properties are objects themselves. The **spec** object contains two properties: **image** of type **string**, and **memory** of special type **int or string**. The **status** object contains one property **state** of type **string**.

Note that you have enabled the **status** subresource by adding the **status** entry in the **subresources** object. You have defined for the CRD three additional printer columns:

image, **memory**, and **age**. The JSON paths for **image** and **memory** point to the fields defined in the schema, and the JSON path for **age** points to a field in the standard **metadata** field.

After applying the CRD again to the cluster, you can define a new resource with these fields, apply the resource definition to the cluster, and get the list of resources with **kubectl**:

```
$ kubectl apply -f myresource.yaml
customresourcedefinition.apiextensions.k8s.io/myresources.mygroup.example.
com configured                                              ❶
```

```
$ cat > myres1.yaml <<EOF
apiVersion: mygroup.example.com/v1alpha1
kind: MyResource
metadata:
  name: myres1
spec:
  image: nginx                                              ❷
  memory: 1024Mi                                            ❸
EOF
```

```
$ kubectl apply -f myres1.yaml                              ❹
myresource.mygroup.example.com/myres1 configured
```

```
$ kubectl get myresources
NAME      IMAGE    MEMORY    AGE
myres1    nginx    1024Mi    12m                            ❺
```

❶ The CRD is updated with the new schema and additional printer columns

❷ A value is given for the field image

❸ A value is given for the field memory; this is a string

❹ The custom resource is updated, with the new fields defined

❺ The output of **kubectl get** now displays the additional columns

Conclusion

In this chapter, you have seen that the list of resources served by the Kubernetes API is extendable by creating **CustomResourceDefinition** (CRD) resources in the cluster. You have seen the structure in Go of this CRD resource and how to manipulate CRD resources using the dedicated Clientset.

Following that you have seen how to write a CRD in YAML and how to deploy it to the cluster using **kubectl**. Some fields then have been added to the CRD scheme, as well as some additional printer columns so as to display these fields in the output of **kubectl get**.

Finally, you have seen that as soon as the CRD is created in the cluster, you can start working with resources of the new associated kind.

CHAPTER 9

Working with Custom Resources

In the previous chapter, you have seen how to declare a new custom resource to be served by the Kubernetes API using **CustomResourceDefinition** resources, and how to create new instances of this custom resource using **kubectl**. But for the moment, you do not have any Go library that allows you to work with instances of custom resources.

This chapter explores the various possibilities to work with custom resources in Go:

- Generating code for a dedicated Clientset for the custom resource.

- Using the **unstructured** package of the API Machinery Library and the **dynamic** package of the Client-go Library.

Generating a Clientset

The repository `https://github.com/kubernetes/code-generator` contains the Go code generators. Chapter 3's "Content of a Package" section contains a very quick overview of these generators, where the content of the API Library was explored.

To use these generators, you will need to first write the Go structures for the kinds defined by the custom resource. In this example, you will write structures for the **MyResource** and **MyResourceList** kinds.

To stick with the organization found in the API Library, you will write these types in a **types.go** file, placed in the directory **pkg/apis/<group>/<version>/**.

Likewise, to work correctly with the generators, the root directory of your project must be in a directory named after the Go package after the Go package of your project. For example, if the package of the project is **github.com/myid/myproject** (defined in the first line of the project's **go.mod** file), the root directory of the project must be in the directory **github.com/myid/myproject/**.

© Philippe Martin 2023
P. Martin, *Kubernetes Programming with Go*, https://doi.org/10.1007/978-1-4842-9026-2_9

As an example, let's start a new project. You can execute these commands from the directory of your choice, generally a directory containing all your Go projects.

```
$ mkdir -p github.com/myid/myresource-crd
$ cd github.com/myid/myresource-crd
$ go mod init github.com/myid/myresource-crd
$ mkdir -p pkg/apis/mygroup.example.com/v1alpha1/
$ cd pkg/apis/mygroup.example.com/v1alpha1/
```

Then, in this directory, you can create the **types.go** file that contains the definitions of the structures for the kinds. Here are the definitions of the structures that match the schema defined in the CRD in the previous chapter.

```
package v1alpha1

import (
    metav1 "k8s.io/apimachinery/pkg/apis/meta/v1"
    "k8s.io/apimachinery/pkg/util/intstr"
)

type MyResource struct {
    metav1.TypeMeta   `json:",inline"`
    metav1.ObjectMeta `json:"metadata,omitempty"`

    Spec MyResourceSpec `json:"spec"`
}

type MyResourceSpec struct {
    Image  string            `json:"image"`
    Memory resource.Quantity `json:"memory"`
}

type MyResourceList struct {
    metav1.TypeMeta `json:",inline"`
    metav1.ListMeta `json:"metadata,omitempty"`

    Items []MyResource `json:"items"`
}
```

Now, you need to run two generators:

- **deepcopy-gen** – this will generate a **DeepCopyObject()** method for each Kind structure, which is needed for these types to implement the **runtime.Object** interface.

- **client-gen** – this will generate the clientset for the group/version.

Using deepcopy-gen

Installing deepcopy-gen

To install the **deepcopy-gen** executable, you can use the **go install** command:

```
go install k8s.io/code-generator/cmd/deepcopy-gen@v0.24.4
```

You can use either the **@latest** tag to use the latest revision of the Kubernetes code or select a specific version.

Adding Annotations

The **deepcopy-gen** generator needs annotations to work. It first needs the // **+k8s:deepcopy-gen=package** annotation to be defined at the package level. This annotation asks **deepcopy-gen** to generate **deepcopy** methods for *all* structures of the package.

For this, you can create a **doc.go** file in the directory in which **types.go** resides, to add this annotation:

```
// pkg/apis/mygroup.example.com/v1alpha1/doc.go
// +k8s:deepcopy-gen=package
package v1alpha1
```

By default, **deepcopy-gen** will generate the **DeepCopy()** and **DeepCopyInto()** methods, but no **DeepCopyObject()**. For this, you need to add another annotation (// **+k8s:deepcopy-gen:interfaces=k8s.io/apimachinery/pkg/runtime.Object**) before each kind structure.

```
// +k8s:deepcopy-gen:interfaces=k8s.io/apimachinery/pkg/runtime.Object
type MyResource struct {
[...]
```

```
// +k8s:deepcopy-gen:interfaces=k8s.io/apimachinery/pkg/runtime.Object
type MyResourceList struct {
[...]
```

Running deepcopy-gen

The generator needs a file that contains the text (generally the license) added at the beginning of the generated files. For this, you can create an empty file (or with the content you prefer, do not forget that the text should be Go comments) named **hack/boilerplate.go.txt**.

You need to run **go mod tidy** for the generator to work (or **go mod vendor** if you prefer to vendor Go dependencies). Finally, you can run the deepcopy-gen command, which will generate a file pkg/apis/mygroup.example.com/v1alpha1/zz_generated.deepcopy.go:

```
$ go mod tidy
$ deepcopy-gen --input-dirs github.com/myid/myresource-crd/pkg/apis/
mygroup.example.com/v1alpha1
        -O zz_generated.deepcopy
        --output-base ../../..
        --go-header-file ./hack/boilerplate.go.txt
```

Note the "../../.." as output-base. It will place the output base in the directory from which you created the directory for the project:

```
$ mkdir -p github.com/myid/myresource-crd
```

You will need to adapt this to the number of subdirectories you created if different from the three.

At this point, you should have the following file structure for your project:

```
├── go.mod
├── hack
│   └── boilerplate.go.txt
├── pkg
│   └── apis
```

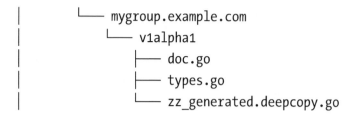

```
|          └── mygroup.example.com
|                └── v1alpha1
|                      ├── doc.go
|                      ├── types.go
|                      └── zz_generated.deepcopy.go
|
```

Using client-gen

Installing client-go

To install the **client-gen** executable, you can use the **go install** command:

```
go install k8s.io/code-generator/cmd/client-gen@v0.24.4
```

You can use either the **@latest** tag to use the latest revision of the Kubernetes code or select a specific version if you want to run the command in a reproducible way.

Adding Annotations

You need to add annotations to the structures, defined in the **types.go** file, to indicate for which types you want to define a Clientset. The annotation to use is // **+genclient**.

- // **+genclient** (with no option) will ask **client-gen** to generate a Clientset for a namespaced resource.

- // **+genclient:nonNamespaced** will generate a Clientset for a non-namespaced resource.

- **+genclient:onlyVerbs=create,get** will generate these verbs only, instead of generating all verbs by default.

- **+genclient:skipVerbs=watch** will generate all verbs except these ones, instead of all verbs by default.

- **+genclient:noStatus** – if a **Status** field is present in the annotated structure, an **updateStatus** function will be generated. With this option, you can disable the generation of the **updateStatus** function (note that it is not necessary if the **Status** field does not exist).

The custom resource you are creating is namespaced so you can use the annotation without an option:

```
// +k8s:deepcopy-gen:interfaces=k8s.io/apimachinery/pkg/runtime.Object
// +genclient
type MyResource struct {
[...]
```

Adding AddToScheme Function

The generated code relies on an **AddToScheme** function defined in the package of the resource. To stick with the convention found in the API Library, you will write this function in a **register.go** file, placed in the directory **pkg/apis/<group>/<version>/**.

By getting as boilerplate, the **register.go** file from a native Kubernetes resource from the Kubernetes API Library, you will obtain the following file. The only changes are to the group name (❶),version name (❷), and the list of resources (❸) to register to the scheme.

```
package v1alpha1

import (
    metav1 "k8s.io/apimachinery/pkg/apis/meta/v1"
    "k8s.io/apimachinery/pkg/runtime"
    "k8s.io/apimachinery/pkg/runtime/schema"
)

const GroupName = "mygroup.example.com"          ❶

var SchemeGroupVersion = schema.GroupVersion{
    Group: GroupName,
    Version: "v1alpha1",                         ❷
}

var (
    SchemeBuilder       = runtime.NewSchemeBuilder(addKnownTypes)
    localSchemeBuilder = &SchemeBuilder
    AddToScheme         = localSchemeBuilder.AddToScheme
)
```

```
func addKnownTypes(scheme *runtime.Scheme) error {
    scheme.AddKnownTypes(SchemeGroupVersion,
        &MyResource{},                          ❸
        &MyResourceList{},
    )
    metav1.AddToGroupVersion(scheme, SchemeGroupVersion)
    return nil
}
```

Running client-go

The **client-gen** needs a file containing the text (generally the license) added at the beginning of generated files. You will use the same file as with **deepcopy-gen**: **hack/boilerplate.go.txt**.

You can run the **client-gen** command, which will generate files in the directory **pkg/clientset/clientset**:

```
client-gen \
    --clientset-name clientset
    --input-base ""
    --input github.com/myid/myresource-crd/pkg/apis/mygroup.example.com/
      v1alpha1
    --output-package github.com/myid/myresource-crd/pkg/clientset
    --output-base ../../..
    --go-header-file hack/boilerplate.go.txt
```

Note the "../../.." as output-base. It will place the output base in the directory from which you created the directory for the project:

```
$ mkdir -p github.com/myid/myresource-crd
```

You will need to adapt this to the number of subdirectories you created if different from the three.

Note that you will need to run this command again when you update the definition of your custom resource. It is recommended to place this command in a **Makefile** to automatically run it every time the files defining the custom resource are modified.

Using the Generated Clientset

Now that the Clientset is generated and the types implement the **runtime.Object** interface, you can work with the custom resource the same way you work with the native Kubernetes resources. For example, this code will use the dedicated Clientset to list the custom resources on the *default* namespace:

```
import (
    "context"
    "fmt"

    "github.com/myid/myresource-crd/pkg/clientset/clientset"
    metav1 "k8s.io/apimachinery/pkg/apis/meta/v1"
    "k8s.io/client-go/tools/clientcmd"
)

config, err :=
    clientcmd.NewNonInteractiveDeferredLoadingClientConfig(
        clientcmd.NewDefaultClientConfigLoadingRules(),
        nil,
    ).ClientConfig()
if err != nil {
    return err
}

clientset, err := clientset.NewForConfig(config)
if err != nil {
    return err
}

list, err := clientset.MygroupV1alpha1().
    MyResources("default").
    List(context.Background(), metav1.ListOptions{})
if err != nil {
```

```
        return err
}

for _, res := range list.Items {
        fmt.Printf("%s\n", res.GetName())
}
```

Using the Generated *fake* Clientset

The **client-gen** tool also generates a *fake* Clientset that you can use the same way you use the *fake* Clientset from the Client-go Library. For more information, see Chapter 7's "Fake Clientset" section.

Using the Unstructured Package and Dynamic Client

The **Unstructured** and **UnstructuredList** types are defined in the **unstructured** package of the API Machinery Library. The import to use is the following:

```
import (
    "k8s.io/apimachinery/pkg/apis/meta/v1/unstructured"
)
```

These types can be used to represent any Kubernetes *Kind*, either a list or a nonlist.

The Unstructured Type

The **Unstructured** type is defined as a structure containing a unique **Object** field:

```
type Unstructured struct {
    // Object is a JSON compatible map with
    // string, float, int, bool, []interface{}, or
    // map[string]interface{}
    // children.
    Object map[string]interface{}
}
```

Using this type, it is possible to define any Kubernetes resource without having to use the typed structures (e.g., the **Pod** structure, found in the API Library).

Getters and **Setters** methods are defined for this type to access generic fields from the **TypeMeta** and **ObjectMeta** fields, common to all structures representing Kubernetes *Kinds*.

Getters and Setters to Access TypeMeta Fields

The **APIVersion** and **Kind** Getters/Setters can be used to directly get and set the **apiVersion** and *Kind* fields of the **TypeMeta**.

The **GroupVersionKind** Getters/Setters can be used to convert the **apiVersion** and kind specified in the object to and from a **GroupVersionKind** value.

```
GetAPIVersion() string
GetKind() string
GroupVersionKind() schema.GroupVersionKind

SetAPIVersion(version string)
SetKind(kind string)
SetGroupVersionKind(gvk schema.GroupVersionKind)
```

Getters and Setters to Access ObjectMeta Fields

Getters and Setters are defined for all fields of the **ObjectMeta** structure. The details of the structure can be found in Chapter 3's "The **ObjectMeta** Fields" section.

As an example, the getter and setter to access the **Name** field are `GetName() string` and `SetName(name string)`.

Methods for Creating and Converting

- `NewEmptyInstance() runtime.Unstructured` – this returns a new instance with only the **apiVersion** and **kind** fields copied from the receiver.

- `MarshalJSON() ([]byte, error)` – this returns the JSON representation of the receiver.

- `UnmarshalJSON(b []byte) error` – this populates the receiver with the passed JSON representation.

- UnstructuredContent() map[string]interface{} - this returns the value of the **Object** field of the receiver.

- SetUnstructuredContent(

    content map[string]interface{},

)

  - this sets the value of the **Object** field of the receiver,].

- IsList() bool - this returns true if the receiver describes a list, by checking if an **items** field exists, and is an array.

- ToList() (*UnstructuredList, error) - this converts the receiver to an **UnstructuredList**.

Helpers to Access Non-meta Fields

The following helpers can be used to get and set the value of specific fields in the **Object** field of an **Unstructured** instance.

Note that these helpers are functions, and not methods on the **Unstructured** type.

They all accept:

- A first parameter **obj** of type **map[string]interface{}** used to pass the **Object** field of the **Unstructured** instance,

- A last parameter **fields** of type **...string** used to pass the keys to navigate into the object. Note that no array/slice syntax is supported.

The **Setters** accept a second parameter giving the value to the set for the specific field in the given object. The **Getters** return three values:

- The value of the requested field, if possible

- A boolean indicating if the requested field has been found

- An error if the field has been found but is not of the requested type

The names of the helper functions are:

- `RemoveNestedField` – this removes the requested field

- `NestedFieldCopy, NestedFieldNoCopy` – this returns a copy or the original value of the requested field

- `NestedBool, NestedFloat64, NestedInt64, NestedString, SetNestedField` - this gets and sets bool / float64 / int64 / string field

- `NestedMap, SetNestedMap` - this gets and sets fields of type **map[string]interface{}**

- `NestedSlice, SetNestedSlice` - this gets and sets fields of type **[]interface{}**

- `NestedStringMap, SetNestedStringMap` - this gets and sets fields of type **map[string]string**

- `NestedStringSlice, SetNestedStringSlice` - this gets and sets fields of type **[]string**

Example

As an example, here is some code that defines a **MyResourc**e instance:

```
import (
    myresourcev1alpha1 "github.com/myid/myresource-crd/pkg/apis/mygroup.
    example.com/v1alpha1"
    "k8s.io/apimachinery/pkg/apis/meta/v1/unstructured"
)

func getResource() (*unstructured.Unstructured, error) {
    myres := unstructured.Unstructured{}
    myres.SetGroupVersionKind(
        myresourcev1alpha1.SchemeGroupVersion.
            WithKind("MyResource"))
    myres.SetName("myres1")
    myres.SetNamespace("default")
    err := unstructured.SetNestedField(
```

```
        myres.Object,
        "nginx",
        "spec", "image",
    )
    if err != nil {
        return err
    }
    // Use int64
    err = unstructured.SetNestedField(
        myres.Object,
        int64(1024*1024*1024),
        "spec", "memory",
    )
    if err != nil {
        return err
    }
    // or use string
    err = unstructured.SetNestedField(
        myres.Object,
        "1024Mo",
        "spec", "memory",
    )
    if err != nil {
        return err
    }
    return &myres, nil
}
```

The UnstructuredList Type

The **UnstructuredList** type is defined as a structure containing an **Object** field and a slice of **Unstructured** instances as items:

```
type UnstructuredList struct {
    Object map[string]interface{}
```

```
    // Items is a list of unstructured objects.
    Items []Unstructured
}
```

Getters and Setters to Access TypeMeta Fields

The **APIVersion** and **Kind** Getters/Setters can be used to directly get and set the apiVersion and kind fields of the **TypeMeta**.

The **GroupVersionKind** Getters/Setters can be used to convert the apiVersion and kind specified in the object to and from a **GroupVersionKind** value.

```
GetAPIVersion() string
GetKind() string
GroupVersionKind() schema.GroupVersionKind

SetAPIVersion(version string)
SetKind(kind string)
SetGroupVersionKind(gvk schema.GroupVersionKind)
```

Getters and Setters to Access ListMeta Fields

These getters and setters are used to get and set values related to the result of **List** operations, in the **ListMeta** field of the List.

```
GetResourceVersion() string
GetContinue() string
GetRemainingItemCount() *int64

SetResourceVersion(version string)
SetContinue(c string)
SetRemainingItemCount(c *int64)
```

Methods for Creating and Converting

- `NewEmptyInstance() runtime.Unstructured` – this creates a new instance of an Unstructured object, using the apiVersion and kind copied from the List receiver.

- `MarshalJSON() ([]byte, error)` – this returns the JSON representation of the receiver.

- UnmarshalJSON(b []byte) error – this populates the receiver with the passed JSON representation.

- UnstructuredContent() map[string]interface{}
  SetUnstructuredContent(content map[string]interface{})
  – this gets the value of the **Object** field of the receiver.

- EachListItem(fn func(runtime.Object) error) error – this executes the **fn** function for each item of the list.

Converting Between Typed and Unstructured Objects

The runtime package of the API Machinery Library provides utilities to convert between typed objects and unstructured objects, objects being either a resource or a list.

```
import (
    "k8s.io/apimachinery/pkg/runtime"
)

converter := runtime.DefaultUnstructuredConverter          ❶

var pod corev1.Pod
converter.FromUnstructured(                                ❷
    u.UnstructuredContent(), &pod,
)

var u unstructured.Unstructured
u.Object = converter.ToUnstructured(&pod)                  ❸
```

   ❶ Get the converter

   ❷ Convert an unstructured object (defining a Pod) to a typed Pod

   ❸ Convert a typed Pod to an unstructured object

The Dynamic Client

As you have seen in Chapter 6, the Client-go provides clients with the ability to work with the Kubernetes API: the Clientset to access typed resources, the REST client to make low-level REST calls to the API, and the Discovery client to get information about the resources served by the API.

It provides another client, the **dynamic** client, to work with untyped resources, described with the **Unstructured** type.

Getting the dynamic Client

The **dynamic** package provides functions to create a dynamic client of the type **dynamic.Interface**.

- func NewForConfig(c *rest.Config) (Interface, error) – this function returns a dynamic client, using the provided **rest.Config** built with one of the methods seen in chapter 6, section "Connecting to the cluster".

- func NewForConfigOrDie(c *rest.Config) Interface – this function is like the previous one, but panics in case of error, instead of returning the error. This function can be used with a hard-coded configuration, for which you want to assert the validity.

- NewForConfigAndClient(-

      c *rest.Config,

      httpClient *http.Client,

) (Interface, error)

  - this function returns a **dynamic** client, using the provided **rest. Config**, and the provided **httpClient**.

  The previous function **NewForConfig** uses a default HTTP Client built with the function **rest.HTTPClientFor**. If you want to personalize the HTTP Client before building the **dynamic** client, you can use this function instead.

Working with the dynamic Client

The **dynamic** client implements the **dynamic.Interface**, defined as follows:

```
type Interface interface {
    Resource(resource schema.GroupVersionResource)
        NamespaceableResourceInterface
}
```

The only direct method for the **dynamic** client is **Resource(gvr)**, returning an object implementing **NamespaceableResourceInterface**.

```
type NamespaceableResourceInterface interface {
    Namespace(string) ResourceInterface
    ResourceInterface
}
```

It is possible to chain the call to **Resource(gvr)** with a call to the method **Namespace(ns)**, returning an object implementing the **ResourceInterface**. Or, if **Resource(gvr)** is not chained with the **Namespace(ns)** method, it also implements the **ResourceInterface**.

Thanks to this, after calling **Resource(gvr)**, you can either chain with **Namespace(ns)**, if the resource described by **gvr** is a namespaced resource, and you want to define on which namespace to work, or else you can omit this call for non-namespaced resources if you want to make a cluster-wide operation.

The **ResourceInterface** is defined as (the complete signature of functions is omitted for conciseness) follows:

```
type ResourceInterface interface {
    Create(...)
    Update(...)
    UpdateStatus(...)
    Delete(...)
    DeleteCollection(...)
    Get(...)
    List(...)
    Watch(...)
    Patch(...)
    Apply(...)            # starting at v1.25
    ApplyStatus(...)      # starting at v1.25
}
```

These methods work with **Unstructured** and **UnstructuredList** types. For example, the **Create** method accepts an **Unstructured** object as input, and returns the created object as **Unstructured**, and the **List** method returns the list of objects as an **UnstructuredList**:

```
Create(
    ctx context.Context,
    obj *unstructured.Unstructured,
    options metav1.CreateOptions,
    subresources ...string,
) (*unstructured.Unstructured, error)

List(
    ctx context.Context,
    opts metav1.ListOptions,
) (*unstructured.UnstructuredList, error)
```

If we compare the signatures of these methods with the methods provided by the Client-go Clientset, you can see that they are very similar. The following are the changes:

- Typed objects (e.g., **corev1.Pod**) for Clientset are replaced by **Unstructured** for the **dynamic** client.

- A **subresource...** parameter is present for dynamic methods, whereas Clientset provides specific methods for subresources.

You can refer to Chapter 6 for more about the behavior of the various operations.

Example

As an example, here is some code that creates a **MyResource** instance in the cluster:

```
import (
    "context"

    myresourcev1alpha1 "github.com/feloy/myresource-crd/pkg/apis/mygroup.
    example.com/v1alpha1"
    metav1 "k8s.io/apimachinery/pkg/apis/meta/v1"
    "k8s.io/client-go/dynamic"
)
```

```
func CreateMyResource(
    dynamicClient dynamic.Interface,
    u *unstructured.Unstructured,
) (*unstructured.Unstructured, error) {
    gvr := myresourcev1alpha1.
        SchemeGroupVersion.
        WithResource("myresources")
    return dynamicClient.
        Resource(gvr).
        Namespace("default").
        Create(
            context.Background(),
            u,
            metav1.CreateOptions{},
        )
}
```

The *fake* dynamic Client

As you have seen in Chapter 7, the Client-go Library provides *fake* implementations for the Clientset, the discovery client, and the REST client. The library also provides a *fake* implementation for the **dynamic** client.

Like other *fake* implementations, you can register reactors using **PrependReactor** and similar methods on the **dynamicClient.Fake** object, and you can inspect **Actions** of the **dynamicClient.Fake** object after the test is executed.

The function **fake.NewSimpleDynamicClient** is used to create a new *fake* **dynamic** client.

```
func NewSimpleDynamicClient(
    scheme *runtime.Scheme,
    objects ...runtime.Object,
) *FakeDynamicClient)
```

The **objects** parameter indicates the resources to create in the *fake* cluster when creating the *fake* client. As an example, here is a test for a function using the **dynamic** client.

The **NewSimpleDynamicClient** function is called with the resource to create an initial resource. Note that the expected type for initial resources is **runtime.Object**, which is an interface implemented by **Unstructured**.

```go
func TestCreateMyResourceWhenResourceExists(t *testing.T) {
    myres, err := getResource()
    if err != nil {
        t.Error(err)
    }

    dynamicClient := fake.NewSimpleDynamicClient(
        runtime.NewScheme(),
        myres,
    )

    // Not really used, just to show how to use it
    dynamicClient.Fake.PrependReactor(
        "create",
        "myresources",
        func(
            action ktesting.Action,
        ) (handled bool, ret runtime.Object, err error) {
            return false, nil, nil
    })
    _, err = CreateMyResource(dynamicClient, myres)
    if err == nil {
        t.Error("Error should happen")
    }

    actions := dynamicClient.Fake.Actions()
    If len(actions) != 1 {
        t.Errorf("# of actions should be %d but is %d", 1, len(actions)
    }
}
```

Conclusion

This chapter has explored various solutions to work with custom resources in Go.

A first solution is to generate Go code based on the definition of a custom resource, to generate a Clientset dedicated to this specific custom resource definition, so you can work with custom resource instances the same as you have been working with for native Kubernetes resources.

Another solution is to work with the **dynamic** client from the Client-go Library and to rely on the **Unstructured** type to define the custom resources.

Writing Operators with the Controller-Runtime Library

As you have seen in Chapter 1, the *Controller Manager* is an important piece of the Kubernetes architecture. It embeds several *Controllers* and the role of each is to watch for instances of a specific high-level resource (Deployments, etc.) and use low-level resources (Pods, etc.) to implement these high-level instances.

As an example, Kubernetes users can create a Deployment when they want to deploy a stateless application. This deployment defines a *Pod Template* that is used to create Pods in the cluster as well as several specifications. The following are the most important specifications:

- *The number of replicas*: the identical Pods the controller must deploy for a single Deployment instance.

- *The deployment strategy*: the way the Pods are replaced when the pod template is updated.

- *The default strategy*: a *Rolling Update* can be used to update an application to a new version without service interruption, and it accepts various parameters. A simpler strategy, *Recreate*, also exists that will first stop a Pod before starting its replacement.

The *Deployment Controller* will create instances of **ReplicaSet** resources, one for each new version of the Pod Template, and update the number of replicas of these **ReplicaSets** to satisfy the replicas and strategy specifications. You will find **ReplicaSet** with zero replicas for decommissioned versions, and a **ReplicaSet** with a positive number of replicas for the actual version of your application. During a *Rolling Update*,

© Philippe Martin 2023
P. Martin, *Kubernetes Programming with Go*, https://doi.org/10.1007/978-1-4842-9026-2_10

two **ReplicaSets** will have a positive number of replicas (the new one with an increasing number, and the previous one with a decreasing number) so as to be able to transition between the two versions without service interruption.

On its side, the *ReplicaSet Controller* will be responsible for maintaining the requested number of Pod replicas for each **ReplicaSet** instance created by the *Deployment Controller*.

Chapter 8 has shown that it is possible to define new Kubernetes resources to extend the Kubernetes API. Even though the native Controller Manager runs controllers to handle native Kubernetes resources, you need to write controllers to handle custom resources.

Generally, such controllers are called *Operators* that handle third-party resources and reserve the name **Controller** for controllers handling native Kubernetes resources.

The **Client-go** Library provides tools to write Controllers and Operators using the Go language, and the **controller-runtime** Library leverages these tools to provide abstractions around the Controller pattern to help you write Operators. This library can be installed with the following command:

```
go get sigs.k8s.io/controller-runtime@v0.13.0
```

You can obtain the available revisions from the source repository at **github.com/ kubernetes-sigs/controller-runtime/releases**.

The Manager

The first important abstraction provided by the **controller-runtime** Library is the *Manager*, which provides shared resources to all Controllers running within the manager, including:

- A Kubernetes client for reading and writing Kubernetes resources

- A cache for reading Kubernetes resources from a local cache

- A scheme for registering all Kubernetes native and custom resources

To create a *Manager*, you need to use the **New** function provided, as follows:

```
import (
        "flag"

        "sigs.k8s.io/controller-runtime/pkg/client/config"
        "sigs.k8s.io/controller-runtime/pkg/manager"
)

flag.Parse()                            ❶
mgr, err := manager.New(
        config.GetConfigOrDie(),
         manager.Options{},
)
```

❶ Parse the command line flags, as **GetConfigOrDie** to handle
the --**kubeconfig** flag; see the following.

The first parameter is a **rest.Config** object, as seen in Chapter 6's "Connecting to
the Cluster" section. Note that, in this example, the **GetConfigOrDie()** utility function
provided by the **controller-runtime** library has been chosen instead of using functions
from the **Client-go** Library.

The **GetConfigOrDie()** function will try to get a configuration to connect to the
cluster:

- By getting the value of the --**kubeconfig** flag, if defined, and reading
  the **kubeconfig** file at this path. For this, first you need to execute
  flag.Parse()

- By getting the value of the **KUBECONFIG** environment variable, if
  defined, and reading the **kubeconfig** file at this path

- By looking at an in-cluster configuration (see Chapter 6's "In-cluster
  Configuration" section), if defined

- By reading the **$HOME/.kube/config** file

If none of the preceding is possible, the function will make the program exit with a **1**
code. The second argument is a structure for options.

One important option is the **Scheme**. By default, if you do not specify any value for
this option, the **Scheme** provided by the **Client-go** Library will be used. It is sufficient

if the controller needs to access only native Kubernetes resources. If you want the controller to access a custom resource, however, you will need to provide a scheme that is able to resolve the custom resource.

For example, if you want the controller to access the Custom Resource, which was defined in Chapter 9, you will need to run the following code at initialization time:

```
import (
      "k8s.io/apimachinery/pkg/runtime"

      clientgoscheme "k8s.io/client-go/kubernetes/scheme"

      mygroupv1alpha1 "github.com/myid/myresource-crd/pkg/apis/mygroup.
      example.com/v1alpha1"
)
```

```
scheme := runtime.NewScheme()                    ❶
clientgoscheme.AddToScheme(scheme)               ❷
mygroupv1alpha1.AddToScheme(scheme)              ❸

mgr, err := manager.New(
      config.GetConfigOrDie(),
      manager.Options{
            Scheme: scheme,                       ❹
      },
)
```

❶ Create a new empty scheme

❷ Add native Kubernetes resources using the Client-go Library

❸ Add to the scheme the resources from **mygroup/v1alpha1** containing our Custom Resource

❹ Use this scheme from this manager

The Controller

The second important abstraction is the *Controller*. The Controller is responsible for implementing the specifications (Spec) given by the instances of a specific Kubernetes resource. (In the Operator case, the Custom Resource is handled by the Operator.)

For this, the Controller watches for specific resources (at least the associated Custom Resource, which is called the "primary resource" in this section), and receives **Watch** events (i.e., Create, Update, Delete) for these resources. When events happen on resources, the Controller populates a Queue with a *Request* containing the name and namespace of the "primary resource" instance affected by the event.

Note that the objects enqueued are only instances of the primary resource watched by the Operator. If the event is received by an instance of another resource, the primary resource is found by following **ownerReference**. For example, the Deployment controller watches Deployment resources and **ReplicaSet** resources. All **ReplicaSet** instances contain an **ownerReference** to a Deployment instance.

- When a Deployment is created, a **Create** event is received by the controller, and the Deployment instance just created is enqueued,

- When a **ReplicaSet** is modified (e.g., by some user), an **Update** event is received for this **ReplicaSet**, and the Controller finds the Deployment referenced by the updated **ReplicaSet**, using the **ownerReference** contained in the **ReplicaSet**. Then, the referenced Deployment instance is enqueued.

The *Controller* implements a **Reconcile** method, which will be called every time a Request is available in the queue. This **Reconcile** method receives as a parameter the **Request**, containing the name and namespace of the primary resource to *reconcile*.

Note that the event that triggered the request is not part of the request and thus, the **Reconcile** method cannot rely on this information. Further, in case the event happens for an owned resource, only the primary resource is enqueued, and the **Reconcile** method cannot rely on which owned resource triggered the event.

Also, because multiple events can occur in a short time related to the same primary resource, Requests can be batched together to limit the number of Requests enqueued.

Creating a Controller

To create a Controller, you need to use the **New** function provided:

```
import (
      "sigs.k8s.io/controller-runtime/pkg/controller"
)

controller, err = controller.New(
     "my-operator", mgr,
     controller.Options{
             Reconciler: myReconciler,
})
```

The **Reconciler** option is required, and its value is an object that must implement the **Reconciler** interface, defined as:

```
type Reconciler interface {
     Reconcile(context.Context, Request) (Result, error)
}
```

As a facility, the **reconcile.Func** type is provided, which implements the **Reconciler** interface, and is the same type as a function with the same signature as the **Reconcile** method.

```
type Func func(context.Context, Request) (Result, error)

func (r Func) Reconcile(ctx context.Context, o Request) (Result, error) {
return r(ctx, o) }
```

Thanks to this **reconcile.Func** type, you can cast a function with the Reconcile signature and assign it to the **Reconciler** option. For example:

```
controller, err = controller.New(
     "my-operator", mgr,
     controller.Options{
             Reconciler: reconcile.Func(reconcileFunction),
})

func reconcileFunction(
```

```
    ctx context.Context,
    r reconcile.Request,
) (reconcile.Result, error) {
    [...]
    return reconcile.Result{}, nil
}
```

Watching Resources

After the controller is created, you need to indicate to the container which resources to watch, and whether these are the *primary* resource or *owned* resources.

The method **Watch** on the controller is used to add a Watch. The method is defined as follows:

```
Watch(
    src source.Source,
    eventhandler handler.EventHandler,
    predicates ...predicate.Predicate,
) error
```

The first parameter indicates what is the source of the events to watch, and its type is the **source.Source** interface. Two implementations are provided for the **Source** interface by the **controller-runtime** Library:

- The **Kind** source is used to watch for events on Kubernetes objects of a specific kind. The **Type** field of the **Kind** structure is required, and its value is an object of the wanted kind. For example, if we want to watch for Deployment, the value of **src** parameter would be:

  ```
  controller.Watch(
      &source.Kind{
          Type: &appsv1.Deployment{},
      },
      ...
  ```

- The **Channel** source is used to watch for events originating from outside the cluster. The **Source** field of the **Channel** structure is required, and its value is a channel emitting objects of type **event.GenericEvent**.

The second parameter is an event handler, and its type is the **handler.EventHandler** interface. Two implementations are provided for the **EventHandler** interface by the **controller-runtime** Library:

- The **EnqueueRequestForObject** event handler is used for the primary resource handled by the controller. In this case, the controller will place into the queue the object attached to the event. For example, if the controller is an operator handling the custom resource created in Chapter 9, you will write:

```
controller.Watch(
        &source.Kind{
                Type: &mygroupv1alpha1.MyResource{},
        },
        &handler.EnqueueRequestForObject{},
)
```

- The **EnqueueRequestForOwner** event handler is used for resources owned by the primary resource. One field of the **EnqueueRequestForOwner** is required: **OwnerType**. The value for this field is an object of the type of the primary resource; the controller will follow the ownerReferences until it finds an object of this type, and it places this object into the queue.

  For example, if the Controller handles the **MyResource** primary resource and is creating **Pods** to implement **MyResource**, it will want to Watch for **Pod** resources using this event handler and specify a **MyResource** object as **OwnerType**.

  If the field **IsController** is set to true, the Controller will consider only the ownerReferences with **Controller: true**.

```
controller.Watch(
        &source.Kind{
                Type: &corev1.Pod{},
        },
        &handler.EnqueueRequestForOwner{
```

```
        OwnerType: &mygroupv1alpha1.MyResource{},
        IsController: true,
    },
)
```

The third parameter is an optional list of *predicates*, and its type is **predicate. Predicate**. Several implementations are provided for the **Predicate** interface from the **controller-runtime** Library:

- **Funcs** is the most generic implementation. The **Funcs** structure is defined as follows:

```
type Funcs struct {
    // Create returns true if the Create event
    // should be processed
    CreateFunc func(event.CreateEvent) bool

    // Delete returns true if the Delete event
    // should be processed
    DeleteFunc func(event.DeleteEvent) bool

    // Update returns true if the Update event
    // should be processed
    UpdateFunc func(event.UpdateEvent) bool

    // Generic returns true if the Generic event
    // should be processed
    GenericFunc func(event.GenericEvent) bool
}
```

You can pass an instance of this structure to the **Watch** method, as a Predicate.

Nondefined fields will indicate that events of the matching type should be processed.

For non-nil fields, the function matching the event will be called (note that the **GenericFunc** will be called when the source is a Channel; see preceding), and the event will be processed if the function returns true.

Using this implementation of **Predicate**, you can define a specific function for each event type.

- ```
  func NewPredicateFuncs(
  filter func(object client.Object) bool,
  ) Funcs
  ```

  This function accepts a *filter* function and returns a **Funcs** structure for which the filter is applied on all events. Using this function, you can define a single filter applied to all event types.

- **ResourceVersionChangedPredicate** struct will define a filter for the **UpdateEvent** only.

  Using this predicate, all Create, Delete, and Generic events will be processed without filtering, and the **Update** events will be filtered so that only the updates with a **metadata.resourceVersion** change will be processed.

  The **metadata.resourceVersion** field is updated every time a new version of a resource is saved, whatever the change in the resource is.

- **GenerationChangedPredicate** struct defines a filter only for the **Update** event.

  Using this predicate, all Create, Delete, and Generic events will be processed without filtering, and the Update events will be filtered so that only the updates with a **metadata.Generation** increment will be processed.

  The **metadata.Generation** is sequentially incremented by the API Server every time an update of the **Spec** part of the resource occurs.

  Note that some resources do not respect this assumption. For example, Deployment's Generation also is incremented when the Annotations field is updated.

  For Custom Resources, Generation is incremented only if the **Status** sub-resource is enabled.

240
  ```

- **AnnotationChangedPredicate** struct defines a filter only for the **Update** event.

  Using this predicate, all Create, Delete, and Generic events will be processed, and the Update events will be filtered so that only the updates with a **metadata.Annotations** change will be processed.

A First Example

In the first example, you will create a manager and a single controller. The Controller will manage a primary custom resource **MyResource** and watch for this resource as well as Pod resources.

The **Reconcile** function will only display the namespace and name of the **MyResource** instance to reconcile.

```
package main

import (
        "context"
        "fmt"

        corev1 "k8s.io/api/core/v1"
        "k8s.io/apimachinery/pkg/runtime"
        "sigs.k8s.io/controller-runtime/pkg/client/config"
        "sigs.k8s.io/controller-runtime/pkg/controller"
        "sigs.k8s.io/controller-runtime/pkg/handler"
        "sigs.k8s.io/controller-runtime/pkg/manager"
        "sigs.k8s.io/controller-runtime/pkg/reconcile"
        "sigs.k8s.io/controller-runtime/pkg/source"
        clientgoscheme "k8s.io/client-go/kubernetes/scheme"

        mygroupv1alpha1 "github.com/myid/myresource-crd/pkg/apis/mygroup.
        example.com/v1alpha1"
)

func main() {
        scheme := runtime.NewScheme()                        ❶
```

```go
clientgoscheme.AddToScheme(scheme)
mygroupv1alpha1.AddToScheme(scheme)

mgr, err := manager.New(                        ❷
    config.GetConfigOrDie(),
    manager.Options{
        Scheme: scheme,
    },
)
panicIf(err)

controller, err := controller.New(              ❸
    "my-operator", mgr,
    controller.Options{
        Reconciler: &MyReconciler{},
    })
panicIf(err)

err = controller.Watch(                         ❹
    &source.Kind{
        Type: &mygroupv1alpha1.MyResource{},
    },
    &handler.EnqueueRequestForObject{},
)
panicIf(err)

err = controller.Watch(                         ❺
    &source.Kind{
        Type: &corev1.Pod{},
    },
    &handler.EnqueueRequestForOwner{
        OwnerType:    &corev1.Pod{},
        IsController: true,
    },
)
panicIf(err)

err = mgr.Start(context.Background())            ❻
```

```
        panicIf(err)
}

type MyReconciler struct{}                              ❼

func (o *MyReconciler) Reconcile(                       ❽
        ctx context.Context,
        r reconcile.Request,
) (reconcile.Result, error) {
        fmt.Printf("reconcile %v\n", r)
        return reconcile.Result{}, nil
}

// panicIf panic if err is not nil
// Please call from main only!
func panicIf(err error) {
        if err != nil {
                panic(err)
        }
}
```

❶ Create a scheme with native resources and the Custom resource, **MyResource**

❷ Create a Manager using the scheme just created

❸ Create a Controller, attached to manager, passing a **Reconciler** implementation

❹ Start watching **MyResource** instances as a primary resource

❺ Start watching Pod instances as an owned resource

❻ Start the manager. This function is long-running and only will return if an error occurs

❼ A type implementing the **Reconciler** interface

❽ Implementation of the **Reconcile** method. This will display the namespace and name of the instance to reconcile

Using the Controller Builder

A *Controller Builder* is proposed by the **controller-runtime** Library to make the creation of a controller more concise.

```
import (
    "sigs.k8s.io/controller-runtime/pkg/builder"
)

func ControllerManagedBy(m manager.Manager) *Builder
```

The **ControllerManagedBy** function is used to initiate a new **ControllerBuilder**. The built controller will be added to the **m** manager. A fluent interface helps configure the build:

- `For(object client.Object, opts ...ForOption) *Builder` – this method is used to indicate the primary resource handled by the controller. It can be called only once because a controller can have only one primary resource. This will internally call the **Watch** function with the event handler **EnqueueRequestForObject**.

  Predicates can be added for this watch with the **WithPredicates** function the result of which implements the **ForOption** interface.

- `Owns(object client.Object, opts ...OwnsOption) *Builder` – this method is used to indicate a resource owned by the controller. This will internally call the **Watch** function with the event handler **EnqueueRequestForOwner**.

  Predicates can be added for this watch with the **WithPredicates** function the result of which implements the **OwnsOption** interface.

- `Watches(src source.Source, eventhandler handler. EventHandler, opts ...WatchesOption) *Builder` – this method can be used to add more watchers not covered by the **For** or **Owns** methods—for example, watchers with a **Channel** source.

  Predicates can be added for this watch with the **WithPredicates** function thie result of which implements the **WatchesOption** interface.

- `WithEventFilter(p predicate.Predicate) *Builder` – this method can be used to add predicates common to all watchers created with **For**, **Owns**, and **Watch** methods.

- `WithOptions(options controller.Options) *Builder` – this sets the options that will be passed internally to the **controller.New** function.

- `WithLogConstructor(` – this sets the **logConstructo**r option.

  ```
  func(*reconcile.Request) logr.Logger,
  ) *Builder
  ```

- `Named(name string) *Builder` – this sets the name of the constructor. It should use underscores and alphanumeric characters only. By default, it is the lowercase version of the kind of the primary resource.

- `Build(`

  ```
      r reconcile.Reconciler,
  ```

  `) (controller.Controller, error)`

  – this builds and returns the Controller.

- `Complete(r reconcile.Reconciler) error` – this builds the Controller. You generally will not need to access the controller directly, so you can use this method that does not return the controller value, instead of **Build**.

A Second Example Using the ControllerBuilder

In this example, you will build the controller using the **ControllerBuilder**, instead of using the **controller.New** function and the **Watch** method on the Controller.

```
package main

import (
    "context"
    "fmt"

    corev1 "k8s.io/api/core/v1"
    "k8s.io/apimachinery/pkg/runtime"
```

```
    clientgoscheme "k8s.io/client-go/kubernetes/scheme"
    "sigs.k8s.io/controller-runtime/pkg/builder"
    "sigs.k8s.io/controller-runtime/pkg/client"
    "sigs.k8s.io/controller-runtime/pkg/client/config"
    "sigs.k8s.io/controller-runtime/pkg/manager"
    "sigs.k8s.io/controller-runtime/pkg/reconcile"

    mygroupv1alpha1 "github.com/feloy/myresource-crd/pkg/apis/mygroup.
    example.com/v1alpha1"
)

func main() {

    scheme := runtime.NewScheme()
    clientgoscheme.AddToScheme(scheme)
    mygroupv1alpha1.AddToScheme(scheme)

    mgr, err := manager.New(
        config.GetConfigOrDie(),
        manager.Options{
            Scheme: scheme,
},
    )
    panicIf(err)

    err = builder.
        ControllerManagedBy(mgr).
        For(&mygroupv1alpha1.MyResource{}).
        Owns(&corev1.Pod{}).
        Complete(&MyReconciler{})
    panicIf(err)

    err = mgr.Start(context.Background())
    panicIf(err)
}

type MyReconciler struct {}

func (a *MyReconciler) Reconcile(
```

```
    ctx context.Context,
    req reconcile.Request,
) (reconcile.Result, error) {
    fmt.Printf("reconcile %v\n", req)
    return reconcile.Result{}, nil
}

func panicIf(err error) {
    if err != nil {
        panic(err)
    }
}
```

Injecting Manager Resources into the Reconciler

The Manager provides shared resources for the controllers, including a client to read and write Kubernetes resources, a cache to read resources from a local cache, and a scheme to resolve resources. The **Reconcile** function needs access to these shared resources. There are two ways to share them:

Passing the Values When Creating the Reconciler Structure

When the controller is created, you are passing an instance of a **Reconcile** structure, implementing the **Reconciler** interface:

```
type MyReconciler struct {}
```

```
err = builder.
            ControllerManagedBy(mgr).
            For(&mygroupv1alpha1.MyResource{}).
            Owns(&corev1.Pod{}).
            Complete(&MyReconciler{})
```

The manager has been created before this, and you can have access to the shared resources using **Getters** on the manager.

As an example, here is how to get the client, cache, and scheme from the newly created manager:

```
mgr, err := manager.New(
      config.GetConfigOrDie(),
      manager.Options{
            manager.Options{
                  Scheme: scheme,
            },
      },
)
// handle err
mgrClient := mgr.GetClient()
mgrCache := mgr.GetCache()
mgrScheme := mgr.GetScheme()
```

You can add fields to the **Reconciler** structure to pass these values:

```
type MyReconciler struct {
      client client.Client
      cache cache.Cache
      scheme *runtime.Scheme
}
```

Finally, you can pass the values during the creation of the Controller:

```
err = builder.
            ControllerManagedBy(mgr).
            For(&mygroupv1alpha1.MyResource{}).
            Owns(&corev1.Pod{}).
            Complete(&MyReconciler{
      client: mgr.GetClient(),
      cache: mgr.GetCache(),
      scheme: mgr.GetScheme(),
})
```

Using Injectors

The **controller-runtime** Library provides a system of *Injectors* to inject shared resources into the **Reconcilers**, and other structures like your own implementations of **Sources**, **EventHandlers**, and **Predicates**.

The **Reconciler** implementations need to implement the specific injector interfaces from the **inject** package: **inject.Client**, **inject.Cache**, **inject.Scheme**, and so on.

These methods will be called at initialization time, when you call **controller.New** or **builder.Complete**. For this, one method needs to be created for each interface, for example:

```
type MyReconciler struct {
    client client.Client
    cache cache.Cache
    scheme *runtime.Scheme
}

func (a *MyReconciler) InjectClient(
    c client.Client,
) error {
    a.client = c
    return nil
}

func (a *MyReconciler) InjectCache(
    c cache.Cache,
) error {
    a.cache = c
    return nil
}

func (a *MyReconciler) InjectScheme(
    s *runtime.Scheme,
) error {
    a.scheme = s
    return nil
}
```

Using the Client

The client can be used to read and write resources on the cluster and to update the statuses of resources.

The **Read** methods internally use a Cache system, based on *Informers* and *Listers*, to limit the read access to the API Server. Using this cache, all controllers of the same manager have read access to the resources while limiting the requests to the API Server.

You must note that objects returned by Read operations are pointers to values into the Cache. You must **never** modify these objects directly. Instead, you must create a deep copy of the returned objects before modifying them.

The methods of the client are generic: they work with any Kubernetes resource, either native or custom if they are known by the Scheme passed to the manager.

All methods return an error, which are of the same type as the errors returned by the **Client-go** Clientset methods. You can refer to Chapter 6's "Errors and Statuses" section for more information.

Getting Information About a Resource

The **Get** method is used to get information about a resource.

```
Get(
    ctx context.Context,
    key ObjectKey,
    obj Object,
    opts ...GetOption,
) error
```

It gets as a parameter an **ObjectKey** value to indicate the namespace and name of the resource, and an **Object** to indicate the *Kind* of the resource to get and to store the result. The **Object** must be a pointer to a typed resource—for example, a **Pod** or a **MyResource** structure. The **ObjectKey** type is an alias for **types.NamespacedName**, defined in the API Machinery Library.

NamespacedName is also the type of the object embedded in the **Request** passed as parameter to the **Reconcile** function. You can directly pass **req.NamespacedName** as **ObjectKey** to get the resource to reconcile. For example, use the following to get the resource to reconcile:

```
myresource := mygroupv1alpha1.MyResource{}
err := a.client.Get(
    ctx,
    req.NamespacedName,
    &myresource,
)
```

It is possible to pass a specific **resourceVersion** value to the **Get** request, passing a **client.GetOptions** structure instance as the last parameter.

The **GetOptions** structure implements the **GetOption** interface and contains a single **Raw** field having a **metav1.GetOptions** value. For example, to specify a **resourceVersion** with a value "0" to get any version of the resource:

```
err := a.client.Get(
    ctx,
    req.NamespacedName,
    &myresource,
    &client.GetOptions{
        Raw: &metav1.GetOptions{
            ResourceVersion: "0",
        },
    },
)
```

Listing Resources

The **List** method is used to list resources of a specific kind.

```
List(
    ctx context.Context,
    list ObjectList,
    opts ...ListOption,
) error
```

The **list** parameter is an **ObjectList** value indicating the *Kind* of the resource to list and to store the result. By default, the list is performed across all namespaces.

The **List** method accepts zero or more parameters of objects implementing the **ListOption** interface. These types are supported by the following:

- **InNamespace**, alias to **string**, is used to return the resources of a specific namespace.

- **MatchingLabels**, alias to **map[string]string**, is used to indicate the list of labels and their exact value that must be defined for a resource to be returned. The following example builds a **MatchingLabels** structure to filter resources with a label "**app=myapp**".

```
matchLabel := client.MatchingLabels{
    "app": "myapp",
}
```

- **HasLabels**, alias to **[]string**, is used to indicate the list of labels, independently of their value, that must be defined for a resource to be returned. The following example builds a **HasLabels** structure to filter resources with "**app**" and "**debug**" labels.

```
hasLabels := client.HasLabels{"app", "debug"}
```

- **MatchingLabelsSelector**, embedding a **labels.Selector** interface, is used to pass more advanced label selectors. See Chapter 6's "Filtering the Result of a List" section for more information on how to build a **Selector**. The following example builds a **MatchingLabelsSelector** structure that can be used as an option for **List** to filter resources with a label **mykey** different from **ignore**.

```
selector := labels.NewSelector()
require, err := labels.NewRequirement(
    "mykey",
    selection.NotEquals,
    []string{"ignore"},
)
```

```
// assert err is nil
selector = selector.Add(*require)
labSelOption := client.MatchingLabelsSelector{
        Selector: selector,
}
```

- **MatchingFields**, alias to **fields.Set**, itself an alias to **map[string]string**, is used to indicate the fields and their value to match. The following example builds a **MatchingFields** structure to filter resources with the field "**status.phase**" that is "**Running**":

```
matchFields := client.MatchingFields{
        "status.phase": "Running",
}
```

- **MatchingFieldsSelector**, embedding a **fields.Selector**, is used to pass more advanced field selectors. See Chapter 6's "Filtering the Result of a List" section for more information on how to build a **fields.Selector**. The following example builds a **MatchingFieldsSelector** structure to filter resources with a field "**status.phase**" different from "**Running**":

```
fieldSel := fields.OneTermNotEqualSelector(
        "status.phase",
        "Running",
)
fieldSelector := client.MatchingFieldsSelector{
        Selector: fieldSel,
}
```

- **Limit**, alias to **int64** and **Continue**, alias to **string**, is used to paginate the result. These options are detailed in Chapter 2's "Paginating Results" section.

Creating a Resource

The **Create** method is used to create a new resource in the cluster.

```
Create(
    ctx context.Context,
    obj Object,
    opts ...CreateOption,
) error
```

The **obj** passed as a parameter defines the kind of object to create, as well as its definition. The following example will create a Pod in the cluster:

```
podToCreate := corev1.Pod{ [...] }
podToCreate.SetName("nginx")
podToCreate.SetNamespace("default")
err = a.client.Create(ctx, &podToCreate)
```

The following options can be passed as **CreateOption** to parameterize the **Create** request.

- **DryRunAll** value indicates that all the operations should be executed except those persisting the resource to storage.

- **FieldOwner**, alias to **string**, indicates the name of the field manager for the **Create** operation. This information is useful for Server-side Apply operations to work correctly.

Deleting a Resource

The **Delete** method is used to delete a resource from the cluster.

```
Delete(
    ctx context.Context,
    obj Object, k
    opts ...DeleteOption,
) error
```

The **obj** passed as a parameter defines the kind of object to delete, as well as its namespace (if the resource is namespaced) and its name. The following example can be used to delete a Pod.

```
podToDelete := corev1.Pod{}
podToDelete.SetName("nginx")
podToDelete.SetNamespace("prj2")
err = a.client.Delete(ctx, &podToDelete)
```

The following options can be passed as **DeleteOption** to parameterize the **Delete** request.

- **DryRunAll** – this value indicates that all the operations should be executed except those persisting the resource to storage.

- **GracePeriodSeconds**, alias to **int64** – this value is useful when deleting pods only. This indicates the duration in seconds before the pod should be deleted. See Chapter 6's, "Deleting a Resource" section for more details.

- **Preconditions**, alias to **metav1.Preconditions** – this indicates which resource you expect to delete. See Chapter 6's, "Deleting a Resource" section for more details.

- **PropagationPolicy**, alias to **metav1.DeletionPropagation** – this indicates whether and how garbage collection will be performed. See Chapter 6's, "Deleting a Resource" section for more details.

Deleting a Collection of Resources

The **DeleteAllOf** method is used to delete all resources of a given type from the cluster.

```
DeleteAllOf(
    ctx context.Context,
    obj Object,
    opts ...DeleteAllOfOption,
) error
```

The **obj** passed as a parameter defines the kind of object to delete.

The **opts** available for the **DeleteAllOf** operation is the combination of the options for the **List** operation (see "Listing Resources" section) and the **Delete** operation (see "Deleting a Resource" section).

As an example, here is how to delete all deployments from a given namespace:

```
err = a.client.DeleteAllOf(
    ctx,
    &appsv1.Deployment{},
    client.InNamespace(aNamespace))
```

Updating a Resource

The **Update** method is used to update an existing resource in the cluster.

```
Update(
    ctx context.Context,
    obj Object,
    opts ...UpdateOption,
) error
```

The **obj** parameter is used to indicate which resource to update, and its new definition. If the object does not exist in the cluster, the Update operation fails.

The following options can be passed as **UpdateOption** to parameterize the **Update** request.

- **DryRunAll** value indicates that all the operations should be executed except those persisting the resource to storage.

- **FieldOwner**, alias to **string**, indicates the name of the field manager for the **Update** operation. This information is useful for Server-side Apply operations to work correctly.

Patching a Resource

The **Patch** method is used to patch an existing resource. It can also be used to run a Server-Side Apply operation.

```
Patch(
    ctx context.Context,
```

```
    obj Object,
    patch Patch,
    opts ...PatchOption,
) error
```

The following options can be passed as **PatchOption** to parameterize the **Patch** request.

- **DryRunAll** value indicates to execute all the operations except persisting the resource to storage.

- **FieldOwner**, alias to **string**, indicates the name of the field manager for the **Patch** operation.

- **ForceOwnership**, alias to **struct{}**, indicates that the caller will reacquire the conflicting fields owned by other managers. This option is valid only when the patch type is **Apply** (see the following).

Server-side Apply

To use a Server-side Apply operation, you need to specify a **patch** value of **client.Apply**. The **obj** value must be the new object definition. It must include its name, namespace (if the resource is namespaced), group, version, and kind.

The name of the field manager is required and must be specified with the option **client.FieldOwner(name)**. As an example, here is how to Server-side Apply a Deployment:

```
deployToApply := appsv1.Deployment{ [...] }
deployToApply.SetName("nginx")
deployToApply.SetNamespace("default")
deployToApply.SetGroupVersionKind(
    appsv1.SchemeGroupVersion.WithKind("Deployment"),
)
err = a.client.Patch(
    ctx,
    &deployToApply,
    client.Apply,
    client.FieldOwner("mycontroller"),
    client.ForceOwnership,
)
```

Strategic Merge Patch

You have seen in Chapter 2's "Using a Strategic Merge Patch to Update a Resource" section how patching a resource with a strategic merge patch works. Chapter 6's "Using a Strategic Merge Patch to Update a Resource" section has shown how to execute this operation using the C**lient-go** Library.

Using *Client-go*, you must first read a resource from the cluster (with a **Get** or **List** operation), then create a Patch using the **StrategicMergeFrom** function on this resource, then update the resource, and finally call the **Data** method on the patch to compute the JSON patch data.

Using the **controller-runtime** client, some part of the process is done by the client. You still must read the resource from the cluster (with a **Get** or **List** operation), create a Patch using the **StrategicMergeFrom** function, then update the resource. At this point, you can call the **Patch** method with the updated object and the patch as parameters. The call to the **Data** method will be done internally by the client.

Note that the **StrategicMergeFrom** function used here is the same as the one used with the Client-go Library. You can refer to Chapter 6's "Using a Strategic Merge Patch to Update a Resource" section to see the available options for this method.

As an example, here is how to add an environment variable to the first container of a Deployment's **Pod** template.

```
var deploymentRead appsv1.Deployment
err = a.client.Get(                                                    ❶
    ctx,
    key, // an ObjectKey defining the namespace and name
    &deploymentRead)
if err != nil {
    return reconcile.Result{}, err
}

patch :=
  client.StrategicMergeFrom(deploymentRead.DeepCopy())          ❷

depModified := deploymentRead.DeepCopy()
depModified.Spec.Template.Spec.Containers[0].Env =        ❸
  append(
      depModified.Spec.Template.Spec.Containers[0].Env,
```

```
        corev1.EnvVar{
              Name:  "newName",
              Value: "newValue",
        })
err = a.client.Patch(ctx, &depModified, patch)                ❹
```

❶ Get the deployment to patch from the cluster

❷ Create a **Patch** object from a copy of this deployment

❸ Modify the deployment

❹ Execute **Patch**, using the modified deployment and the **Patch** object

Merge Patch

A Merge Patch works in a similar way to a Strategic Merge Patch, except for how the lists are merged. See Chapter 2's "Patching Array Fields" section for more information on how lists are merged using a Strategic Merge Patch. For Merge Patch, the original lists are not considered, and the new list is the list defined in the patch.

Using the **controller-runtime** Library, you just need to replace the call to **client.StrategicMergeFrom** with a call to **client.MergeFrom** at step ❷ in the listing to indicate performance of a Merge Patch.

```
patch := client.MergeFrom(deploymentRead.DeepCopy())          ❷
```

Updating the Status of a Resource

When working on an Operator, you will want to modify values into the Status part of the Custom Resource, to indicate the current state of it.

```
Update(
     ctx context.Context,
     obj Object,
     opts ...UpdateOption,
) error
```

Note that you do not need specific **Create**, **Get**, or **Delete** operations for the Status because you will create the Status as part of the Custom Resource when you create the Custom Resource itself. Also, the **Get** operation for a resource will return the Status part of the resource and deleting a resource will delete its status part.

The API Server, however, forces you to use different **Update** methods for the Status and for the rest of the resource to protect you from modifying both parts at the same time by mistake.

For the Update of the status to work, the Custom Resource Definition must declare the **status** field in the list of sub-resources of the Custom Resource. See Chapter 8's "Definition of the Resource Versions" section to understand how to declare this **status** sub-resource.

This method works like the **Update** method for the resource itself, but to invoke it, you need to call the method on the object returned by **client.Status()**:

```
err = client.Status().Update(ctx, obj)
```

Patching the Status of a Resource

As for the **Update** method, patching the status of a resource needs a dedicated method on the result of **client.Status()**.

```
Patch(
    ctx context.Context,
    obj Object,
    patch Patch,
    opts ...PatchOption,
) error
```

The **Patch** method for the Status works the same as the **Patch** method for the resource itself, except that it will patch the Status part of the resource only.

```
err = client.Status().Patch(ctx, obj, patch)
```

Logging

The Manager leverages a logger system defined in the log package of the **controller-runtime** Library. The logger must be initialized with a call to **SetLogger**. Then, it is possible to use the **Log** variable defined into the log package.

```
import (
        crlog "sigs.k8s.io/controller-runtime/pkg/log"
        "sigs.k8s.io/controller-runtime/pkg/log/zap"
)

func main() {
    log.SetLogger(zap.New())
    log.Log.Info("starting")
    [...]
}
```

The **Log** object, of type **logr.Logger** (from **github.com/go-logr/logr**), has two main methods, **Info** and **Error**.

```
func (l Logger) Info(
    msg string,
    keysAndValues ...interface{},
)

func (l Logger) Error(
    err error,
    msg string,
    keysAndValues ...interface{},
)
```

The **Logger** is a "structured" logging system, in that logs are mostly made of key-value pairs rather than printf-style formatted strings. Whereas printf-style logs are easier to read by humans, structured logs are easier to analyze by tools. The predefined keys for log entries are:

- **level**: the verbosity level of the log; see the following section for a definition of log verbosity

- **ts**: timestamp of the log entry

261

- **logger**: name of the logger for this entry; see the section that follows for a definition of the name of the logger

- **msg**: message associated with the log entry

- **error**: the error associated with the log entry

The **Info** and **Error** methods accept a message and zero or more key-value pairs. The **Error** method also accepts an error value.

Verbosity

The Info messages can be given a *Verbosity* by using **log.V(*n*).Info(...)**. The larger is the *n* verbosity, the less important is the message. **log.Info(...)** is equivalent to **log.V(0). Info(...)**.

Predefined Values

You can build a new logger with predefined key-value pairs by using **WithValues**:

```
func (l Logger) WithValues(
    keysAndValues ...interface{},
) Logger

ctrlLog := log.Log.WithValues("package", "controller")
```

Logger Name

You can build a new logger by appending a name to the logger name by using **WithName**:

```
func (l Logger) WithName(name string) Logger
```

Successive calls to **WithName** will add suffixes to the logger name. For example, the following will set a logger name "**controller.main**":

```
ctrlLog := log.Log.WithName("controller")
[...]
ctrlMainLog = ctrlLog.Log.WithName("main")
```

Getting the Logger from Context

The Manager adds a logger to the Context passed to the different methods, and especially the **Reconcile** function.

You can extract the logger from the Context using the function **FromContext**. Optional parameters can be used to add predefined key-value pairs to the logger:

```
func FromContext(
    ctx context.Context,
    keysAndValues ...interface{},
) logr.Logger {

func (a *MyReconciler) Reconcile(
    ctx context.Context,
    req reconcile.Request,
) (reconcile.Result, error) {
    log := log.FromContext(ctx).WithName("reconcile")
    [...]
}
```

Events

The Kubernetes API provides an **Event** resource, and an *Event* instance is attached to a specific instance of any kind. Events are sent by controllers to inform the user that some event occurred related to an object. These events are displayed when executing **kubectl describe**. For example, you can see the events related to a pod executing:

```
$ kubectl describe pods nginx
[...]
Events:
  Type     Reason      Age         From                 Message
  ----     ------      ----        ----                 -------
  Normal   Scheduled   1s          default-scheduler    Successfully assigned...
  Normal   Pulling     0s          kubelet              Pulling image "nginx"
  Normal   Pulled      <invalid>   kubelet              Successfully pulled...
  Normal   Created     <invalid>   kubelet              Created container nginx
  Normal   Started     <invalid>   kubelet              Started container nginx
```

263

To send such events from the **Reconcile** function, you need to have access to the **EventRecorder** instance provided by the Manager. During initialization, you can get this instance with the **GetEventRecorderFor** method on the Manager, then pass this value when building the **Reconcile** structure:

```go
type MyReconciler struct {
      client          client.Client
      EventRecorder record.EventRecorder
}

func main() {
      [...]
      eventRecorder := mgr.GetEventRecorderFor(
"MyResource",
      )

      err = builder.
            ControllerManagedBy(mgr).
            Named(controller.Name).
            For(&mygroupv1alpha1.MyResource{}).
            Owns(&appsv1.Deployment{}).
            Complete(&controller.MyReconciler{
                  EventRecorder: eventRecorder,
            })
      [...]
}
```

Then, from the **Reconcile** function, you can call the **Event**, **Eventf**, and **AnnotatedEventf** methods.

```go
func (record.EventRecorder) Event(
      object runtime.Object,
      eventtype, reason, message string,
)

func (record.EventRecorder) Eventf(
      object runtime.Object,
      eventtype, reason, messageFmt string,
```

```
    args ...interface{},
)

func (record.EventRecorder) AnnotatedEventf(
    object runtime.Object,
    annotations map[string]string,
    eventtype, reason, messageFmt string,
    args ...interface{},
)
```

The **object** parameter indicates to which object to attach the Event. You will pass the custom resource being reconciled.

The **eventtype** parameter accepts two values, **corev1.EventTypeNormal** and **corev1.EventTypeWarning**.

The **reason** parameter is a short value in **UpperCamelCase** format. The **message** parameter is a human-readable text.

The **Event** method is used to pass a static message, the **Eventf** method can create a message using **Sprintf**, and the **AnnotatedEventf** method also can attach annotations to the event.

Conclusion

In this chapter, you have worked with the **controller-runtime** library to start creating an operator. You have seen how to create a Manager using the appropriate scheme, how to create a controller and declare the **Reconcile** function, and have explored the various functions of the client provided by the library to access the resources in the cluster.

The next chapter explores how to write a **Reconcile** function.

CHAPTER 11

Writing the Reconcile Loop

We have seen in the previous chapter how to bootstrap a new project for writing an Operator, using the **controller-runtime** Library. In this chapter, we will focus on the implementation of the **Reconcile** function, which is an important part of the implementation of an operator.

The Reconcile function contains all the business logic of the Operator. The function will work on a single resource kind—one says the Operator *reconciles* this resource—and can be notified when objects of other types trigger events, by mapping these other types to the reconciled one using *Owner References*.

The role of the **Reconcile** function is to ensure that the state of the system matches what is specified in the resource to be reconciled. For this, it will create "low-level" resources to implement the resource to reconcile. These resources, in turn, will be reconciled by other controllers or operators. When the reconciliation of these resources is completed, their status will be updated to reflect their new state. In addition, the Operator will be able to detect these changes and to adapt the status of the reconciled resource accordingly.

As an example, the Operator you started to implement in the previous chapter reconciles the Custom Resource **MyResource**. The Operator will create **Deployment** instances for implementing **MyResource** instances, and for this reason, the operator also will want to watch for Deployment resources.

When an event is triggered for a Deployment instance, the **MyResource** instance for which the deployment has been created will be reconciled. For example, after the Pods for the Deployment are created, the status of the deployment will be updated to indicate that all replicas are running. At this point, the Operator can modify the status of the reconciled resource to indicate that it is ready.

The *Reconcile Loop* is known as the process of watching for resources and calling the **Reconcile** function when resources are created, modified, or deleted, implementing the reconciled resource with low-level ones, watching for the status of these resources, and updating the status of the reconciled resource accordingly.

© Philippe Martin 2023
P. Martin, *Kubernetes Programming with Go*, https://doi.org/10.1007/978-1-4842-9026-2_11

Writing the Reconcile Function

The **Reconcile** function receives from the queue a resource to reconcile. The first operation to work on is to get the information about this resource to reconcile.

As a matter of fact, only the namespace and name of the resource are received (its kind is known by its design, being the kind to be reconciled by the operator), but you do not receive the complete definition of the resource.

A **Get** operation is used to get the definition of the resource.

Checking Whether the Resource Exists

The resource may have been enqueued for various reasons: it has been created, modified, or deleted (or another owned resource has been created, modified, or deleted). In the first two cases (creation or modification), the **Get** operation will succeed and the **Reconcile** function will know the definition of the resource at this point. In case of deletion, the **Get** operation will fail with a **Notfound** error because the resource is now deleted.

The good practice for an Operator is to add OwnerReferences to resources it creates when reconciling a resource. The primary goal is to be able to reconcile its owner when these created resources are modified, and a result of adding these OwnerReferences is that these owned resources will be deleted by the Kubernetes garbage collector when the owner resource is deleted.

For this reason, when a reconciled object is deleted, there is nothing to do in the cluster because the deletion of the associated created resources will be handled by the cluster.

Implementing the Reconciled Resource

If the resource to reconcile has been found in the cluster, the operator's next step is to create "low-level" resources to implement this resource to reconcile.

Because Kubernetes is a declarative platform, a good way of creating these resources is to declare what the low-level resources should be, independent of what exists, or not, in the cluster, and to rely on the Kubernetes controllers to take over and reconcile these low-level resources.

For this reason, it is not possible to use the **Create** method blindly because we are not sure whether the resources exist or not, and the operation would fail if the resources already exist.

You could check whether resources exist, and create them if they do not, or modify them if they exist. As has been shown in the previous chapters, the Server-side Apply method is perfect for this situation: when running an Apply operation, if the resource does not exist, it is created; and if the resource exists, it is patched, taking care of conflicts in case the resource has been modified by another participant.

Using the Server-side Apply method, the Operator does not need to check whether the resources exist or not, or whether they have been modified by another participant. The Operator only needs to run the Server-side Apply operation with the definitions of the resources from the Operator's point of view.

After the low-level resources are applied, two possibilities should be considered.

> *Case 1:* If the low-level resources already exist and have not been modified by the Apply, no MODIFIED event will be triggered for these resources, and the **Reconcile** function will not be called again (at least for this Apply operation).

> *Case 2:* If the low-level resources have been created or modified, this will trigger CREATED or MODIFIED events for these resources, and the **Reconcile** function will be called again because of these events. This new execution of the function will again Apply the low-level resources and, if nothing has updated these resources in the meantime, the Operator will fall on Case 1.

The new low-level resources will be handled eventually by their respective operators or controllers. In turn, they will reconcile these resources, and update their status to announce their current state.

As soon as the statuses of these low-level resources are updated, MODIFIED events will be triggered for these resources, and the **Reconcile** function will be called again. Once more, the Operator will Apply the resources, and Cases 1 and 2 have to be considered.

The Operator needs, at some point, to read the Statuses of the low-level resources it has created so as to compute the status of the reconciled resource. In simple cases, it can be done just after executing the Server-side Apply of the low-level resources.

Simple Implementation Example

To illustrate, here is a complete **Reconcile** function for an operator that creates a Deployment with the **Image** and **Memory** information provided in a **MyResource** instance.

```go
func (a *MyReconciler) Reconcile(
  ctx context.Context,
  req reconcile.Request,
) (reconcile.Result, error) {
  log := log.FromContext(ctx)

  log.Info("getting myresource instance")

  myresource := mygroupv1alpha1.MyResource{}
  err := a.client.Get(                                      ❶
    ctx,
    req.NamespacedName,
    &myresource,
    &client.GetOptions{},
  )
  if err != nil {
    if errors.IsNotFound(err) {                             ❷
      log.Info("resource is not found")
      return reconcile.Result{}, nil
    }
    return reconcile.Result{}, err
  }

  ownerReference := metav1.NewControllerRef(                ❸
    &myresource,
    mygroupv1alpha1.SchemeGroupVersion.
        WithKind("MyResource"),
  )

  err = a.applyDeployment(                                  ❹
    ctx,
```

```
        &myresource,
        ownerReference,
    )
      if err != nil {
        return reconcile.Result{}, err
      }

      status, err := a.computeStatus(ctx, &myresource)          ❺
      if err != nil {
        return reconcile.Result{}, err
      }
      myresource.Status = *status
      log.Info("updating status", "state", status.State)
      err = a.client.Status().Update(ctx, &myresource)          ❻
      if err != nil {
        return reconcile.Result{}, err
      }

      return reconcile.Result{}, nil
}
```

❶ Get the definition of the resource to reconcile

❷ If resource does not exist, return immediately

❸ Build the **ownerReference** pointing to the resource to reconcile

❹ Use Server-side Apply for the "low-level" deployment

❺ Compute the status of the resource based on the "low-level" deployment

❻ Update the status of the resource to reconcile

Here is an example of an implementation of the Server-side Apply operation for the deployment created by the operator:

```
func (a *MyReconciler) applyDeployment(
  ctx context.Context,
  myres *mygroupv1alpha1.MyResource,
  ownerref *metav1.OwnerReference,
```

```
) error {
  deploy := createDeployment(myres, ownerref)
  err := a.client.Patch(                                    ❼
    ctx,
    deploy,
    client.Apply,
    client.FieldOwner(Name),
    client.ForceOwnership,
  )
  return err
}

func createDeployment(
  myres *mygroupv1alpha1.MyResource,
  ownerref *metav1.OwnerReference,
) *appsv1.Deployment {
  deploy := &appsv1.Deployment{
    ObjectMeta: metav1.ObjectMeta{
      Labels: map[string]string{
        "myresource": myres.GetName(),
      },
    },
    Spec: appsv1.DeploymentSpec{
      Selector: &metav1.LabelSelector{
        MatchLabels: map[string]string{
          "myresource": myres.GetName(),
        },
      },
      Template: corev1.PodTemplateSpec{
        ObjectMeta: metav1.ObjectMeta{
          Labels: map[string]string{
            "myresource": myres.GetName(),
          },
        },
        Spec: corev1.PodSpec{
          Containers: []corev1.Container{
```

```
        {
          Name:  "main",
          Image: myres.Spec.Image,                        ❽
          Resources: corev1.ResourceRequirements{
            Requests: corev1.ResourceList{
              corev1.ResourceMemory:      myres.Spec.Memory,    ❾
            },
          },
        },
      },
    },
  },
}
deploy.SetName(myres.GetName() + "-deployment")
deploy.SetNamespace(myres.GetNamespace())
deploy.SetGroupVersionKind(
  appsv1.SchemeGroupVersion.WithKind("Deployment"),
)
deploy.SetOwnerReferences([]metav1.OwnerReference{    ❿
  *ownerref,
})
return deploy
}
```

❼ Use the **Patch** method to execute the Server-side Apply operation

❽ Use the **Image** defined in the resource to reconcile

❾ Use the **Memory** defined in the resource to reconcile

❿ Set the **OwnerReference** to point to the resource to reconcile

Then, here is an example of how the computation and update of the Status can be implemented:

```go
const (
  _buildingState = "Building"
  _readyState    = "Ready"
)

func (a *MyReconciler) computeStatus(
  ctx context.Context,
  myres *mygroupv1alpha1.MyResource,
) (*mygroupv1alpha1.MyResourceStatus, error) {

  logger := log.FromContext(ctx)
  result := mygroupv1alpha1.MyResourceStatus{
    State: _buildingState,
  }

  deployList := appsv1.DeploymentList{}
  err := a.client.List(
    ctx,
    &deployList,
    client.InNamespace(myres.GetNamespace()),
    client.MatchingLabels{
      "myresource": myres.GetName(),
    },
  )
  if err != nil {
    return nil, err
  }

  if len(deployList.Items) == 0 {
    logger.Info("no deployment found")
    return &result, nil
  }

  if len(deployList.Items) > 1 {
    logger.Info(
```

❶

```
                "too many deployments found", "count",
        len(deployList.Items),
)
    return nil, fmt.Errorf(
            "%d deployment found, expected 1",
        len(deployList.Items),
)
  }

  status := deployList.Items[0].Status              ⓬
  logger.Info(
        "got deployment status",
        "status", status,
)
  if status.ReadyReplicas == 1 {
    result.State = _readyState                      ⓭
  }

  return &result, nil
}
```

❶❶ Get the deployment created for this resource to reconcile

⓬ Get the status of the unique Deployment found

⓭ When replicas is **1**, set status **Ready** for the reconciled resource

Conclusion

This chapter has shown how to implement the **Reconcile** function for a simple operator that creates a Deployment using information from the Custom Resource.

Real operators generally will be more complex than this simple example by creating several resources having more complex lifecycle, but it demonstrates the main points to know when starting to write an operator: The declarative nature of the **Reconcile** loop, the use of Owner References, the use of Server-side Apply, and how the status is updated.

The next chapter will show how to test the **Reconcile** loop.

CHAPTER 12

Testing the Reconcile Loop

The previous chapter described how to implement a simple, but complete, **Reconcile** function for an Operator reconciling a Custom Resource.

To test the **Reconcile** function you have written in the previous chapter, you will use **ginkgo**, which is a Testing Framework for Go; and the **envtest** package from the **controller-runtime** Library, which provides a Kubernetes environment for testing.

The envtest Package

The **controller-runtime** Library provides an **envtest** package. This package provides a Kubernetes environment by starting a simple local control plane.

By default, the package uses local binaries for **etcd** and **kube-apiserver** located in **/usr/local/kubebuilder/bin**, and you can provide your own path to find these binaries. You can install **setup-envtest** to obtain these binaries for various Kubernetes versions.

Installing envtest Binaries

The **setup-envtest** tool can be used to install binaries used by **envtest**. To install the tool, you must run:

```
$ go install sigs.k8s.io/controller-runtime/tools/setup-envtest@latest
```

Then, you can install the binaries for a specific Kubernetes version using the following command:

```
$ setup-envtest use 1.23
Version: 1.23.5
OS/Arch: linux/amd64
Path: /path/to/kubebuilder-envtest/k8s/1.23.5-linux-amd64
```

© Philippe Martin 2023
P. Martin, *Kubernetes Programming with Go*, https://doi.org/10.1007/978-1-4842-9026-2_12

The output of the command will inform you in which directory the binaries have been installed. If you want to use these binaries from the default directory, **/usr/local/ kubebuilder/bin**, you can create a symbolic link to access them from there:

```
$ sudo mkdir /usr/local/kubebuilder
$ sudo ln -s /path/to/kubebuilder-envtest/k8s/1.23.5-linux-amd64 /usr/
local/kubebuilder/bin
```

Or, if you prefer to use the **KUBEBUILDER_ASSETS** environment variable to define the directory containing the binaries, you can execute:

```
$ source <(setup-envtest use -i -p env 1.23.5)
$ echo $KUBEBUILDER_ASSETS
/path/to/kubebuilder-envtest/k8s/1.23.5-linux-amd64
```

This will define and export the **KUBEBUILDER_ASSETS** variable with the path containing the binaries for Kubernetes 1.23.5.

Using envtest

The control plane will only run the API Server and **etcd**, but no controller. This means that when the operator you want to test will create Kubernetes resources, no controller will react. For example, if the operator creates a Deployment, no pod will be created, and the deployment status will never be updated.

This can be surprising at first, but this will help you test your operator only, not the Kubernetes controllers. To create the Test Environment, you first need to create an instance of an **envtest.Environment** structure.

Using default values for the **Environment** structure will start a local control plane using binaries in **/usr/local/kubebuilder/bin** or from the directory defined in the **KUBEBUILDER_ASSETS** environment variable.

If you are writing an operator reconciling a custom resource, you will need to add the Custom Resource Definition (CRD) for this custom resource. For this, you can use the **CRDDirectoryPaths** field to pass the list of directories containing CRD definitions in YAML or JSON format. All these definitions will be applied to the local cluster when initializing the environment.

The field **ErrorIfCRDPathMissing** is useful if you want to be altered when the CRD directories do not exist. As an example, here is how an **Environment** structure can be created, with the CRD YAML or JSON files located in the **../../crd** directory:

```
import (
  "path/filepath"

  "sigs.k8s.io/controller-runtime/pkg/envtest"
)

testEnv = &envtest.Environment{
  CRDDirectoryPaths:    []string{
    filepath.Join("..", "..", "crd"),
  },
  ErrorIfCRDPathMissing: true,
}
```

To start the environment, you can use the **Start** method on this **Environment**:

```
cfg, err := testEnv.Start()
```

This method returns a **rest.Config** value, which is the **Config** value to be used to connect to the local cluster launched by the **Environment**. At the end of the test, the **Environment** can be stopped using the **Stop** method:

```
err := testEnv.Stop()
```

Once the environment is started and you have a **Config**, you can create the Manager and the Controller and start the Manager, as described in Chapter 10.

Defining a ginkgo Suite

To start the tests for the **Reconcile** function, you can use a **go** test function to start **ginkgo** specs:

```
import (
    "testing"

    . "github.com/onsi/ginkgo/v2"
    . "github.com/onsi/gomega"
)
```

```
func TestMyReconciler_Reconcile(t *testing.T) {
    RegisterFailHandler(Fail)
    RunSpecs(t,
        "Controller Suite",
    )
}
```

Then, you can declare **BeforeSuite** and **AfterSuite** functions, which are used to start and stop the **Environment** and the Manager.

Here is an example for these functions, which will create an environment with the CRD for **MyResource** loaded. The Manager is started in a **Go** routine at the end of the **BeforeSuite** function, so the tests can be executed on the main **Go** routine.

Note that you are creating a *Cancelable Context*, which is used when starting the Manager, so you can stop the Manager by canceling the context from the **AfterSuite** function.

```
import (
    "context"
    "path/filepath"
    "testing"

    . "github.com/onsi/ginkgo/v2"
    . "github.com/onsi/gomega"

    appsv1 "k8s.io/api/apps/v1"
    "k8s.io/apimachinery/pkg/runtime"
    clientgoscheme "k8s.io/client-go/kubernetes/scheme"

    "sigs.k8s.io/controller-runtime/pkg/builder"
    "sigs.k8s.io/controller-runtime/pkg/client"
    "sigs.k8s.io/controller-runtime/pkg/envtest"
    "sigs.k8s.io/controller-runtime/pkg/log"
    "sigs.k8s.io/controller-runtime/pkg/log/zap"
    "sigs.k8s.io/controller-runtime/pkg/manager"

    mygroupv1alpha1 "github.com/feloy/myresource-crd/pkg/apis/mygroup.
    example.com/v1alpha1"
)
```

```go
var (
    testEnv    *envtest.Environment                          ❶
    ctx        context.Context
    cancel     context.CancelFunc
    k8sClient client.Client                                  ❷
)

var _ = BeforeSuite(func() {
    log.SetLogger(zap.New(
        zap.WriteTo(GinkgoWriter),
        zap.UseDevMode(true),
    ))

    ctx, cancel = context.WithCancel(                        ❸
        context.Background(),
    )

    testEnv = &envtest.Environment{                          ❹
        CRDDirectoryPaths:     []string{
            filepath.Join("..", "..", "crd"),
        },
        ErrorIfCRDPathMissing: true,
    }

    var err error
    // cfg is defined in this file globally.
    cfg, err := testEnv.Start()                              ❺
    Expect(err).NotTo(HaveOccurred())
    Expect(cfg).NotTo(BeNil())

    scheme := runtime.NewScheme()                            ❻
    err = clientgoscheme.AddToScheme(scheme)
    Expect(err).NotTo(HaveOccurred())
    err = mygroupv1alpha1.AddToScheme(scheme)
    Expect(err).NotTo(HaveOccurred())

    mgr, err := manager.New(cfg, manager.Options{            ❼
        Scheme: scheme,
    })
```

```
    Expect(err).ToNot(HaveOccurred())
    k8sClient = mgr.GetClient()                             ❽

    err = builder.                                          ❾
        ControllerManagedBy(mgr).
        Named(Name).
        For(&mygroupv1alpha1.MyResource{}).
        Owns(&appsv1.Deployment{}).
        Complete(&MyReconciler{})

    go func() {
        defer GinkgoRecover()
        err = mgr.Start(ctx)                                ❿
        Expect(err).ToNot(
            HaveOccurred(),
            "failed to run manager",
)
    }()
})

var _ = AfterSuite(func() {
    cancel()                                                ⓫
    err := testEnv.Stop()                                   ⓬
    Expect(err).NotTo(HaveOccurred())
})
```

❶ **testEnv**, **ctx**, and **cancel** will be used in **BeforeSuite** and **AfterSuite**

❷ **k8sClient** will be used in tests

❸ Create a cancelable context

❹ Create the **testEnv** environment

❺ Start the **testEnv** environment

❻ Build the scheme to pass to the Manager

❼ Build the Manager

❽ Get the **k8sClient** from the Manager to use for tests

❾ Build the Controller

❿ Start the Manager from a **Go** routine

⓫ Cancel the context, which will terminate the Manager

⓬ Terminate the **testEnv** environment

Writing the Tests

Now that you have a suite that starts and stops the environment, you can write the tests. The tests will start by creating a **MyResource** instance to verify that the **Reconcile** function creates the expected "low-level" resources, with the expected definition.

Then, when the low-level resources are created, the tests will update the status of the low-level resources (remember that no Controller is deployed in the cluster, so you have to do these changes from the tests instead) to verify that the status of the **MyResource** instance is updated accordingly.

The plan for the tests will be the following. Note that each **It** test will be executed separately, and for each **It**, all preceding **BeforeEach** will be executed before the test, and all preceding **AfterEach** will be executed after the test.

```
var _ = Describe("MyResource controller", func() {
  When("creating a MyResource instance", func() {
    BeforeEach(func() {
      // Create the MyResource instance
    })

    AfterEach(func() {
      // Delete the MyResource instance
    })

    It("should create a deployment", func() {
      // Check that the deployment
      // is eventually created
    })

    When("deployment is found", func() {
```

```
BeforeEach(func() {
  // Wait for the deployment
  // to be eventually created
})

It("should be owned by the MyResource instance", func() {
  // Check ownerReference in Deployment
  // references the MyResource instance
})

It("should use the image specified in MyResource instance", func() {
})

When("deployment ReadyReplicas is 1", func() {
  BeforeEach(func() {
    // Update the Deployment status
    // to ReadyReplicas=1
  })

  It("should set status ready for MyResource instance", func() {
    // Check the status of MyResource instance
    // is eventually Ready
  })
})
})
})
})
```

To clearly show the unfolding of the tests, here is how the four **It** tests will be executed, with the **BeforeEach** and **AfterEach** displayed.

Test 1

When: creating a MyResource instance

Before: // Create the MyResource instance

It: should create a deployment

After: // Delete the MyResource instance

Test 2

When: creating a MyResource instance

Before: // Create the MyResource instance

When: deployment is found

Before: // Wait deployment eventually created

It: should be owned by the MyResource instance

After: // Delete the MyResource instance

Test 3

When: creating a MyResource instance

Before: // Create the MyResource instance

When: deployment is found

Before: // Wait deployment eventually created

It: should use image specified in MyResource instance

After: // Delete the MyResource instance

Test 4

When: creating a MyResource instance

Before: // Create the MyResource instance

When: deployment is found

Before: // Wait deployment eventually created

When: deployment ReadyReplicas is 1

Before: // Update Deployment status to ReadyReplicas=1

It: should set status ready for MyResource instance

After: // Delete the MyResource instance

Finally, the complete source code of the tests follows after the next paragraphs. Note that you are creating the MyResource instance with a random name, so the created resources are not in conflict between the tests.

As a matter of fact, tests are executed one after the other, so resources remaining from the previous tests could interfere with the subsequent tests.

In this implementation, you can finish the test by removing the MyResource instance, but because no Controller is running in the cluster, the Deployment is not deleted by the garbage collector, despite that it references the deleted MyResource instance as owner. Because of this, if you execute all the tests with the same MyResource instance name, the Deployment from the first test would be used for the tests that follow.

```go
import (
  "fmt"
  "math/rand"

  . "github.com/onsi/ginkgo/v2"
  . "github.com/onsi/gomega"
  appsv1 "k8s.io/api/apps/v1"
  metav1 "k8s.io/apimachinery/pkg/apis/meta/v1"
  "k8s.io/apimachinery/pkg/types"
  "sigs.k8s.io/controller-runtime/pkg/client"

  mygroupv1alpha1 "github.com/feloy/myresource-crd/pkg/apis/mygroup.
  example.com/v1alpha1"
)

var _ = Describe("MyResource controller", func() {
  When("When creating a MyResource instance", func() {
    var (
      myres       mygroupv1alpha1.MyResource
      ownerref    *metav1.OwnerReference
      name        string
      namespace   = "default"
      deployName  string
      image       string
    )

    BeforeEach(func() {
```

```go
// Create the MyResource instance
image = fmt.Sprintf("myimage%d", rand.Intn(1000))
myres = mygroupv1alpha1.MyResource{
  Spec: mygroupv1alpha1.MyResourceSpec{
    Image: image,
  },
}
name = fmt.Sprintf("myres%d", rand.Intn(1000))
myres.SetName(name)
myres.SetNamespace(namespace)
err := k8sClient.Create(ctx, &myres)
Expect(err).NotTo(HaveOccurred())
ownerref = metav1.NewControllerRef(
  &myres,
  mygroupv1alpha1.SchemeGroupVersion.
    WithKind("MyResource"),
)
deployName = fmt.Sprintf("%s-deployment", name)
})

AfterEach(func() {
  // Delete the MyResource instance
  k8sClient.Delete(ctx, &myres)
})

It("should create a deployment", func() {
  // Check that the deployment
  // is eventually created
  var dep appsv1.Deployment
  Eventually(
    deploymentExists(deployName, namespace, &dep),
    10, 1
  ).Should(BeTrue())
})

When("deployment is found", func() {
  var dep appsv1.Deployment
```

```
BeforeEach(func() {
  // Wait for the deployment
  // to be eventually created
  Eventually(
    deploymentExists(deployName, namespace, &dep),
    10, 1,
  ).Should(BeTrue())
})

It("should be owned by the MyResource instance", func() {
  // Check ownerReference in Deployment
  // references the MyResource instance
  Expect(dep.GetOwnerReferences()).
    To(ContainElement(*ownerref))
})

It("should use the image specified in MyResource instance", func() {
  Expect(
    dep.Spec.Template.Spec.Containers[0].Image,
  ).To(Equal(image))
})

When("deployment ReadyReplicas is 1", func() {
  BeforeEach(func() {
    // Update the Deployment status
    // to ReadyReplicas=1
    dep.Status.Replicas = 1
    dep.Status.ReadyReplicas = 1
    err := k8sClient.Status().Update(ctx, &dep)
    Expect(err).NotTo(HaveOccurred())
  })

  It("should set status ready for MyResource instance", func() {
    // Check the status of MyResource instance
    // is eventually Ready
    Eventually(
      getMyResourceState(name, namespace), 10, 1,
```

```go
      ).Should(Equal("Ready"))
    })
   })
  })
 })
})

func deploymentExists(
  name, namespace string, dep *appsv1.Deployment,
) func() bool {
  return func() bool {
    err := k8sClient.Get(ctx, client.ObjectKey{
      Namespace: namespace,
      Name:      name,
    }, dep)
    return err == nil
  }
}

func getMyResourceState(
  name, namespace string,
) func() (string, error) {
  return func() (string, error) {
    myres := mygroupv1alpha1.MyResource{}
    err := k8sClient.Get(ctx, types.NamespacedName{
      Namespace: namespace,
      Name:      name,
    }, &myres)
    if err != nil {
      return "", err
    }
    return myres.Status.State, nil
  }
}
```

Conclusion

This chapter concludes the presentation of the various concepts and libraries that can be used to write Kubernetes Operators.

Chapter 8 introduced the Custom Resources, permitting extension of the Kubernetes API by adding new resources to the list of served resources. Chapter 9 presented various ways to work with Custom Resources using the Go language, either by generating a Clientset for this resource, or by using the **DynamicClient**.

Chapter 10 introduced the **controller-runtime** Library, useful for implementing an Operator to manage a Custom Resource lifecyle. Chapter 11 focused on writing the business logic of the Operator, and Chapter 12 is used to test this logic.

The next chapter describes the **kubebuilder** SDK, a framework using the tools introduced in the previous chapters. This framework facilitates the development of Operators, by generating code for new custom resource definitions and associated Operators, and by providing tools to build and to deploy these custom resource definitions and Operators to the cluster.

CHAPTER 13

Creating an Operator with Kubebuilder

You have seen in the previous chapters how to define new resources to be served by the API Server using Custom Resources Definitions (CRD), and how to build Operators, using the controller-runtime library.

The Kubebuilder SDK is dedicated to help you create new resources and their related Operators. It provides commands to bootstrap a project defining a Manager, and to add resources and their related controllers to the project.

Once the source code for new custom resources and controllers is generated, you will need to implement the missing parts, depending on the business domain of the resources. The Kubebuilder SDK then provides tools to build and deploy the Custom Resource Definitions and the Manager to the cluster.

Installing Kubebuilder

Kubebuilder is provided as a single binary. You can download the binary from the Release page of the project[1] and install it in your PATH. Binaries are provided for Linux and MacOS systems.

Creating a Project

The first step is to create a project. The project initially will contain:

- Go source code defining a Manager (without any Controller for the moment)

---

[1] https://github.com/kubernetes-sigs/kubebuilder/releases

© Philippe Martin 2023
P. Martin, *Kubernetes Programming with Go*, https://doi.org/10.1007/978-1-4842-9026-2_13

- A Dockerfile to build an image containing the manager binary to deploy to the cluster

- Kubernetes manifests to help deploy the Manager to the cluster

- A Makefile defining commands to help you test, build, and deploy the manager

To create a project, first create an empty directory and **cd** into it, then execute the following **kubebuilder init** command:

```
$ mkdir myresource-kb
$ cd myresource-kb
$ kubebuilder init
    --domain myid.dev                          ❶
    --repo github.com/myid/myresource           ❷
```

> ❶ Domain name, used as a suffix to the name of the GVK groups. Custom resources defined in this project can belong to various groups, but all groups will belong to the same domain. For example, **mygroup1.myid.dev** and **mygroup2.myid.dev**
>
> ❷ Name of the Go module for the generated Go code for the Manager

You can examine the commands available from the Makefile by running the following command:

```
$ make help
```

You can build the binary for the Manager with the following command:

```
$ make build
```

Then, you can run the Manager locally:

```
$ make run
```

or

```
$ ./bin/manager
```

At this point, it is interesting to initiate a source control project (e.g., a git project), and create a first revision with the files generated. This way, you will be able to examine the changes made by the next executed **kubebuilder** commands. For example, if you use git:

```
$ git init
$ git commit -am 'kubebuilder init --domain myid.dev --repo github.com/
myid/myresource'
```

Adding a Custom Resource to the Project

For the moment, the Manager does not manage any Controller. Even if you can build and run it, you cannot do anything with it.

The next **kubebuilder** command to execute is **kubebuilder create api** to add a Custom Resource and its related Controller to the project. The command will ask you whether you want to create the Resource and the Controller. Reply **y** to each question.

```
$ kubebuilder create api
    --group mygroup              ❶
    --version v1alpha1           ❷
    --kind MyResource            ❸
Create Resource [y/n]
y
Create Controller [y/n]
y
```

> ❶ The group of the custom resource. It will be suffixed with the domain to form the complete GVK group
>
> ❷ The version of the resource
>
> ❸ The kind of the resource

You can see the changes made by the command by running the following **git** command:

```
$ git status
On branch main
Changes not staged for commit:
```

```
(use "git add <file>..." to update what will be committed)
(use "git restore <file>..." to discard changes in working directory)
    modified:   PROJECT
    modified:   go.mod
    modified:   go.sum
    modified:   main.go

Untracked files:
  (use "git add <file>..." to include in what will be committed)
    api/
    config/crd/
    config/rbac/myresource_editor_role.yaml
    config/rbac/myresource_viewer_role.yaml
    config/samples/
    controllers/

no changes added to commit (use "git add" and/or "git commit -a")
```

The **PROJECT** file contains the definition of the project. It originally contained the domain and **repo** provided as flags to the **init** command. It now also contains the definition of a first resource. The **main.go** file and the **controllers** directory define a Controller for the custom resource.

The **api/v1alpha1** directory has been created and contains the definition of the custom resource using Go structures, as well as code generated by **deepcopy-gen** (see Chapter 8's "Running **deepcopy-gen**" section), with the help of the **controller-gen** tool. It also contains the definition of the **AddToScheme** function, useful for adding this new custom resource to a Scheme.

The **config/samples** directory contains a new file, defining an instance of the custom resource, in YAML format. The **config/rbac** directory contains two new files, defining two new **ClusterRole** resources—one for viewing and one for editing MyResource instances. The **config/crd** directory contains kustomize files to build the CRD.

Building and Deploying Manifests

The following command builds manifests to be deployed to the cluster:

```
$ make manifests
```

This command build two manifests:

- `config/rbac/role.yaml` – the ClusterRole that will be affected to the service account used by the Manager, giving access to the custom resource.

- `config/crd/bases/mygroup.myid.dev_myresources.yaml` – the definition of the Custom Resource.

The following command will deploy the manifest defining the CRD:

```
$ make install
[...]
bin/kustomize build config/crd | kubectl apply -f -
customresourcedefinition.apiextensions.k8s.io/myresources.mygroup.myid.
dev created
```

Running the Manager Locally

This time, the Manager is handling a Controller, reconciling the MyResource instances. The **Reconcile** function generated by **kubebuilder** does nothing but return directly without error:

```
func (r *MyResourceReconciler) Reconcile(ctx context.Context, req ctrl.
Request) (ctrl.Result, error) {
    _ = log.FromContext(ctx)

    // TODO(user): your logic here

    return ctrl.Result{}, nil
}
```

Let's add a log when the **Reconcile** function is called:

```
-      _ = log.FromContext(ctx)
+      log := log.FromContext(ctx)
+      log.Info("reconcile")
```

The following command will execute the Manager locally. It will use your **kubeconfig** file to connect to the cluster, with the associated permissions:

```
$ make run
[...]
INFO       setup        starting manager
INFO       Starting server      [...]
INFO       Starting server      [...]
INFO       Starting EventSource      [...]
INFO       Starting Controller      [...]
INFO       Starting workers      [...]
```

From another terminal, you can create a MyResource instance using the provided sample:

```
$ kubectl apply -f config/samples/mygroup_v1alpha1_myresource.yaml
```

In the first terminal, a new log should appear, indicating that the **Reconcile** function has been called:

```
$ make run
[...]
INFO       reconcile            [...]
```

Personalizing the Custom Resource

The **kubebuilder create api** command has created as a template a resource with **Spec** and **Status** fields, the Spec containing a **Foo** field and the Status being empty.

In this section, you will find out how to update this template to add the necessary fields.

Editing the Go Structures

You can edit the file **api/v1alpha1/myresource_types.go** to personalize the custom resource. In this example, you will use the **Image** and **Memory** fields for the **Spec**, and a **State** field for the **Status**:

```
// MyResourceSpec defines the desired state of MyResource
type MyResourceSpec struct {
    Image   string              `json:"image"`
    Memory resource.Quantity `json:"memory"`
}

// MyResourceStatus defines the observed state of MyResource
type MyResourceStatus struct {
    State string `json:"state"`
}
```

Enabling the Status Subresource

You can see the annotations in the comments preceding the **MyResource** structure.

The first annotation //+kubebuilder:object:root=true indicates that **MyResource** is a *Kind*. With this annotation, **kubebuilder** will generate the **DeepCopyObject()** method for this structure. See Chapter 9's "Adding Annotations" section for more details.

The second annotation //+kubebuilder:subresource:status indicates that the **status** subresource must be enabled for **MyResource**. With this annotation, **kubebuilder** will add the status as subresource in the YAML definition of the CRD in **config/crd/bases/**. See Chapter 8's "Definition of the Resource Versions" section for more details.

The **Status** is being enabled by default, so you do not have to make any changes to these annotations.

Defining Printer Columns

Chapter 8's "Additional Printer Columns" section has shown how to declare printer columns for a custom resource by editing the YAML definition of the CRD.

Using **kubebuilder**, the YAML definition of the CRD is autogenerated, so you cannot edit it directly. Instead, you can use the +**kubebuilder:printcolumn** annotation. Each annotation accepts **name**, **type**, and **JSONPath** values, similar to the **additionalPrinterColumns** entries in the YAML definition.

As an example, adding the following annotations will define **Image**, **State**, and **Age** printer columns:

```
// +kubebuilder:printcolumn:name="Image",type=string,
JSONPath=`.spec.image`
// +kubebuilder:printcolumn:name="State",type=string,
JSONPath=`.status.state`
// +kubebuilder:printcolumn:name="Age",type="date",
JSONPath=".metadata.creationTimestamp"
```

Regenerating the Files

To regenerate the **DeepCopy** methods, reflecting the changes made to the structures, you need to run the following command:

```
$ make
```

To regenerate the YAML definition of the CRD with the new fields, this command must be executed:

```
$ make manifests
```

You also can edit the sample file to adapt the sample resource. The file is **config/samples/mygroup_v1alpha1_myresource.yaml**, and you can adapt the content with:

```
$ cat > config/samples/mygroup_v1alpha1_myresource.yaml <<EOF
apiVersion: mygroup.myid.dev/v1alpha1
kind: MyResource
metadata:
  labels:
    app.kubernetes.io/name: myresource
    app.kubernetes.io/instance: myresource-sample
    app.kubernetes.io/part-of: myresource-kb
    app.kuberentes.io/managed-by: kustomize
    app.kubernetes.io/created-by: myresource-kb
  name: myresource-sample
```

```
spec:
  image: nginx
  memory: 512Mi
EOF
```

Now the CRD and sample are compatible, so you can apply the CRD to the cluster and update the sample resource:

```
$ make install
[...]
bin/kustomize build config/crd | kubectl apply -f -
customresourcedefinition.apiextensions.k8s.io/myresources.mygroup.myid.dev
configured

$ kubectl apply -f
    config/samples/mygroup_v1alpha1_myresource.yaml
myresource.mygroup.myid.dev/myresource-sample configured
```

Implementing the Reconcile Function

Because **kubebuilder** generates code based on the **controller-runtime** Library, you can reuse with very minor changes the code that was written for the **Reconcile** function in Chapter 11. Also, you can reuse the source code for testing the **Reconcile** function written in Chapter 12.

Adding RBAC Annotations

When running the Operator locally, the operator uses your **kubeconfig** file, with the authorizations specific to this **kubeconfig**. If you are connected using a **cluster-admin** account, the Operator will have all authorizations on the cluster and will be able to do any operations.

When the Operator is deployed on the cluster, however, it is running with a specific Kubernetes Service Account and is given restricted authorizations. These authorizations are defined in the **ClusterRole** built and deployed by **kubebuilder**.

To help Kubebuilder build this **ClusterRole**, annotations are present in the generated comments of the **Reconcile** function (line breaks have been added for clarity):

```
//+kubebuilder:rbac:
    groups=mygroup.myid.dev,
    resources=myresources,
    verbs=get;list;watch;create;update;patch;delete
//+kubebuilder:rbac:
    groups=mygroup.myid.dev,
    resources=myresources/status,
    verbs=get;update;patch
//+kubebuilder:rbac:
    groups=mygroup.myid.dev,
    resources=myresources/finalizers,
    verbs=update
```

These rules will give full access to the MyResource resource, but no access to other resources.

The **Reconcile** function needs to have read and write access to the Deployment resource as soon as watching it; for this reason, you will need to add this new annotation (line breaks have been added):

```
//+kubebuilder:rbac:
    groups=apps,
    resources=deployments,
    verbs=get;list;watch;create;update;patch;delete
```

Deploying the Operator on the Cluster

To be able to deploy the Operator to a cluster, you need to build the container image and deploy it to a container image registry (e.g., **DockerHub**, **Quay.io**, or many others).

The first step is to create a new repository in your preferred container image registry to contain the image of the Operator container. Let's say you have created a repository named **myresource** in **quay.io/myid**, the full name of the image will be **quay.io/myid/myresource**.

For each build, you will need to use a different tag for the image so that the update of the container will be done correctly. The build the image locally, you need to run the following command (note the tag **v1alpha1-1**):

```
$ make docker-build
    IMG=quay.io/myid/myresource:v1alpha1-1
```

To deploy it to the registry, the following command must be executed:

```
$ make docker-push
    IMG=quay.io/myid/myresource:v1alpha1-1
```

Finally, to deploy the Operator to the cluster:

```
$ make deploy
    IMG=quay.io/myid/myresource:v1alpha1-1
```

This will create a new namespace, **myresource-kb-system**, containing a new deployment that will execute the Operator. You can examine the logs of the Operator with the following command:

```
$ kubectl logs
    deployment/myresource-kb-controller-manager
    -n myresource-kb-system
```

Creating a New Version of the Resource

The Kubernetes API supports versioned resources, and a mechanism to convert resources between versions. The conversion between any versions must not lose any information. For the moment, you have created the custom resource MyResource with the version **v1alpha1**. The **Spec** of the resource contains **Image** and **Memory** fields.

You want to create a **v1beta1** version, change the field **Memory**, and rename it to **MemoryRequest** to remove any ambiguity. You will be able to convert between these two versions by affecting the Memory value to the appropriate field.

Defining a New Version

To create the new version, you need to invoke the **kubebuilder create api** command again, with the same group and kind, but with a new version. Also, because the resource already exists and the Controller is already declared, you can reply with an **n** when asked whether you want to create a Resource and a Controller.

```
$ kubebuilder create api --group mygroup --version v1beta1 --kind
MyResource
Create Resource [y/n]
n
Create Controller [y/n]
n
```

This command has created a new directory, **api/v1beta1**, containing the default definition of the resource. You will need to update these files to declare the definition of the custom resource for the new version. You can copy the file **api/v1alpha1/myresource_types.go** into **api/v1beta1** and make the necessary changes:

- The name of the package at the beginning of the file, from **v1alpha1** to **v1beta1**

- The name of the Memory field, from **Memory** to **MemoryRequest**, and the **yaml** field name from **Memory** to **MemoryRequest**

```
package v1beta1
[...]

// MyResourceSpec defines the desired state of MyResource
type MyResourceSpec struct {
  Image         string            `json:"image"`
  MemoryRequest resource.Quantity `json:"memoryRequest"`
}
```

Because you now have several versions, you have to declare on which format the resource will be stored in **etcd**. You can choose to use the format of **v1alpha1**. For this, you can use the annotation **+kubebuilder:storageversion** in the comments preceding the definition of the **MyResource** structure in the **v1alpha1** package.

```
package v1alpha1

[...]
// +kubebuilder:object:root=true
// +kubebuilder:subresource:status
// +kubebuilder:storageversion

// MyResource is the Schema for the myresources API
type MyResource struct {
    [...]
}
```

Implementing Hub and Convertible

A *Conversion* system is provided by the **controller-runtime** Library. This system relies on two interfaces:

- The **Hub** interface to mark the version used for the storage

- The **Convertible** interface to provide converters to and from the storage version

```
type Hub interface {
    runtime.Object
    Hub()
}

type Convertible interface {
    runtime.Object
    ConvertTo(dst Hub) error
    ConvertFrom(src Hub) error
}
```

You have chosen the version **v1alpha1** for the storage and need to make **v1alpha1. MyResource** implement the **Hub** interface:

```
package v1alpha1

// Hub marks this type as a conversion hub.
func (*MyResource) Hub() {}
```

All other types, in this case, the **v1beta1.MyResource** must implement the **Convertible** interface and provide code to convert to and from the **Hub** version:

```
package v1beta1

import (
    "github.com/myid/myresource/api/v1alpha1"
    "sigs.k8s.io/controller-runtime/pkg/conversion"
)

func (src *MyResource) ConvertTo(
    dstRaw conversion.Hub,
) error {
    dst := dstRaw.(*v1alpha1.MyResource)
    dst.Spec.Memory = src.Spec.MemoryRequest
    // Copy other fields
    dst.ObjectMeta = src.ObjectMeta
    dst.Spec.Image = src.Spec.Image
    dst.Status.State = src.Status.State
    return nil
}

func (dst *MyResource) ConvertFrom(
    srcRaw conversion.Hub,
) error {
    src := srcRaw.(*v1alpha1.MyResource)
    dst.Spec.MemoryRequest = src.Spec.Memory
    // Copy other fields
    dst.ObjectMeta = src.ObjectMeta
    dst.Spec.Image = src.Spec.Image
    dst.Status.State = src.Status.State
    return nil
}
```

Setting Up the webhook

The **kubebuilder create webhook** command is used to set up webhooks. Several webhook types are supported:

- *Conversion Webhook* to help convert between resource versions (flag **--conversion**)

- *Mutating Admission Webhook* to help set default values on new objects (flag **--defaulting**)

- *Validating Admission Webhook* to help validate the created or updated objects (flag **--programmatic-validation**)

In this example, you will create a **Conversion** webhook for **MyResource** in version **v1beta1** (the version that needs to be converted):

```
$ kubebuilder create webhook
    --group mygroup
    --version v1beta1
    --kind MyResource
    --conversion
```

This will add code to the **main** function to set up the Conversion webhook:

```
(&mygroupv1beta1.MyResource{}).
    SetupWebhookWithManager(mgr)
```

Then, create new code in the **v1beta1** package, to be called from **main**:

```
package v1beta1

func (r *MyResource) SetupWebhookWithManager(
    mgr ctrl.Manager,
) error {
    return ctrl.NewWebhookManagedBy(mgr).
        For(r).
        Complete()
}
```

305

Updating kustomization Files

You need to enable the **webhook** in the deployment manifests by uncommenting sections related to **[WEBHOOK]** and **[CERTMANAGER]** in the files **config/default/ kustomization.yaml** and **config/crd/kustomization.yaml**.

If you are not using any other webhooks (i.e., conversion or mutating), you also will need to comment on the lines:

- "- manifests.yaml" in the file config/webhook/kustomization.yaml

- "- webhookcainjection_patch.yaml" in the file **config/default/ kustomization.yaml**

You also will need to install cert-manager[2] to generate certificates based on annotations added by **kubebuilder** to the CRD.

Using Various Versions

After deploying the new version, as described in the "Deploying the Operator on the Cluster" section, you can create MyResource instances in version **v1alpha1** or **v1beta1**. As an example, you can create two sample resources in the **config/sample** directory:

config/samples/mygroup_v1alpha1_myresource.yaml:

```
apiVersion: mygroup.myid.dev/v1alpha1
kind: MyResource
metadata:
  name: myresource-sample-alpha
spec:
  image: nginx
  memory: 512Mi
```

config/samples/mygroup_v1beta1_myresource.yaml:

```
apiVersion: mygroup.myid.dev/v1beta1
kind: MyResource
metadata:
  name: myresource-sample-beta
```

---

[2] https://cert-manager.io/docs/installation/

```
spec:
  image: nginx
  memoryRequest: 256Mi
```

Then, you can create the resources in the cluster using **kubectl**:

```
$ kubectl apply
    -f config/samples/mygroup_v1alpha1_myresource.yaml
$ kubectl apply
    -f config/samples/mygroup_v1beta1_myresource.yaml
```

Finally, when listing the resources, you will get the definition in the **v1beta1** format, using the **memoryRequest** field:

```
$ kubectl get myresources.mygroup.myid.dev -o yaml
apiVersion: v1
kind: List
items:
- apiVersion: mygroup.myid.dev/v1beta1
  kind: MyResource
  metadata:
    name: myresource-sample-alpha
  spec:
    image: nginx
    memoryRequest: 512Mi
  status:
    state: Ready
- apiVersion: mygroup.myid.dev/v1beta1
  kind: MyResource
  metadata:
    name: myresource-sample-beta
  spec:
    image: nginx
    memoryRequest: 256Mi
  status:
    state: Ready
```

Note that you get the definition in **v1beta1** because **kubectl** returns you to the preferred version (the most recent one) of the requested resource.

If you want to get the result in the **v1alpha1** format, you can specify it when invoking **kubectl get**:

```
$ kubectl get myresources.v1alpha1.mygroup.myid.dev
    -o yaml
```

This command will return the resources using the **Memory** field.

Conclusion

This chapter has used the Kubebuilder SDK to help write and deploy Operators more easily than if you had to write the code and the Kubernetes manifests yourselves.

Note that the Operator SDK[3] is another framework to build operators. Operator SDK can manage Go, Helm, and Ansible projects. For the Go projects, Operator SDK makes use of **kubebuilder** to generate the code and the Kubernetes manifests.

Operator SDK provides more functionalities on top of **kubebuilder** to integrate the built operator with the Operator Lifecycle Manager[4] and Operator Hub.[5]

As these extra functionalities are out of the scope of this book, Operator SDK will not be covered here. But you can run through this chapter again by replacing the command **kubebuilder** with **operator-sdk** to build your Operator with this framework instead.

---

[3] https://sdk.operatorframework.io/
[4] https://github.com/operator-framework/operator-lifecycle-manager
[5] https://operatorhub.io/

Index

© Philippe Martin 2023
P. Martin, *Kubernetes Programming with Go*, https://doi.org/10.1007/978-1-4842-9026-2

P, Q

R

Printed in the United States
by Baker & Taylor Publisher Services